BENCHMARK SERIES

Microsoft® WORD

EXPERT CERTIFICATION

2002

MICROSOFT OFFICE
Microsoft®
OFFICE
USER SPECIALIST

APPROVED COURSEWARE

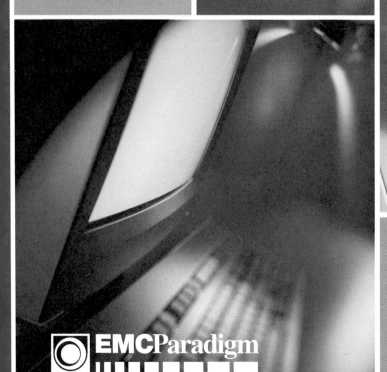

Pierce College at Puyallup
Puyallup, Washington

EMCParadigm

NITA RUTKOSKY

Senior Developmental Editor	Sonja M. Brown
Special Projects Coordinator	Joan D'Onofrio
Senior Designer	Jennifer Wreisner
Editorial Assistant	Susan Capecchi
Copy Editor	Sharon O'Donnell
Proofreader	Joy McComb
Indexer	Nancy Fulton

Publishing Team—George Provol, Publisher; Janice Johnson, Director of Product Development; Tony Galvin, Acquisitions Editor; Lori Landwer, Marketing Manager; Shelley Clubb, Electronic Design and Production Manager

Acknowledgments—The author and publisher wish to thank the following reviewers for their technical and academic assistance in testing exercises and assessing instruction:

- Kay M. Newton, Commonwealth Business College, LaPorte, Indiana
- Michael Gookins, Converse, Tennessee

Special thanks to Professor Stephanie Fells of Berkeley College, Woodbridge, New Jersey, for preparing Internet Projects and Job Study scenarios as part of the Unit Performance Assessment sections.

Library of Congress Cataloging-in-Publication Data
    Rutkosky, Nita Hewitt.
        Microsoft Word 2002: expert certification / Nita Rutkosky.
           p.cm. – (Benchmark series)
        ISBN 0-7638-1464-4
           1. Microsoft Word. 2. Word processing. I. Title. II. Benchmark series
    (Saint Paul, Minn.)

Z52.5.M52 R944 2002
652.5'5369—dc21   2001033791

Care has been taken to verify the accuracy of information presented in this book. However, the author, editor, and publisher cannot accept any responsibility for Web, e-mail, newsgroup, or chat room subject matter or content, or for consequences from application of the information in this book, and make no warranty, expressed or implied, with respect to its content.

Trademarks: Some of the product names and company names included in this book have been used for identification purposes only and may be trademarks or registered trademarks of their respective manufacturers and sellers. The author, editor, and publisher disclaim any affiliation, association, or connection with, or sponsorship or endorsement by, such owners.

Text: ISBN 0-7638-1464-4
Order Number: 05553

© 2002 by Paradigm Publishing Inc.
    Published by **EMC**Paradigm
    875 Montreal Way
    St. Paul, MN 55102

    (800) 535-6865
    E-mail: educate@emcp.com
    Web site: www.emcp.com

Printed in the United States of America
10 9 8 7 6 5 4 3 2 1

CONTENTS

Chapter 6
Creating Specialized Tables and Indexes — E213

Chapter 7
Preparing and Protecting Forms — E243

Chapter 8
Sharing Data — E273

Expert Unit 2
Performance Assessments — E299

WELCOME

You are about to begin working with a textbook that is part of the Benchmark Office XP Series. The word *Benchmark* in the title holds a special significance in terms of *what* you will learn and *how* you will learn. *Benchmark*, according to *Webster's Dictionary*, means "something that serves as a standard by which others may be measured or judged." In this text, you will learn the Microsoft Office User Specialist (MOUS) skills required for certification on the Core and/or Expert level of one or more major applications within the Office XP suite. These skills are benchmarks by which you will be evaluated, should you choose to take one or more certification exams.

The design and teaching approach of this textbook also serve as a benchmark for instructional materials on software programs. Features and commands are presented in a clear, straightforward way, and each short section of instruction is followed by an exercise that lets you practice using the new feature. Gradually, as you move through each chapter, you will build your skills to the point of mastery. At the end of a chapter, you are offered the opportunity to demonstrate your newly acquired competencies—to prove you have met the benchmarks for using the Office suite or an individual program. At the completion of the text, you are well on your way to becoming a successful computer user.

EMCParadigm's Office XP Benchmark Series includes textbooks on Office XP, Word 2002, Excel 2002, Access 2002, PowerPoint 2002, Publisher 2002, Outlook 2002, and FrontPage 2002. Note that the programs include the year 2002 in their name, while the suite itself is called Office XP (for "experience"). Each book includes a Student CD, which contains prekeyed documents and files required for completing the exercises. A CD icon and folder name displayed on the opening page of each chapter indicates that you need to copy a folder of files from the CD before beginning the chapter exercises. *(See the inside back cover for instructions on copying a folder.)*

Introducing Microsoft Office XP

Microsoft Office XP, released in May 2001, is a suite of programs designed to improve productivity and efficiency in workplace, school, and home settings. A suite is a group of programs that are sold as a package and are designed to be used together, making it possible to exchange files among the programs. The major applications included in Office are Word, a word processing program; Excel, a spreadsheet program; Access, a database management program; PowerPoint, a slide presentation program; and Outlook, a desktop information management program.

Using the Office suite offers significant advantages over working with individual programs developed by different software vendors. The programs in the Office suite use similar toolbars, buttons, icons, and menus, which means that once you learn the basic features of one program, you can use those same features in the other programs. This easy transfer of knowledge decreases the learning time and allows you to concentrate on the unique commands and options within each program. The compatibility of the programs creates seamless integration of data within and between programs and lets the operator use the program most appropriate for the required tasks.

The number of programs in the Office XP suite varies by the package, or edition. Four editions are available:

- **Standard:** Word, Excel, Outlook, PowerPoint
- **Professional:** Word, Excel, Outlook, PowerPoint, and Access
- **Professional Special Edition:** All Professional package programs plus FrontPage, Publisher, and SharePoint. This edition is available only for a limited time and only to current Office users.
- **Developer:** All Professional package programs (except SharePoint) plus Developer tools

New Features in Office XP

Users of previous editions of Office will find that the essential features that have made Office popular still form the heart of the suite. New enhancements focus on collaboration, or the ability for multiple users to work together on the same document from different locations over the Internet. Another highlight is the Smart Tag feature, which is an icon that when clicked offers a list of commands that are especially useful for the particular job being done. In Word, for example, a Smart Tag might offer the ability to turn off automatic capitalization or other types of automatic formatting. A more comprehensive kind of targeted assistance is offered in a new Task Pane, which is a narrow window that appears at the right of the screen to display commands relevant to the current task. Speech recognition technology is available with this edition, offering users the ability to dictate text into any Office program. This feature must be installed separately.

Structure of the Benchmark Textbooks

Users of the Core Certification texts and the complete application textbooks may begin their course with an overview of computer hardware and software, offered in the *Getting Started* section at the beginning of the book. Your instructor may also ask you to complete the *Windows 2000* and the *Internet Explorer* sections so you become familiar with the computer's operating system and the essential tools for using the Internet.

Instruction on the major programs within the Office suite is presented in units of four chapters each. Both the Core and Expert levels contain two units, which culminate with performance assessments to check your knowledge and skills. Each chapter contains the following sections:

- performance objectives that identify specifically what you are expected to learn
- instructional text that introduces and explains new concepts and features
- step-by-step, hands-on exercises following each section of instruction
- a chapter summary
- a knowledge self-check called Concepts Check
- skill assessment exercises called Skills Check

Exercises offered at the end of units provide writing and research opportunities that will strengthen your performance in other college courses as well as on the job. The final activities simulate interesting projects you could encounter in the workplace.

Benchmark Series Ancillaries

The Benchmark Series includes some important resources that will help you succeed in your computer applications courses:

Online Resource Center

Internet Resource Centers hosted by EMC/Paradigm provide additional material for students and teachers using the Benchmark books. Online you will find Web links, updates to textbooks, study tips, quizzes and assignments, and supplementary projects.

Class Connection

Available for both the WebCT and Blackboard e-learning platforms, EMC/Paradigm's Class Connection is a course management tool for traditional and distance learning. The Class Connection allows students to access the course syllabus and assignment schedule online, provides self-quizzes and study aids, and facilitates communication among students and instructors via e-mail and e-discussions.

MOUS CERTIFICATION

APPROVED COURSEWARE

What Does This Logo Mean?

It means this courseware has been approved by the Microsoft® Office User Specialist Program to be among the finest available for learning Microsoft Word 2002. It also means that upon completion of this courseware, you may be prepared to become a Microsoft Office User Specialist.

What Is a Microsoft Office User Specialist?

A Microsoft Office User Specialist is an individual who has certified his or her skills in one or more of the Microsoft Office desktop applications of Microsoft Word, Microsoft Excel, Microsoft PowerPoint®, Microsoft Outlook® or Microsoft Access, or in Microsoft Project. The Microsoft Office User Specialist Program typically offers certification exams at the "Core" and "Expert" skill levels. * The Microsoft Office User Specialist Program is the only Microsoft approved program in the world for certifying proficiency in Microsoft Office desktop applications and Microsoft Project. This certification can be a valuable asset in any job search or career advancement.

More Information

- To learn more about becoming a Microsoft Office User Specialist, visit www.mous.net.
- To purchase a Microsoft Office User Specialist certification exam, visit www.DesktopIQ.com.
- To learn about other Microsoft Office User Specialist approved courseware from EMC/Paradigm, visit www.emcp.com/college_division/MOUS_ready.php.

EMC/Paradigm Publishing is independent from Microsoft Corporation and not affiliated with Microsoft in any manner. This publication may be used in assisting students to prepare for a Microsoft office User Specialist Exam. Neither Microsoft, its designated review company, nor EMC/Paradigm Publishing warrants that use of this publication will ensure passing the relevant exam.

---

* The availability of Microsoft Office User Specialist certification exams varies by application, application version and language. Visit www.mous.net for exam availability.

Microsoft, the Microsoft Office User Specialist Logo, PowerPoint and Outlook are either registered trademarks or trademarks of Microsoft Corporation in the United States and/or other countries.

WORD

EXPERT LEVEL UNIT 1: MANAGING DATA AND DOCUMENTS

Merging Documents and Sorting and Selecting Data

Formatting with Special Features

Adding Visual Appeal to Documents

Formatting with Macros and Styles

MICROSOFT® WORD 2002

EXPERT BENCHMARK MOUS SKILLS-UNIT 1

Reference No.	Skill	Pages
W2002e-1	**Customizing Paragraphs**	
W2002e-1-1	Control pagination	
	Insert a manual line break; insert a column break	E49; E73-E74
	Turn on/off widow/orphan control	E50, E52
	Keep paragraphs together on page	E50-E53
W2002e-1-2	Sort paragraphs in lists and tables	
	Sort text in paragraph	E22-E25
	Sort text in columns	E25-E29
	Sort text in tables	E29-E30
	Sort records in a data source	E30-E32
	Select records	E32-E36
W2002e-2	**Formatting Documents**	
W2002e-2-1	Create and format document sections	
	Format document sections	E69-E74
	Display paragraph formatting with Reveal Formatting	E51-E53
	Clear formatting	E149-E150
W2002e-2-2	Create and apply character and paragraph styles	
	Create, apply, and modify styles	E140-E146
	Assign a shortcut key combination to a style	E146-E149
W2002e-2-4	Create cross-references	E151-E152
W2002e-2-5	Add and revise endnotes and footnotes	
	Create and print footnotes and endnotes	E62-E66
	View, edit, move, copy, and delete footnotes and endnotes	E67-E69
W2002e-2-7	Move within documents	
	Navigate in Outline view	E152-E153
	Navigate with Document Map	E153-E154
	Navigate using bookmarks	E155-E156
W2002e-4	**Creating and Modifying Graphics**	
W2002e-4-1	Create, modify, and position graphics	
	Insert, size, move, and format an image	E83-E95
	Draw shapes, lines, and autoshapes	E95-E102
	Create, size, move, and customize WordArt	E103-E109
W2002e-4-3	Align text and graphics	E87-E90
W2002e-5	**Customizing Word**	
W2002e-5-1	Create, edit, and run macros	
	Record and run a macro	E122-E127
	Pause, resume, and delete a macro	E127
	Assign a macro a keyboard command and to a toolbar	E127-E131
	Edit a macro with Visual Basic	E134-E136
W2002e-5-2	Customize menus and toolbars	E111-E116
W2002e-7	**Using Mail Merge**	
W2002e-7-1	Merge letters with a Word, Excel, or Access data source	
	Complete a merge with the Mail Merge Wizard	E3-E9
	Prepare envelopes using the Mail Merge Wizard	E9-E11
	Prepare a directory using the Mail Merge Wizard	E12-E14
	Edit merge documents	E15-E21
W2002e-7-2	Merge labels with a Word, Excel, or Access data source	E11-E12
W2002e-7-3	Use Outlook data as mail merge data source	E14-E15

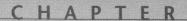

CHAPTER 1

MERGING DOCUMENTS AND SORTING AND SELECTING DATA

PERFORMANCE OBJECTIVES

Upon successful completion of chapter 1, you will be able to:
- **Use the Mail Merge Wizard to create letters, envelopes, labels, and a directory**
- **Create custom fields for a merge**
- **Edit main documents and data source files**
- **Input text during a merge**
- **Sort text in paragraphs, columns, and tables**
- **Sort records in a data source file**
- **Sort on more than one field**
- **Select specific records in a data source file for merging**

Word Chapter 01E

Word includes a Mail Merge Wizard you can use to create customized letters, envelopes, labels, directories, e-mail messages, and faxes. The Mail Merge Wizard guides you through six steps to create customized documents including steps on selecting a document type to executing the final merge. The Mail Merge Wizard presents a Mail Merge Task Pane for each step. This allows you to work in your document without having to close the Wizard.

Word includes some basic database functions you can use to alphabetize information, arrange numbers numerically, and select specific records from a document. In addition, you can sort text in paragraphs, columns, tables, and data sources and select specific records from a document.

Completing a Merge with the Mail Merge Wizard

A merge generally takes two files—the *data source* file and the *main document*. The data source file contains the variable information that will be inserted in the main document. Before creating a data source file, determine what type of correspondence you will be creating and the type of information you will need to insert in the correspondence. Word provides predetermined field names that can be used when creating the data source file. Use these field names if they represent the data you are creating. Variable information in a data source file is saved as a *record*. A record contains all of the information for one unit (for example, a person, family, customer, client, or business). A series of fields makes one record, and a series of records makes a data source file. The main document contains standard text along with fields identifying where variable information is inserted during the merge process.

The Mail Merge Wizard guides you through the merge process and presents six task panes. Begin the Wizard by clicking Tools, pointing to Letters and Mailings, and then clicking Mail Merge Wizard. The options in each task pane may vary depending on the type of merge you are performing. Generally, you complete the following steps at each of the six task panes:

Step 1: Identify the type of document you are creating (letter, e-mail message, envelope, label, or directory).

Step 2: Specify whether you want to use the current document window to create the document, start from a template, or start from an existing document.

Step 3: Specify whether you are using an existing list (for the variable information), selecting from an Outlook contacts list, or typing a new list. Depending on the choice you make, you may need to select a specific data source file or create a new data source file.

Step 4: Use the items in this task pane to help you prepare the main document. For example, if you are creating a letter, click the *Address block* hyperlink and the Wizard inserts the required codes in the main document for merging names and addresses. Click the *Greeting* hyperlink and the Wizard inserts codes for a greeting.

Step 5: Preview the merged documents.

Step 6: Complete the merge. At this step, you can send the merged document to the printer and/or edit the merged document.

HINT

If you want merged data formatted, you must format the merge fields at the main document.

HINT

View the merged document before printing to ensure that the merged data is correct.

If you choose to type a new list at step 3, the Mail Merge Wizard saves the completed list in the *My Data Sources* folder as an Access database file. Microsoft Word looks for data source files in this folder. In a multi-user environment, such as a school, you may want to specify a different location for your list. The Mail Merge Wizard provides a variety of predesigned fields. If these fields do not provide all variable information in a main document, you can create your own custom field. For exercise 1, you will prepare a data source file using predesigned fields as well as a custom field. You will also prepare a main document and then merge the documents to create form letters. In exercises 2, 3, and 4, you will use the data source file created in exercise 1 to prepare envelopes, labels, and a directory.

(Before completing computer exercises, copy to your disk the Word Chapter 01E *subfolder from the* Word 2002 Expert *folder on the CD that accompanies this textbook. Steps explaining how to copy a folder are presented on the inside of the back cover of this textbook.)*

1. At a clear document screen, click Tools, point to Letters and Mailings, and then click Mail Merge Wizard.
2. At the first Mail Merge Task Pane, make sure the Letters option is selected in the Select document type section of the task pane, and then click the *Next: Starting document* hyperlink located toward the bottom of the task pane.
3. At the second Mail Merge Task Pane, make sure the Use the current document option is selected in the Select starting document section of the task pane, and then click the *Next: Select recipients* hyperlink located toward the bottom of the task pane.
4. At the third Mail Merge Task Pane, click *Type a new list* in the Select recipients section of the task pane.
5. Click the *Create* hyperlink that displays in the Type a new list section of the task pane.
6. At the New Address List dialog box, the Mail Merge Wizard provides you with a number of predesigned fields. Delete the fields you do not need by completing the following steps:
   a. Click the Customize button.
   b. At the Customize Address List dialog box, click *Company Name* to select it, and then click the Delete button.
   c. At the message asking if you are sure you want to delete the field, click the Yes button.
   d. Complete steps similar to those in 6b and 6c to delete the following fields:
      Country
      Home Phone
      Work Phone
      E-mail Address
   e. Insert a custom field by completing the following steps:
      1) At the Customize Address List box, click the Add button.
      2) At the Add Field dialog box, key **Fund** and then click OK.

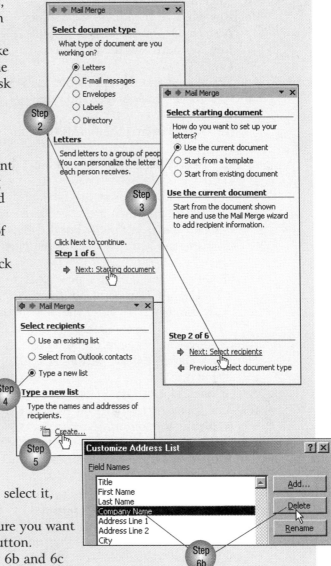

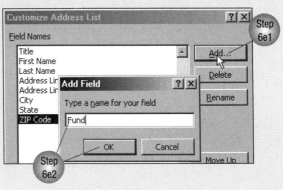

f. Click the OK button to close the Customize Address List dialog box.

7. At the New Address List dialog box, enter the information for the first client shown in figure 1.1 by completing the following steps:
   a. Click in the Title text box.
   b. Key **Mr.** and then press the Tab key. (This moves the insertion point to the *First Name* field. You can also press Shift + Tab to move to the previous field.)
   c. Key **Kenneth** and then press the Tab key.
   d. Key **Porter** and then press the Tab key.
   e. Key **7645 Tenth Street** and then press the Tab key.
   f. Key **Apt. 314** and then press the Tab key.
   g. Key **New York** and then press the Tab key.
   h. Key **NY** and then press the Tab key.
   i. Key **10192** and then press the Tab key.
   j. Key **Mutual Investment Fund** and then press the Tab key. (This makes the New Entry button active.)

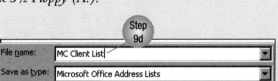

   k. Press the Enter key and a new blank record form displays in the dialog box.
   l. With the insertion point positioned in the *Title* field, complete steps similar to those in 7b through 7k to enter the information for the three other clients shown in figure 1.1.

8. After entering all of the information for the last client in figure 1.1 (Mrs. Wanda Houston), click the Close button located in the bottom right corner of the New Address List dialog box.

9. At the Save Address List dialog box, specify that you want the data source file saved in the *Word Chapter 01E* folder on your disk in drive A and then name the data source file by completing the following steps:
   a. Click the down-pointing triangle at the right of the Save in option box.
   b. At the drop-down list that displays, click *3½ Floppy (A:)*.
   c. Double-click the *Word Chapter 01E* folder.
   d. Click in the File name text box and then key **MC Client List**.
   e. Press Enter or click the Save button.
   f. At the Mail Merge Recipients dialog box, check to make sure all four entries are correct and then click the OK button.

Step 9d

File name:	MC Client List
Save as type:	Microsoft Office Address Lists

10. Move to the next step by clicking the *Next: Write your letter* hyperlink that displays toward the bottom of the task pane.

11. At the fourth Mail Merge Task Pane, create the letter shown in figure 1.2 by completing the following steps:
   a. Press the Enter key six times, key **February 19, 2003**, and then press the Enter key five times.
   b. Insert the address fields by clicking the *Address block* hyperlink located in the Write your letter section of the task pane.

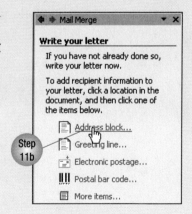

c. At the Insert Address Block dialog box, click the OK button.

d. Press the Enter key twice and then click the *Greeting line* hyperlink located in the Write your letter section of the task pane.

e. At the Greeting Line dialog box, click the down-pointing triangle at the right of the option box containing the comma (the box to the right of the box containing *Mr. Randall*).

f. At the drop-down list that displays, click the colon.

g. Click OK to close the Greeting Line dialog box.

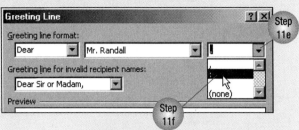

h. Press the Enter key twice.

i. Key the letter to the point where «Fund» displays and then insert the «Fund» field by completing the following steps:

   1) Click the *More items* hyperlink in the Write your letter section of the task pane.

   2) At the Insert Merge Field dialog box, click *Fund* in the *Fields* list box.

   3) Click the *Insert* button and then click the Close button.

j. Key the letter to the point where the «Title» field displays and then insert the «Title» field by completing steps similar to those in 11i1 through 11i3. Press the spacebar and then insert the «Last_Name» field by completing steps similar to those in 11i1 through 11i3.

k. Key the remainder of the letter shown in figure 1.2. (Insert your initials instead of the *XX* at the end of the letter.)

12. When you are finished keying the letter, click the *Next: Preview your letters* hyperlink located toward the bottom of the task pane.

13. At the fifth Mail Merge Task Pane, look over the letter that displays in the document window and make sure the information was merged properly. If you want to see the letters for the other recipients, click the button in the Mail Merge Task Pane containing the two right-pointing arrows.

14. Click the *Next: Complete the merge* hyperlink that displays toward the bottom of the task pane.

15. At the sixth Mail Merge Task Pane, click the *Edit individual letters* hyperlink that displays in the Merge section of the task pane.

16. At the Merge to New Document dialog box, make sure All is selected, and then click the OK button.

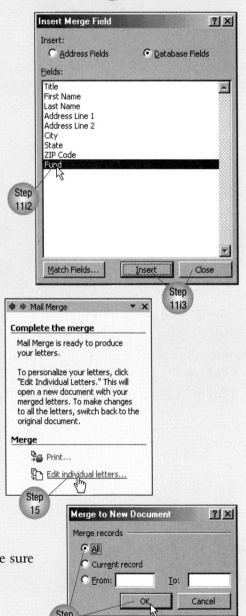

17. Save the merged letters in the normal manner in the *Word Chapter 01E* folder on your disk in drive A and name the document MC Client Letters.
18. Print MC Client Letters. (This document will print four letters.)
19. Close MC Client Letters.
20. At the sixth Mail Merge Task Pane, save the main document in the normal manner in the *Word Chapter 01E* folder on your disk in drive A and name it MC Main Doc.
21. Close MC Main Doc.

FIGURE

1.1 *Information for Data Source Fields*

Title	=	**Mr.**
First Name	=	**Kenneth**
Last Name	=	**Porter**
Address Line 1	=	**7645 Tenth Street**
Address Line 2	=	**Apt. 314**
City	=	**New York**
State	=	**NY**
Zip Code	=	**10192**
Fund	=	**Mutual Investment Fund**

Title	=	**Ms.**
First Name	=	**Carolyn**
Last Name	=	**Renquist**
Address Line 1	=	**13255 Meridian Street**
Address Line 2	=	(leave this blank)
City	=	**New York**
State	=	**NY**
Zip Code	=	**10435**
Fund	=	**Quality Care Fund**

Title	=	**Dr.**
First Name	=	**Amil**
Last Name	=	**Ranna**
Address Line 1	=	**433 South 17th**
Address Line 2	=	**Apt. 17-D**
City	=	**New York**
State	=	**NY**
Zip Code	=	**10322**
Fund	=	**Priority One Fund**

Title	=	**Mrs.**
First Name	=	**Wanda**
Last Name	=	**Houston**
Address Line 1	=	**566 North 22nd Avenue**
Address Line 2	=	(leave this blank)
City	=	**New York**
State	=	**NY**
Zip Code	=	**10634**
Fund	=	**Quality Care Fund**

WORD

FIGURE

1.2 *Main Document*

February 19, 2003

««AddressBlock»»

««GreetingLine»»

McCormack Funds is lowering its expense charges beginning May 1, 2003. The reductions in expense charges mean that more of your account investment performance in the «Fund» is returned to you, «Title» «Last_Name». The reductions are worth your attention because most of our competitors' fees have gone up.

Lowering expense charges is noteworthy because before the reduction, McCormack expense deductions were already among the lowest, far below most mutual funds and variable annuity accounts with similar objectives. At the same time, services for you, our client, will continue to expand. If you would like to discuss this change, please call us at (212) 555-2277. Your financial future is our main concern at McCormack.

Sincerely,

Jodie Langstrom
Director, Financial Services

XX:MC Client Letters

Preparing Envelopes Using the Mail Merge Wizard

If you create a letter as a main document and then merge it with a data source file, more than likely you will need envelopes properly addressed in which to send the letters. The Mail Merge Wizard guides you through the steps for creating and printing envelopes. For exercise 2, you will create and print envelopes for the letters you created and printed in exercise 1.

1. At a clear document screen, click <u>T</u>ools, point to L<u>e</u>tters and Mailings, and then click <u>M</u>ail Merge Wizard.
2. At the first Mail Merge Task Pane, click *Envelopes* in the Select document type section.
3. Click the <u>*Next: Starting document*</u> hyperlink.
4. At the second Mail Merge Task Pane, make sure the Change document layout option is selected in the Select starting document section, and then click the <u>*Next: Select recipients*</u> hyperlink located toward the bottom of the task pane.
5. At the Envelope Options dialog box, make sure the envelope size is 10, and then click OK.
6. At the third Mail Merge Task Pane, make sure the Use an existing list option is selected in the Select recipients section.
7. Click the <u>*Browse*</u> hyperlink located in the Use an existing list section.
8. At the Select Data Source dialog box, complete the following steps:
   a. Change the Look <u>i</u>n option to *3½ Floppy (A:)*.
   b. Double-click the *Word Chapter 01E* folder.
   c. Double-click *MC Client List* in the Select Data Source list box. (Notice that MC Client List is an Access database file and an Access icon displays before the file name.)
   d. At the Mail Merge Recipients dialog box, click OK.
9. Click the <u>*Next: Arrange your envelope*</u> hyperlink located toward the bottom of the third Mail Merge Task Pane.
10. At the fourth Mail Merge Task Pane, complete the following steps:
    a. Click in the approximate location in the envelope in the document window where the recipient's address will appear. (This causes a box with a dashed gray border to display. If you do not see this box, try clicking in a different location on the envelope.)

    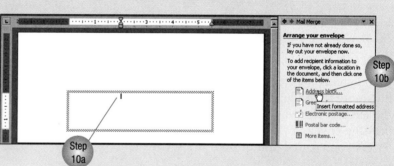

    b. Click the <u>*Address block*</u> hyperlink located in the Arrange your envelope section of the task pane.
    c. At the Insert Address Block dialog box, click OK. (This inserts the field «AddressBlock» inside the box on the envelope.)
11. Click the <u>*Next: Preview your envelopes*</u> hyperlink located toward the bottom of the fourth Mail Merge Task Pane.

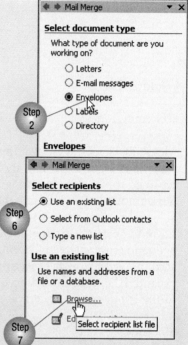

12. At the fifth Mail Merge Task Pane, view the first merged envelope. (To view the other envelopes, click the button located toward the top of the task pane containing the two right-pointing arrows.)
13. Click the *Next: Complete the merge* hyperlink located toward the bottom of the task pane.
14. At the sixth Mail Merge Task Pane, click the *Edit individual envelopes* hyperlink that displays in the Merge section of the task pane.
15. At the Merge to New Document dialog box, make sure All is selected, and then click the OK button.
16. Save the merged envelopes in the normal manner in the *Word Chapter 01E* folder on your disk in drive A and name the document MC Client Envs.
17. Print MC Client Envs. (This document will print four envelopes. Check with your instructor about specific steps for printing envelopes. You may need to hand feed envelopes in your printer.)
18. Close MC Client Envs.
19. At the sixth Mail Merge Task Pane, save the envelope main document in the normal manner in the *Word Chapter 01E* folder on your disk in drive A and name it MC Env Main Doc.
20. Close MC Env Main Doc.

Preparing Labels Using the Mail Merge Wizard

Create mailing labels for records in a data source file in much the same way that you create envelopes. Use the Mail Merge Wizard to guide you through the steps for preparing mailing labels.

exercise 3

PREPARING LABELS USING THE MAIL MERGE WIZARD

1. At a clear document screen, click Tools, point to Letters and Mailings, and then click Mail Merge Wizard.
2. At the first Mail Merge Task Pane, click the Labels option in the Select document type section.
3. Click the *Next: Starting document* hyperlink.
4. At the second Mail Merge Task Pane, make sure the Change document layout option is selected in the Select starting document section.
5. Click the *Label options* hyperlink in the Change document layout section of the task pane.
6. At the Label Options dialog box, complete the following steps:
   a. Make sure *Avery standard* displays in the Label products option box.
   b. Scroll down the Product number list box until *5260 - Address* is visible, and then click it.
   c. Click OK to close the dialog box.

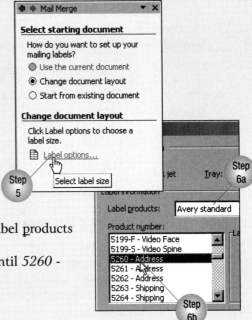

7. Click the *Next: Select recipients* hyperlink located toward the bottom of the task pane.
8. At the third Mail Merge Task Pane, make sure the Use an existing list option is selected in the Select recipients section.
9. Click the *Browse* hyperlink located in the Use an existing list section.
10. At the Select Data Source dialog box, complete the following steps:
    a. Change the Look in option to *3½ Floppy (A:)*.
    b. Double-click the *Word Chapter 01E* folder.
    c. Double-click *MC Client List* in the Select Data Source list box.
    d. At the Mail Merge Recipients dialog box, click OK.
11. Click the *Next: Arrange your labels* hyperlink located toward the bottom of the third Mail Merge Task Pane.
12. At the fourth Mail Merge Task Pane, complete the following steps:
    a. Click the *Address block* hyperlink located in the Arrange your labels section of the task pane.

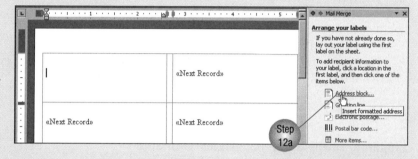

    b. At the Insert Address Block dialog box, click OK. (This inserts «AddressBlock» in the first label. The other labels contain the «Next Record» field.)
    c. Click the Update all labels button in the task pane. (This adds the «AddressBlock» field after each «Next Record» field in the second and subsequent labels.)
13. Click the *Next: Preview your labels* hyperlink located toward the bottom of the fourth Mail Merge Task Pane. (You may need to click the down-pointing triangle at the bottom of the task pane to display the *Next: Preview your labels* hyperlink.)
14. At the fifth Mail Merge Task Pane, view the first merged labels. (Only four labels will contain names and addresses since you only have four records in the MC Client List data source file.)
15. Click the *Next: Complete the merge* hyperlink located toward the bottom of the task pane.
16. At the sixth Mail Merge Task Pane, save the merged labels document in the normal manner in the *Word Chapter 01E* folder on your disk in drive A and name the document MC Client Labels.
17. Print MC Client Labels. (Check with your instructor about specific steps for printing labels. You may need to hand feed paper into the printer.)
18. Close MC Client Labels.

Preparing a Directory Using the Mail Merge Wizard

When merging letters, envelopes, or mailing labels, a new form is created for each record. For example, if there are eight records in the data source file that is merged with a letter, eight letters are created. If there are twenty records in a data source file that is merged with a mailing label, twenty labels are created. In some situations, you may want merged information to remain on the same page. This is useful, for example, when creating a list such as a directory or address list. Use the Mail Merge Wizard to create a merged directory. In exercise 4, you will create a directory that displays the last name, first name, and Zip Code for the four records in the MC Client List.

exercise 4

PREPARING A DIRECTORY LIST USING THE MAIL MERGE WIZARD

1. At a clear document screen, set left tabs at the 1-inch mark, the 2.5-inch mark, and the 4-inch mark on the Ruler, and then press the Tab key. (This moves the insertion point to the tab set at the 1-inch mark.)
2. Click Tools, point to Letters and Mailings, and then click Mail Merge Wizard.
3. At the first Mail Merge Task Pane, click the Directory option in the Select document type section.
4. Click the *Next: Starting document* hyperlink.
5. At the second Mail Merge Task Pane, make sure the Use the current document option is selected in the Select starting document section.
6. Click the *Next: Select recipients* hyperlink located toward the bottom of the task pane.
7. At the third Mail Merge Task Pane, make sure the Use an existing list option is selected in the Select recipients section.
8. Click the *Browse* hyperlink located in the Use an existing list section.
9. At the Select Data Source dialog box, complete the following steps:
   a. Change the Look in option to *3½ Floppy (A:)*.
   b. Double-click the Word Chapter 01E folder.
   c. Double-click *MC Client List* in the Select Data Source list box.
   d. At the Mail Merge Recipients list box, click OK.
10. Click the *Next: Arrange your directory* hyperlink located toward the bottom of the third Mail Merge Task Pane.
11. At the fourth Mail Merge Task Pane, complete the following steps:
    a. Click the *More items* hyperlink located in the Arrange your directory section of the task pane.
    b. At the Insert Merge Field dialog box, click *Last Name* in the list box, and then click the Insert button. (This inserts the «Last_Name» field in the document.)
    c. Click the Close button to close the Insert Merge Field dialog box.

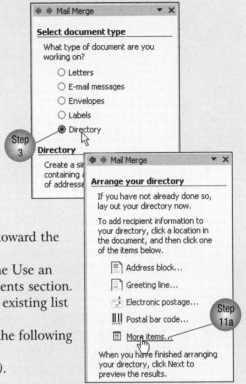

Step 3

Step 11a

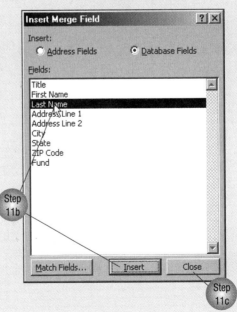

Step 11b

Step 11c

d. Press the Tab key to move the insertion point to the tab set at the 2.5-inch mark.

e. Click the *More items* hyperlink.

f. At the Insert Merge Field dialog box, click *First Name* in the list box, and then click the Insert button. (This inserts the «First_Name» field in the document.)

g. Click the Close button to close the Insert Merge Field dialog box.

h. Press the Tab key to move the insertion point to the tab set at the 4-inch mark.

i. Click the *More items* hyperlink.

j. At the Insert Merge Field dialog box, click *ZIP Code* in the list box, and then click the Insert button. (This inserts the «ZIP_Code» field in the document.)

k. Click the Close button to close the Insert Merge Field dialog box.

l. Press the Enter key once.

12. Click the *Next: Preview your directory* hyperlink located toward the bottom of the fourth Mail Merge Task Pane.

13. At the fifth Mail Merge Task Pane, view the first merged record. (Only the first record displays at this step.)

14. Click the *Next: Complete the merge* hyperlink located toward the bottom of the task pane.

15. At the sixth Mail Merge Task Pane, click the *To New Document* hyperlink located in the Merge section of the task pane.

16. At the Merge to New Document dialog box, make sure All is selected, and then click OK.

17. At the document (with the four records displayed), make the following changes:

a. Press the Enter key twice.

b. Press Ctrl + Home to move the insertion point back to the beginning of the document.

c. Turn on bold.

d. Press the Tab key and then key **Last Name**.

e. Press the Tab key and then key **First Name**.

f. Press the Tab key and then key **Zip Code**.

18. Save the directory list document in the normal manner in the *Word Chapter 01E* folder on your disk in drive A and name the document MC Directory.

19. Print MC Directory.

20. Close MC Directory.

21. At the sixth Mail Merge Task Pane, save the directory list main document in the normal manner in the *Word Chapter 01E* folder on your disk in drive A and name it MC List Main Doc.

22. Close MC List Main Doc.

Completing a Merge Using Outlook Information as the Data Source

If you maintain a contacts list in Microsoft Outlook, you can use the list as the data source to merge with a main document to create form letters, envelopes, labels, directories, and/or e-mail messages. The specific steps for preparing a merge using Outlook information vary depending on your system configuration and contacts data in Outlook. To create and distribute an e-mail message using an Outlook contacts list, you would complete the following basic steps. Check with your instructor to determine if you have access to Outlook and an Outlook contacts list and to obtain specific information on completing the steps.

WORD

STEPS TO CREATE AN E-MAIL MESSAGE MERGED WITH AN OUTLOOK CONTACT LIST (OPTIONAL EXERCISE)

1. At a clear document screen click Tools, point to Letters and Mailings, and then click Mail Merge Wizard.
2. At the first Mail Merge Task Pane, click *E-mail messages* in the Select document type section, and then click the *Next: Starting document* hyperlink.
3. At the second Mail Merge Task Pane, make sure the Use the current document option is selected in the Select starting document section of the task pane, and then click the *Next: Select recipients* hyperlink.
4. At the third Mail Merge Task Pane, click *Select from Outlook contacts* in the Select recipients section of the task pane.
5. Click the *Choose Contacts Folder* hyperlink.
6. At the Select Contact List folder dialog box, click the desired contact list, and then click OK.
7. At the Mail Merge Recipients dialog box, click OK. (If you do not want all individuals in the Mail Merge Recipients dialog box to receive the e-mail, remove the check mark preceding the name.)
8. Move to the next step by clicking the *Next: Write your e-mail message* hyperlink.
9. At the fourth Mail Merge Task Pane, create the e-mail message in the document screen.
10. When the e-mail message is complete, click the *Next: Preview your e-mail message* hyperlink.
11. At the fifth Mail Merge Task Pane, make sure the information is merged properly, and then click the *Next: Complete the merge* hyperlink.
12. At the sixth Mail Merge Task Pane, click the *Electronic Mail* hyperlink.
13. At the Merge to E-mail dialog box, specify the distribution settings and then click OK.

Editing Merge Documents

Edit a main document in the normal manner. Open the document, make the required changes, and then save the document. Since a data source is actually an Access database file, you cannot open it in the normal manner. Edit a data source file using the Mail Merge Wizard or with buttons on the Mail Merge toolbar.

Editing Merge Documents Using the Mail Merge Wizard

When you complete the six Mail Merge Wizard steps, you create a data source file and a main document. The data source file is associated with the main document. If you need to edit the main document, open it in the normal manner, make the required changes, and then start the Mail Merge Wizard. With a main document open, the Mail Merge Wizard begins with the third step. At this step, click the *Edit recipient list* hyperlink. At the Mail Merge Recipients dialog box, click the Edit button and then make the necessary edits to the fields in the records. Changes you make to the data source file are automatically saved. If you want to save edits made to a main document, you must save the changes.

1. Open MC Main Doc.
2. Make the following changes to the document:
   a. Change the date *February 19, 2003* to *February 26, 2003*.
   b. Select and then delete the last sentence in the second paragraph of text in the body of the letter. (This is the sentence that begins *Your financial future is our...*)
3. Start the Mail Merge Wizard by clicking Tools, pointing to Letters and Mailings, and then clicking Mail Merge Wizard. (Since a main document is open, the Mail Merge Wizard begins with step 3 instead of step 1.)
4. Edit the data source file by completing the following steps:
   a. Click the *Edit recipient list* hyperlink that displays in the Use an existing list section of the third Mail Merge Task Pane.
   b. At the Mail Merge Recipients dialog box, click the Edit button. (This displays the fields for the record for Kenneth Porter.)
   c. Click the Next button. (This displays the record for Carolyn Renquist.)
   d. Select the current address in the *Address Line 1* field and then key **7651 South 22nd**.
   e. Click the New Entry button.
   f. Key the following in the specified fields:

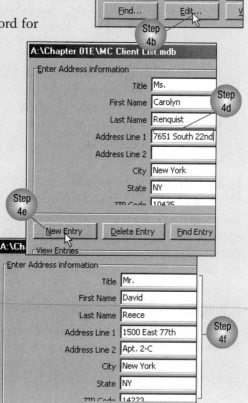

Title	=	**Mr.**
First Name	=	**David**
Last Name	=	**Reece**
Address Line 1	=	**1500 East 77th**
Address Line 2	=	**Apt. 2-C**
City	=	**New York**
State	=	**NY**
ZIP Code	=	**14223**
Fund	=	**Mutual Investment Fund**

   g. Delete the record for Wanda Houston by completing the following steps:
      1) Click the Previous button until the record for Wanda Houston displays.
      2) Click the Delete Entry button.
      3) At the message asking if you want to delete the entry, click the Yes button.
   h. Click the Close button.
   i. At the Mail Merge Recipients dialog box, click OK.
5. Click the *Next: Write your letter* hyperlink located toward the bottom of the third Mail Merge Task Pane.
6. At the fourth Mail Merge Task Pane, click the *Next: Preview your letters* hyperlink located toward the bottom of the task pane.

7. At the fifth Mail Merge Task Pane, click the *Next: Complete the merge* hyperlink located toward the bottom of the task pane.
8. At the sixth Mail Merge Task Pane, click the *Edit individual letters* hyperlink located in the Merge section of the task pane.
9. At the Merge to New Document dialog box, click OK.
10. Save the merged letters in the normal manner in the *Word Chapter 01E* folder on your disk in drive A and name the document MC Client Edited Ltrs 01.
11. Print MC Client Edited Ltrs 01. (This document will print four letters.)
12. Close MC Client Edited Ltrs 01.
13. At the sixth Mail Merge Task Pane, save the edited main document with the same name (MC Main Doc).
14. Close MC Main Doc.

Editing Merge Documents Using the Mail Merge Toolbar

The Mail Merge toolbar shown in figure 1.3 provides buttons you can use to edit a main document and/or a data source file. Display this toolbar by clicking View, pointing to Toolbars, and then clicking Mail Merge. The Mail Merge toolbar displays toward the top of the screen, generally between the Standard and Formatting toolbars (this location may vary).

HINT

With buttons on the Mail Merge toolbar, you can prepare merged documents without using the Mail Merge Wizard.

FIGURE

1.3 *Mail Merge Toolbar Buttons*

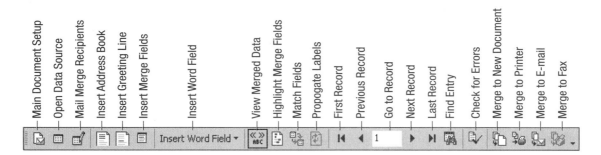

To edit a main document, open the document in the normal manner. You can insert additional fields in a main document by clicking the Insert Merge Fields button on the Mail Merge toolbar. At the Insert Merge Field dialog box, click the desired field, click the Insert button, and then click the Close button.

Insert Merge Fields

After editing the main document, you can merge it with the associated data source file. Click the Merge to New Document button on the Mail Merge toolbar and the main document is merged with the data source file to a new document. You can also merge the main document with the data source file directly to the printer by clicking the Merge to Printer button on the Mail Merge toolbar.

Merge to New Document

Edit a data source file by clicking the Mail Merge Recipients button on the Mail Merge toolbar. At the Mail Merge Recipients dialog box, click the Edit button, and then make the desired edits to the data source records.

Merge to Printer

Mail Merge Recipients

1. Open the MC Main Doc document in the normal manner. (This was the main document you created in exercise 1 and edited in exercise 5.)
2. Display the Mail Merge toolbar by clicking View, pointing to Toolbars, and then clicking Mail Merge.
3. Change the date in the letter from *February 26, 2003* to *March 6, 2003*.
4. Edit the MC Client List data source by completing the following steps:
   a. Click the Mail Merge Recipients button on the Mail Merge toolbar.
   b. At the Mail Merge Recipients dialog box, click the Edit button. (This displays the fields for the record for Kenneth Porter.)
   c. Click the Next button. (This displays the record for Carolyn Renquist.)
   d. Change the last name from *Renquist* to *Fanshaw*.
   e. Display the record for Dr. Amil Ranna and then delete the record.
   f. Click the Close button.
   g. At the Mail Merge Recipients dialog box, click OK.
5. Merge the edited data source file with MC Main Doc by completing the following steps:
   a. Click the Merge to New Document button on the Mail Merge toolbar.
   b. At the Merge to New Document dialog box, make sure All is selected, and then click OK.
6. Save the merged document in the *Word Chapter 01E* folder on your disk in drive A and name it MC Client Edited Ltrs 02.
7. Print and then close MC Client Edited Ltrs 02. (Three letters will print.)
8. Save and then close MC Main Doc.

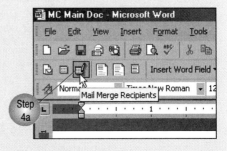

Inputting Text during a Merge

Word's Merge feature contains a large number of Word fields that can be inserted in a main document. In this chapter, you will learn about the *Fill-in* field that is used for information input at the keyboard during a merge. For more information on the other Word fields, please refer to the on-screen help.

Insert Word Field ▾

Insert Word Field

Situations may arise in which you do not need to keep all variable information in a data source file. For example, there may be variable information that changes on a regular basis such as a customer's monthly balance, a product price, and so on. Word lets you input variable information into a document during the merge using the keyboard. A Fill-in field is inserted in a main document by clicking the Insert Word Field button on the Mail Merge toolbar and then clicking Fill-in at the drop-down list. A document can contain any number of Fill-in fields.

To insert a Fill-in field, open a main document, and position the insertion point at the location in the document where you want the field to display. Click the Insert Word Field button on the Mail Merge toolbar and then click Fill-in at the drop-down list that displays. At the Insert Word Field: Fill-in dialog box shown in figure 1.4, key a short message indicating what should be entered at the keyboard, and then click OK. At the Microsoft Word dialog box with the message you entered displayed in the upper left corner, key text you want to display in the document, and then click OK. When the Fill-in field or fields are added, save the main document in the normal manner.

FIGURE

1.4 *Insert Word Field: Fill-In Dialog Box*

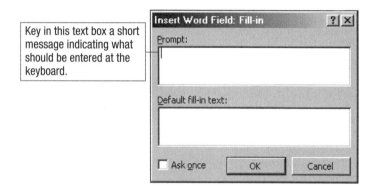

Key in this text box a short message indicating what should be entered at the keyboard.

To merge the main document with the data source file, click the Merge to New Document button on the Mail Merge toolbar or the Merge to Printer button. When Word merges the main document with the first record in the data source file, the Microsoft Word dialog box displays with the message you entered displayed in the upper left corner. Key the required information for the first record in the data source file and then click the OK button. If you are using the keyboard, key the required information, press the Tab key to make the OK button active, and then press Enter.

Word displays the dialog box again. Key the required information for the second record in the data source file and then click OK. Continue in this manner until the required information has been entered for each record in the data source file. Word then completes the merge.

HINT
Press Alt + Shift + N to display the Merge to New Document dialog box.

HINT
Press Alt + Shift + M to display the Merge to Printer dialog box.

exercise *7*

1. Edit the MC Main Doc main document so it
   includes Fill-in fields by completing the following
   steps:
   a. Open MC Main Doc.
   b. Turn on the display of the Mail Merge toolbar.
   c. Change the second paragraph in the body of
      the letter to the paragraph shown in figure 1.5.
      Insert the first Fill-in field (representative's
      name) by completing the following steps:
      1) Click the Insert Word Field button on the
         Mail Merge toolbar.
      2) At the drop-down menu that displays, click
         Fill-in.
      3) At the Insert Word Field: Fill-in dialog box,
         key **Insert rep name** in the Prompt text
         box.
      4) Click OK.
      5) At the Microsoft Word dialog box with *Insert
         rep name* displayed in the upper left corner,
         key **(representative's name)**, and then click
         OK.
   d. Complete steps
      similar to those in
      1c to insert the
      second Fill-in field
      (phone number),
      except key **Insert
      phone number** in
      the Prompt text
      box at the Insert Word Field: Fill-in dialog box and key **(phone number)** at the
      Microsoft Word dialog box.

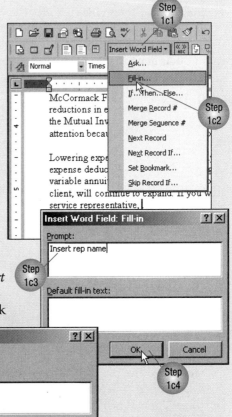

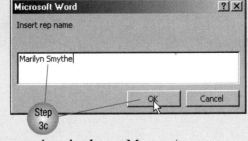

2. When the paragraph is completed, save the document with Save As and name it MC
   Main Doc Ltr2.
3. Merge the main document with the data source file by completing the following steps:
   a. Click the Merge to New Document button on the Mail Merge toolbar.
   b. At the Merge to New Document dialog box, make sure All is selected, and then click OK.
   c. When Word merges the main document
      with the first record, a dialog box displays
      with the message *Insert rep name* and the
      text *(representative's name)* selected. At this
      dialog box, key **Marilyn Smythe**, and then
      click OK.
   d. At the dialog box with the message *Insert
      phone number* and *(phone number)* selected,
      key **(646) 555-8944**, and then click OK.
   e. At the dialog box with the message *Insert rep name*, key **Anthony Mason** (over
      Marilyn Smythe), and then click OK.

WORD

     f. At the dialog box with the message *Insert phone number*, key **(646) 555-8901** (over the previous number), and then click OK.

     g. At the dialog box with the message *Insert rep name*, key **Faith Ostrom** (over *Anthony Mason*), and then click OK.

     h. At the dialog box with the message *Insert phone number*, key **(646) 555-8967** (over the previous number), and then click OK.

4. Save the merged document and name it EWd C01 Ex07.
5. Print and then close EWd C01 Ex07.
6. Save and then close MC Main Doc Ltr02.

<u>F I G U R E</u>

1.5   *Exercise 7*

Lowering expense charges is noteworthy because before the reduction, McCormack expense deductions were already among the lowest, far below most mutual funds and variable annuity accounts with similar objectives. At the same time, services for you, our client, will continue to expand. If you would like to discuss this change, please call our service representative, **(representative's name)**, at **(phone number)**.

Sorting Text

In Word, you can sort text in paragraphs, text in rows in tables, or records in a data source. Sorting can be done alphabetically, numerically, or by date. You can also select specific records from a data source to be merged with a main document. Word can perform the three types of sorts shown in figure 1.6.

<u>F I G U R E</u>

1.6   *Types of Sorts*

Alphanumeric: In an alphanumeric sort, Word arranges the text in the following order: special symbols such as @ and # first, numbers second, and letters third. You can tell Word to sort text in all uppercase letters first, followed by words beginning with uppercase letters, and then words beginning with lowercase letters.

Numeric: In a numeric sort, Word arranges the text in numeric order and ignores any alphabetic text. Only the numbers 0 through 9 and symbols pertaining to numbers are recognized. These symbols include $, %, ( ), a decimal point, a comma, and the symbols for the four basic operations: + (addition), - (subtraction, * (multiplication), and / (division).

Date: In a date sort, Word sorts dates that are expressed in common date format, such as 05-15-02; 05/15/02; May 15, 2002; or 15 May 2002. Word does not sort dates that include abbreviated month names without periods. Dates expressed as months, days, or years by themselves are also not sorted.

Sorting Text in Paragraphs

Text arranged in paragraphs can be sorted by the first character of the paragraph. This character can be a number, a symbol (such as $ or #), or a letter. The paragraphs to be sorted can be keyed at the left margin or indented with the Tab key. Unless you select paragraphs to be sorted, Word sorts the entire document.

Paragraphs can be sorted alphanumerically, numerically, or by date. In an alphanumeric sort, punctuation marks or special symbols are sorted first, followed by numbers, and then text. If you sort paragraphs either alphanumerically or numerically, dates are treated as regular numbers.

To sort text in paragraphs, open the document containing the paragraphs to be sorted. (If the document contains text you do not want sorted with the paragraphs, select the paragraphs.) Click Table and then Sort and the Sort Text dialog box displays as shown in figure 1.7. At this dialog box, make sure *Paragraphs* displays in the Sort by option and the Ascending option is selected, and then click OK or press Enter.

F I G U R E

1.7 *Sort Text Dialog Box*

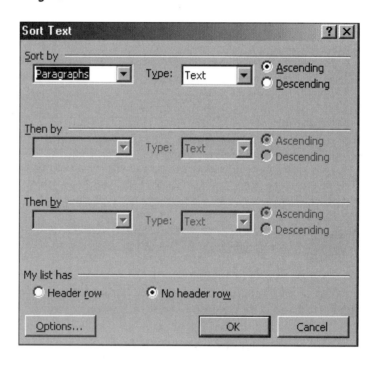

The Sort by option at the Sort Text dialog box has a default setting of *Paragraphs*. This default setting changes depending on the text in the document. For example, if you are sorting a table, the Sort by option has a default setting of *Column 1*. If you are sorting only the first word of each paragraph in the document, leave the Sort by option at the default of *Paragraphs*.

The Type option at the Sort Text dialog box has a default setting of *Text*. This can be changed to *Number* or *Date*. Figure 1.6 specifies how Word will sort numbers and dates.

When Word sorts paragraphs that are separated by two hard returns (two strokes of the Enter key), the hard returns are removed and inserted at the beginning of the document. If you want the sorted text separated by hard returns, you will need to insert the hard returns by positioning the insertion point where you want the hard return, and then pressing the Enter key.

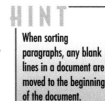

HINT

When sorting paragraphs, any blank lines in a document are moved to the beginning of the document.

exercise

SORTING PARAGRAPHS ALPHABETICALLY

1. Open Word Bibliography.
2. Save the document with Save As and name it EWd C01 Ex08.
3. Sort the paragraphs alphabetically by the last name by completing the following steps:

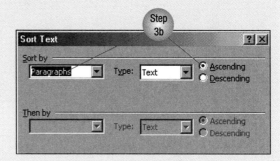
Step 3b

   a. Click Table and then Sort.
   b. At the Sort Text dialog box, make sure *Paragraphs* displays in the Sort by option box and the Ascending option is selected.
   c. Click OK.
   d. Deselect the text.
   e. Delete the hard returns at the beginning of the document.
   f. Add space below each paragraph by completing the following steps:
      1) Press Ctrl + A to select the entire document.
      2) Click Format and then Paragraph.
      3) At the Paragraph dialog box with the Indents and Spacing tab selected, click the up-pointing triangle at the right side of the After text box (in the Spacing section) until *12 pt* displays in the text box.
      4) Click OK to close the dialog box.
   g. Deselect the text.
4. Save, print, and then close EWd C01 Ex08.

Changing Sort Options

The Sort by options will also vary depending on selections at the Sort Options dialog box shown in figure 1.8. To display the Sort Options dialog box, open a document containing text to be sorted and click Table and then Sort. At the Sort Text dialog box, click the Options button.

1.8 Sort Options Dialog Box

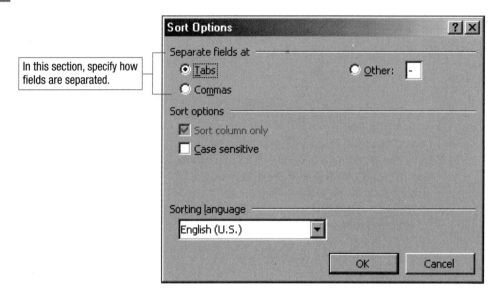

In this section, specify how fields are separated.

The Separate fields at section of the dialog box contains three options. The first option, Tabs, is selected by default. At this setting, Word assumes that text to be sorted is divided by tabs. This can be changed to Commas or Other. With the Other setting, you can specify the character that divides text to be sorted. For example, suppose a document contains first and last names in paragraphs separated by a space and you want to sort by the last name. To do this, you would click Other at the Sort Options dialog box, and then press the spacebar. (This inserts a space, which is not visible, in the Other text box.) If names are separated by a comma, click Commas as the separator.

The Sort Options dialog box contains two choices in the Sort options section. The first choice, Sort column only, sorts only the selected column. This choice is dimmed unless a column of text is selected. If a check mark appears in the Case sensitive check box, Word will sort text so that a word whose first letter is a capital letter is sorted before any word with the same first letter in lowercase. This option is available only if *Text* is selected in the Type option box at the Sort Text dialog box.

When you make changes at the Sort Options dialog box, the choices available with the Sort by option at the Sort Text dialog box will vary. For example, if you click Other at the Sort Options dialog box, and then press the spacebar, the choices for the Sort by option at the Sort Text dialog box will include *Word 1, Word 2, Word 3*, and so forth.

exercise

1. Open Word Document 01.
2. Save the document with Save As and name it EWd C01 Ex09.
3. Sort the text alphabetically by first name by completing the following steps:
   a. Click T̲able and then S̲ort.
   b. At the Sort Text dialog box, make sure *Paragraphs* displays in the S̲ort by option box and the A̲scending option is selected.
   c. Click OK or press Enter.
   d. Deselect the text.
4. Save and then print EWd C01 Ex09.
5. With EWd C01 Ex09 still displayed, sort the text by the last name (second word) by completing the following steps:
   a. Click T̲able and then S̲ort.
   b. At the Sort Text dialog box, click the O̲ptions button.
   c. At the Sort Options dialog box, click Other, and then press the spacebar.
   d. Click OK or press Enter.
   e. At the Sort Text dialog box, click the down-pointing triangle at the right side of the S̲ort by option box (contains the word *Paragraphs*), and then click *Word 2* at the drop-down list.
   f. Make sure the A̲scending option is selected.
   g. Click OK or press Enter.
   h. Deselect the text.
6. Save, print, and then close EWd C01 Ex09.

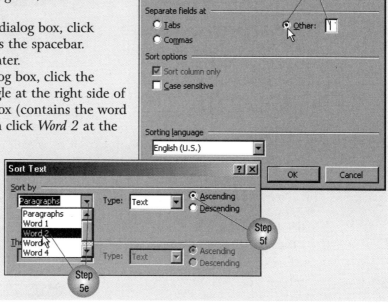

Sorting Text in Columns

Text arranged in columns with tabs between the columns can be sorted alphabetically or numerically. Text in columns must be separated with tabs. When sorting text in columns, Word sorts by *fields*. Text keyed at the left margin is considered *Field 1*, text keyed at the first tab stop is considered *Field 2,* and so on. To sort text arranged in columns, display the Sort Text dialog box, and then click the O̲ptions button. At the Sort Options dialog box, make sure T̲abs is selected in the Separate fields at section of the dialog box, and then click OK or press Enter. At the Sort Text dialog box, display the appropriate field number in the S̲ort by option box, and then click OK or press Enter.

HINT

Columns of text to be sorted must be separated by tabs.

When sorting text in columns, only one tab can be inserted between columns when keying the text. If you press the Tab key more than once between columns, Word recognizes each tab as a separate column. In this case, the field number you specify may correspond to an empty column rather than the desired column.

1. Open Word Tab 01.
2. Save the document with Save As and name it EWd C01 Ex10.
3. Sort the first column alphabetically by last name by completing the following steps:
   a. Select the text in all three columns except the headings.
   b. Click Table and then Sort.
   c. At the Sort Text dialog box, click the Options button.
   d. At the Sort Options dialog box, click the Tabs option in the Separate fields at section.
   e. Click OK to close the Sort Options dialog box.
   f. At the Sort Text dialog box, click the down-pointing triangle at the right side of the Sort by option box, and then click *Field 2* at the drop-down list. (Field 2 is the first tab stop.)
   g. Make sure Ascending is selected.
   h. Click OK or press Enter.
   i. Deselect the text.

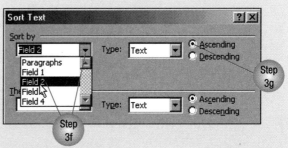

4. Save and then print EWd C01 Ex10.
5. With EWd C01 Ex10 still open, sort the third column of text numerically by completing the following steps:
   a. Select the text in all three columns except the headings.
   b. Click Table and then Sort.
   c. At the Sort Text dialog box, click the Options button.
   d. At the Sort Options dialog box, click the Tabs option in the Separate fields at section.
   e. Click OK to close the Sort Options dialog box.
   f. At the Sort Text dialog box, click the down-pointing triangle at the right side of the Sort by option box, and then click *Field 4* at the drop-down list. (Field 4 is the third tab stop.)
   g. Click the down-pointing triangle at the right side of the Type option box, and then click *Number* at the drop-down list.
   h. Make sure Ascending is selected.
   i. Click OK or press Enter.
   j. Deselect the text.

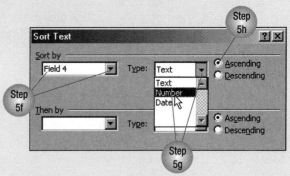

6. Save, print, and then close EWd C01 Ex10.

Sorting on More than One Field

When sorting text, you can sort on more than one field. For example, in the text shown in the columns in figure 1.9, you can sort the text alphabetically by department and then tell Word to sort the last names alphabetically within the departments. To do this, you would tell Word to sort on Field 3 (the second tab stop) and then sort on Field 2 (the first tab stop). Word sorts the second column of text (Field 3) alphabetically by department, and then sorts the names in the first column of text (Field 2) by last name. This results in the columns displaying as shown in figure 1.10.

HINT

When sorting on two fields, Word sorts on the first field and then sorts the second field within the first.

FIGURE

1.9 *Columns*

Employee	Department	Ext.
Thomas, Megan	Financial Services	474
Dey, Richard	Administrative Services	122
Lattin, Kim	Financial Services	430
Ebsen, William	Administrative Services	153
Blanchett, Jan	Financial Services	436

FIGURE

1.10 *Sorted Columns*

Employee	Department	Ext.
Dey, Richard	Administrative Services	122
Ebsen, William	Administrative Services	153
Blanchett, Jan	Financial Services	436
Lattin, Kim	Financial Services	430
Thomas, Megan	Financial Services	474

Notice that the departments in the second column in figure 1.10 are alphabetized and that the last names *within* the departments are alphabetized. For example, *Dey* is sorted before *Ebsen* within *Administrative Services*.

exercise 11

SORTING ON TWO FIELDS

1. Open Word Tab 01.
2. Save the document with Save As and name it EWd C01 Ex11.
3. Sort the text in columns alphabetically by department and then alphabetically by last name by completing the following steps:
   a. Select the text in all three columns except the headings.
   b. Click Table and then Sort.
   c. At the Sort Text dialog box, click the Options button.

d. At the Sort Options dialog box, click the <u>T</u>abs option in the Separate fields at section.
e. Click OK or press Enter to close the Sort Options dialog box.
f. At the Sort Text dialog box, click the down-pointing triangle at the right side of the <u>S</u>ort by option box, and then click *Field 3* at the drop-down list. (Field 3 is the second tab stop.)
g. Click the down-pointing triangle at the right side of the <u>T</u>hen by option box and then click *Field 2* from the drop-down list.
h. Make sure <u>A</u>scending is selected on both fields.
i. Click OK or press Enter.
j. Deselect the text.
4. Save, print, and then close EWd C01 Ex11.

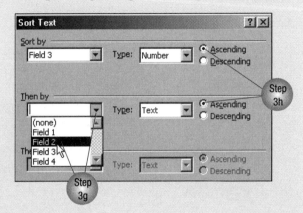

Specifying a Header Row

The Sort Text dialog box contains the option Header <u>r</u>ow in the My list has section. If a document contains only columns of text with headings, you can use this option to tell Word to sort all text except for the headings of the columns.

exercise 12

1. Open Word Tab 01.
2. Save the document with Save As and name it EWd C01 Ex12.
3. Sort the third column of text numerically by the extension number by completing the following steps:
   a. With the columns displayed on the document screen, position the insertion point anywhere within the document.
   b. Click <u>T</u>able and then <u>S</u>ort.
   c. At the Sort Text dialog box, make sure the Header <u>r</u>ow in the My list has section of the dialog box is selected.
   d. Click the <u>O</u>ptions button.
   e. At the Sort Options dialog box, click the <u>T</u>abs option in the Separate fields at section.
   f. Click OK to close the Sort Options dialog box.
   g. At the Sort Text dialog box, click the down-pointing triangle at the right side of the <u>S</u>ort by option box, and then click *Ext.* at the drop-down list.
   h. Make sure <u>A</u>scending is selected.

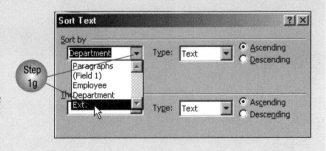

i. If there is any text displayed in the <u>T</u>hen by option box, click the down-pointing triangle to the right of the box, and then click *(none)* at the drop-down list.

j. Click OK or press Enter.

k. Deselect the text.

4. Save, print, and then close EWd C01 Ex12.

Sorting Text in Tables

Sorting text in columns within tables is very similar to sorting columns of text separated by tabs. The same principles that apply to sorting columns of text also apply to sorting text within table columns. If a table contains a header row, you can tell Word not to include the header row when sorting by clicking Header <u>r</u>ow at the Sort dialog box. (The Sort Text dialog box becomes the Sort dialog box when sorting a table.) You can also select the cells in the table except the header row and then complete the sort.

If Header <u>r</u>ow is selected at the Sort dialog box, the information in the header row becomes the <u>S</u>ort by options. For example, in the table shown in figure 1.11, if Header <u>r</u>ow is selected, the <u>S</u>ort by options are *Salesperson, January Sales,* and *February Sales.*

FIGURE

1.11 *Table*

Salesperson	January Sales	February Sales
Underwood, Gary	214,368.10	208,438.50
Russell, Felicia	243,655.00	230,541.65
Meyers, Alan	198,560.15	187,240.75
Epstein, Byron	215,466.35	204,233.45

exercise 13

SORTING TEXT ALPHABETICALLY IN A TABLE

1. Open Word Table 01.
2. Save the document with Save As and name it EWd C01 Ex13.
3. Sort the text alphabetically in the first column by completing the following steps:
   a. Position the insertion point anywhere within the table.
   b. Click T<u>a</u>ble and then <u>S</u>ort.
   c. At the Sort dialog box, make sure the Header <u>r</u>ow in the My list has section of the dialog box is selected.
   d. Make sure *Salesperson* displays in the <u>S</u>ort by option box.
   e. Make sure <u>A</u>scending is selected.
   f. Click OK or press Enter.
4. Save, print, and then close EWd C01 Ex13.

In exercise 13, the Header row option at the Sort dialog box was selected. You can also sort text in a table by first selecting the cells you want sorted and then displaying the Sort dialog box.

| | SORTING NUMBERS IN A TABLE IN DESCENDING ORDER |

1. Open Word Table 01.
2. Save the document with Save As and name it EWd C01 Ex14.
3. Sort the numbers in the second column in descending order by completing the following steps:
   a. Select all of the cells in the table except the cells in the first row.
   b. Click Table and then Sort.
   c. At the Sort dialog box, click the down-pointing triangle at the right side of the Sort by option, and then click *Column 2* at the drop-down list.
   d. Click Descending.
   e. Click OK or press Enter.
4. With the insertion point positioned anywhere in the table, display the Table AutoFormat dialog box, and then apply the *Table 3D effects 3* table style.
5. Save, print, and then close EWd C01 Ex14.

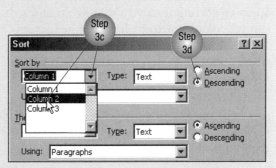

Sorting Records in a Data Source

To sort records in a data source, open the main document, display the Mail Merge toolbar, and then click the Mail Merge Recipients button. This displays the Mail Merge Recipients dialog box shown in figure 1.12 where you can sort the various fields in the data source and/or perform advanced sorts.

F I G U R E

1.12 *Mail Merge Recipients Dialog Box*

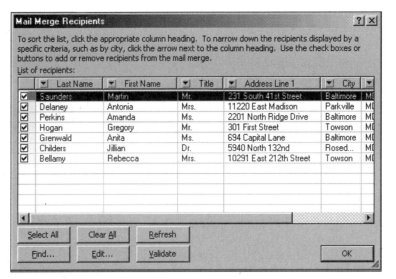

Click the column heading to sort data in a specific column in ascending order. To perform additional types of sorts, click the down-pointing triangle at the left of the column heading, and then click *(Advanced...)* at the drop-down list. This displays the Filter and Sort dialog box. At this dialog box, click the S<u>o</u>rt Records tab and the dialog box displays as shown in figure 1.13. The options at the Filter and Sort dialog box with the S<u>o</u>rt Records tab selected are similar to the options available at the Sort Text (and Sort) dialog box.

HINT

Decide the order in which you want your merged documents printed and then sort the data before merging.

FIGURE

1.13 *Filter and Sort Dialog Box with S<u>o</u>rt Records Tab Selected*

exercise **15**

SORTING DATA IN A DATA SOURCE

1. Open LFS Main Doc. (If a message displays telling you that Word cannot find the data source, click the <u>F</u>ind Data Source button. At the Select Data Source dialog box, change the Look <u>i</u>n option to the *Word Chapter 01E* folder on your disk and then double-click *LFS Clients* in the list box.)

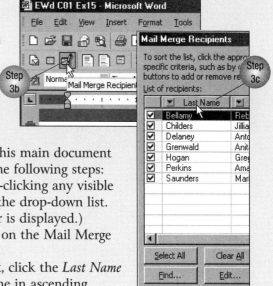

2. Save the document with Save As and name it EWd C01 LFS Main Doc.
3. Sort records in the data source attached to this main document alphabetically by last name by completing the following steps:
   a. Display the Mail Merge toolbar by right-clicking any visible toolbar and then clicking *Mail Merge* at the drop-down list. (Skip this step if the Mail Merge toolbar is displayed.)
   b. Click the Mail Merge Recipients button on the Mail Merge toolbar.
   c. At the Mail Merge Recipients dialog box, click the *Last Name* column heading. (This sorts the last name in ascending alphabetical order.)
   d. Scroll to the right to display the *ZIP Code* field and then click the *ZIP Code* column heading. (This sorts the Zip Codes in order from lowest to highest.)

WORD

e. Sort by Zip Codes and then by last name by completing the following steps:
   1) Click the down-pointing triangle at the left side of the *ZIP Code* column heading.
   2) Click *(Advanced...)* at the drop-down list.
   3) At the Filter and Sort dialog box, click the Sort Records tab.
   4) Make sure *ZIP Code* displays in the Sort by option box and Ascending is selected.
   5) Make sure *Last Name* displays in the Then by option box and Ascending is selected (located to the right of the Then by option box).
   6) Click OK to close the Filter and Sort dialog box.
   7) Click OK to close the Mail Merge Recipients dialog box.
f. View the first merged letter (for Mr. Martin Saunders) and then click the Next Record button on the Mail Merge toolbar.
g. Continue clicking the Next Record button to view the sorted letters. (The order of the letters should be— *Saunders, Bellamy, Hogan, Grenwald, Childers, Delaney,* and *Perkins*.)
   (Optional: If you want to print the merged document, click the Merge to Printer button on the Mail Merge toolbar and then click OK at the Merge to Printer dialog box.)
4. Save the document with Save As and name it EWd C01 Ex15.
5. Close EWd C01 Ex15.

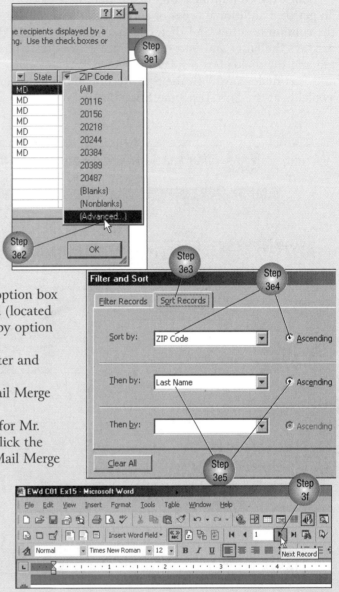

Selecting Records

If you have created a main document and a data source file to create personalized form letters, situations may arise where you want to merge the main document with specific records in the data source. For example, you may want to send a letter to customers with a specific Zip Code or who live in a certain city.

One method for selecting specific records is to display the Mail Merge Recipients dialog box and then insert or remove check marks from specific records. For example, to select records for a specific city, remove check marks from

any record that does not contain the desired city. To remove or insert a check mark, click the check box that displays at the beginning of the record. If you will be selecting only a few check boxes, click the Clear All button. This removes the check marks from all of the check boxes. If you will be selecting most of the records in the data source, leave the marks in the check boxes (or click the Select All button to insert check marks in all check boxes).

	SELECTING RECORDS FOR A SPECIFIC CITY

1. Open EWd C01 LFS Main Doc.
2. Save the document with Save As and name it EWd C01 Ex16.
3. Click the Mail Merge Recipients button on the Mail Merge toolbar.
4. At the Mail Merge Recipients dialog box, select the records of those individuals living in the city of Rosedale by completing the following steps:

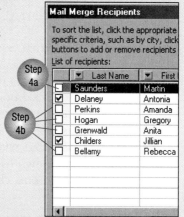

   a. Click the check box preceding the last name *Saunders*. (This removes the check mark from the check box.)
   b. Click the check box before the following last names— *Perkins*, *Hogan*, *Grenwald*, and *Bellamy*. (The only records that should be checked are those for *Delaney* and *Childers*. These individuals live in the city of Rosedale.)
   c. Click OK to close the Mail Merge Recipients dialog box.
   d. View the first merged letter and then click the Next Record to view the next letter. Click the Next Record and/or Previous Record button to view the two merged letters. *(Optional: If you want to print the merged document, click the Merge to Printer button on the Mail Merge toolbar and then click OK at the Merge to Printer dialog box.)*
5. Save and then close EWd C01 Ex16.

Using check boxes to select specific records is useful in a data source containing a limited number of records, but may not be practical in a data source containing many records. In a large data source, use options from the Filter and Sort dialog box with the Filter Records tab selected, shown in figure 1.14, to select specific records for merging with the main document that meet certain criteria. For example, in exercise 17, you will select records of clients with a Zip Code higher than 20300.

1.14 Filter and Sort Dialog Box with Filter Records Tab Selected

Filter and Sort

Filter Records | Sort Records

Field: | Comparison: | Compare to:

Clear All | OK | Cancel

When you select a field from the Field drop-down list, Word automatically inserts *Equal to* in the Comparison option box. You can make other comparisons. Clicking the down-pointing triangle to the right of the Comparison option box causes a drop-down list to display with these additional options: *Not equal to, Less than, Greater than, Less than or equal, Greater than or equal, is blank*, and *is not blank*. Use one of these options to create a select equation. For example, select all customers with a Zip Code higher than 90543 by clicking *ZIP Code* at the Field drop-down list. Click the down-pointing triangle at the right of the Comparison option box, click *Greater than*, and then key **90543** in the Compare to text box.

exercise 17

SELECTING RECORDS WITH SPECIFIC ZIP CODES

1. Open EWd C01 LFS Main Doc.
2. Save the document with Save As and name it EWd C01 Ex17.
3. Select the records with a Zip Code higher than 20300 by completing the following steps:
   a. Click the Mail Merge Recipients button on the Mail Merge toolbar.
   b. Scroll to the right until the ZIP Code field is visible, click the down-pointing triangle at the left of the *ZIP Code* column heading, and then click *(Advanced...)* at the drop-down list.
   c. At the Filter and Sort dialog box with the Filter Records tab selected, click the down-pointing triangle at the right side of the Field option box, and then click *ZIP Code* at the drop-down list. (You will need to scroll down the list to display *ZIP Code*. When *ZIP Code* is inserted in the Field option box, *Equal to* is inserted in the Comparison option box and the insertion point is positioned in the Compare to text box.)

   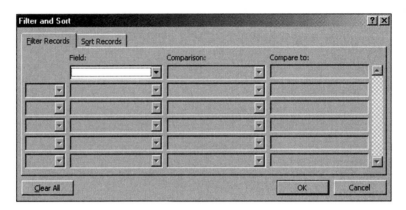

   Step 3c
   Step 3e
   Step 3d

   Filter and Sort
   Filter Records | Sort Records
   Field: | Comparison: | Compare to:
   ZIP Code | Equal to | 20300
   And | | Equal to
   | | Not equal to
   | | Less than
   | | Greater than
   | | Less than or equal
   | | Greater than or equal
   | | Is blank
   | | Is not blank
   | | Contains
   | | Does not contain

   d. Key **20300** in the Compare to text box.
   e. Click the down-pointing triangle at the right of the Comparison option box and then click *Greater than* at the drop-down list.

    f. Click OK to close the Filter and Sort dialog box.
    g. Click OK to close the Mail Merge Recipients dialog box.
    h. View the letters merged with the selected records.
        *(Optional: If you want to print the merged document, click the Merge to Printer button on the
        Mail Merge toolbar and then click OK at the Merge to Printer dialog box.)*
4. Save and then close EWd C01 Ex17.

When a field is selected from the Field option box, Word automatically
inserts *And* in the first box at the left side of the dialog box. This can be changed,
if needed, to *Or*. With the *And* and *Or* options, you can specify more than one
condition for selecting records. For example, in exercise 18, you will select all
records of clients living in the cities of *Rosedale* or *Towson*. If the data source file
contained another field such as a specific financial plan for each customer, you
could select all customers in a specific city that subscribe to a specific financial
plan. For this situation, you would use the *And* option.

If you want to clear the current options at the Filter and Sort dialog box with
the Filter Records tab selected, click the Clear All button. This clears any text
from text boxes and leaves the dialog box on the screen. Click Cancel if you want
to close the Filter and Sort dialog box without specifying any records.

 exercise 18

SELECTING RECORDS CONTAINING SPECIFIC CITIES

1. Open EWd C01 LFS Main Doc.
2. Save the document with Save As and name it EWd C01 Ex18.
3. Select the records that contain *Rosedale* or *Towson* by completing the following steps:
    a. Click the Mail Merge Recipients button on the Mail Merge toolbar.
    b. Click the down-pointing triangle at the left of the *Last Name* column heading and
        then click *(Advanced...)* at the drop-down list.
    c. At the Filter and Sort dialog box with the Filter Records tab selected, click the down-
        pointing triangle to the right of the Field option box, and then click *City* at the drop-
        down list. (You will need to scroll down the list to display this field.)
    d. With the insertion point positioned in the Compare to text box, key **Rosedale**.
    e. Click the down-pointing triangle to the right of the option box containing the word
        And (at the left side of the dialog box) and then click *Or* at the drop-down list.
    f. Click the down-pointing triangle to the right of the second Field option box and then
        click *City* at the drop-down list. (You will need to scroll down the list to display this
        field.)
    g. With the insertion point
        positioned in the second
        Compare to text box
        (the one below the box
        containing *Rosedale*), key
        Towson.
    h. Click OK to close the
        Filter and Sort dialog
        box.

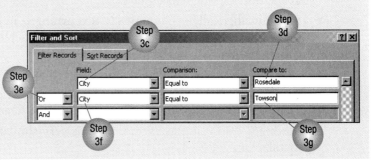

i. Click OK to close the Mail Merge Recipients dialog box.
j. View the letters merged with the selected records.
(Optional: If you want to print the merged document, click the Merge to Printer button on the Mail Merge toolbar and then click OK at the Merge to Printer dialog box.)
4. Save and then close EWd C01 Ex18.

CHAPTER summary

➤ Word includes a Mail Merge Wizard you can use to create letters, envelopes, labels, directories, e-mail messages, and faxes, all with personalized information.

➤ Generally, a merge takes two documents—the data source file containing the variable information and the main document containing standard text along with fields identifying where variable information is inserted during the merge process.

➤ Variable information in a data source file is saved as a record. A record contains all of the information for one unit. A series of fields makes one record, and a series of records makes a data source file.

➤ The Mail Merge Wizard guides you through six steps for merging documents and presents a Mail Merge Task Pane for each step.

➤ You can create your own custom field at the Customize Address List dialog box.

➤ Edit a main document in the normal manner. Edit a data source file using the Mail Merge Wizard or with buttons on the Mail Merge toolbar.

➤ The Mail Merge toolbar contains buttons you can use to edit a main document and/or a data source file.

➤ Word lets you input variable information with the keyboard into a document during the merge. This Fill-in field is inserted in a main document by clicking the Insert Word Field button on the Mail Merge toolbar, and then clicking Fill-in at the drop-down list.

➤ You can sort text in paragraphs, text in table rows, or records in a data source. You can also select specific records from a data source to be merged with a main document.

➤ Word can perform these three types of sorts: alphanumeric, numeric, and date.

➤ Sort text arranged in paragraphs by the first character of the paragraph at the Sort Text dialog box.

➤ The Sort by option at the Sort Text dialog box has a default setting of *Paragraphs*. This default setting changes depending on the text in the document and the options specified at the Sort Options dialog box.

➤ Sort alphabetically or numerically text arranged in columns with tabs between the columns. Text keyed at the left margin is considered *Field 1*, text keyed at the first tab is considered *Field 2*, and so on.

➤ When sorting text, you can sort on more than one field.

➤ Use the option Header row in the My list has section of the Sort Text dialog box to tell Word to sort all text in columns except for the headings of the columns.

➤ Sorting text in columns within tables is very similar to sorting columns of text separated by tabs.

➤ Sort records in a data source at the Mail Merge Recipients dialog box. To display this dialog box, open the main document, display the Mail Merge toolbar, and then click the Mail Merge Recipients button on the Mail Merge toolbar.

➤ At the Mail Merge Recipients dialog box, click the column heading to sort the data in a specific field in ascending order.

➤ Sort records at the Filter and Sort dialog box with the Sort Records tab selected.

➤ Select specific records for merging with the main document with options at the Mail Merge Recipients dialog box or with options at the Filter and Sort dialog box with the Filter Records tab selected.

COMMANDS review

Command	Mouse/Keyboard
Begin Mail Merge Wizard	Tools, Letters and Mailings, Mail Merge Wizard
Display Mail Merge toolbar	View, Toolbars, Mail Merge
Display Sort Text dialog box	Table, Sort
Display Sort Options dialog box	Click Options button at Sort Text dialog box
Display Mail Merge Recipients dialog box	With main document open, click Mail Merge Recipients button on Mail Merge toolbar

CONCEPTS check

Completion: On a blank sheet of paper, indicate the correct term, command, or number for each item.

1. The Mail Merge Wizard guides you through this number of steps to prepare merge documents.
2. Generally, a merge takes two documents: the data source file and this document.
3. Variable information in a data source file is saved as this, which contains all of the information for one unit.
4. A data source file created using the Mail Merge Wizard is created and saved as this type of database file.
5. This inserts records on the same page, rather than creating a new form for each record.
6. Open a main document, start the Mail Merge Wizard, and the Wizard begins with this step.
7. Click this button on the Mail Merge toolbar and the main document is merged with the data source file to a new document.
8. Edit a data source by clicking this button on the Mail Merge toolbar.
9. This field is used for information input at the keyboard during a merge.
10. With the sorting feature, you can sort text in paragraphs, text in rows in tables, or records in this type of file.

11. These three types of sorts can be performed by Word's sort feature: alphanumeric, numeric, and this.
12. At this dialog box, you can sort text in paragraphs.
13. When sorting columns, text keyed at the first tab is considered to be this field number.
14. Click this option at the Sort Text dialog box to tell Word not to include the column headings in the sort.
15. With the insertion point positioned in a table, clicking Table and then Sort causes this dialog box to display.
16. At the Mail Merge Recipients dialog box, click this option to sort data in a specific column in ascending order.
17. Use options from this dialog box with the Filter Records tab selected to select specific records for merging with the main document.

SKILLS check

Assessment 1

1. Look at the information shown in figures 1.15 and 1.16.
2. Use the Mail Merge Wizard to prepare four letters using the information shown in figures 1.15 and 1.16. When completing the steps, consider the following:
   a. At step 3, create a data source file using the information shown in figure 1.15. Save the data source file in the *Word Chapter 01E* folder on your disk and name it SF Client List.
   b. At step 6, complete the following steps:
      1) Click the *Edit individual letters* hyperlink in the task pane.
      2) At the Merge to New Document dialog box, make sure All is selected, and then click the OK button.
      3) Save the merged letters in the normal manner in the *Word Chapter 01E* folder on your disk and name the document SF Client Letters.
      4) Print SF Client Letters. (This document will print four letters.)
      5) Close SF Client Letters.
      6) Save the main document in the normal manner in the Word Chapter 01E folder on your disk and name it SF Main Doc.

FIGURE

1.15 *Assessment 1*

Mr. and Mrs. Tony Benedetti
13114 East 203rd Street
Apt. 402
New Rochelle, NY 10342
Supplemental Retirement Plan

Ms. Theresa Dusek
12044 Ridgway Drive
(leave this blank)
New York, NY 10233
Firstline Retirement Plan

Mrs. Mary Arguello	Mr. Preston Miller
2554 Country Drive	120 South Broadway
Suite 105	(leave this blank)
Mount Vernon, NY 10539	New York, NY 10123
Personal Pension Plan	Supplemental Retirement Plan

FIGURE

1.16 *Assessment 1*

(current date)

««AddressBlock»»

««GreetingLine»»

Last year, «Title» «Last_Name», a law went into effect that changes the maximum amounts that may be contributed to defined contribution pension and tax-deferred annuity plans, such as those using Stradford Funds annuities. Generally, the changes slow down the rate at which the maximums will increase in the future. A likely result is that more people will reach the maximum and, if they wish to save more for their retirement, they will have to use after-tax savings instruments.

The amount of money you can voluntarily contribute to your «Plan» was expected to rise above the current maximum. The amendments will delay any cost-of-living adjustments, and the limit will probably not go up for several years. The changes in the law will have an effect on your next annuity statement. If you want to increase or decrease the amount you contribute to your «Plan», please let us know.

Sincerely,

Chris Warren
Director of Financial Services

XX:SF Client Letters

Assessment 2

1. Use the Mail Merge Wizard to prepare envelopes for the letters created in assessment 1.
2. Specify SF Client List as the data source file.
3. Save the merged envelope document in the *Word Chapter 01E* folder on your disk and name the document SF Client Envs.
4. Print the SF Client Envs document.
5. Do not save the envelope main document.

Assessment 3

1. Use the Mail Merge Wizard to prepare mailing labels for the names and addresses in the SF Client List.
2. Save the label document in the *Word Chapter 01E* folder on your disk and name the document SF Client Labels.
3. Print the SF Client Labels document.

Assessment 4

1. Open the SF Main Doc document.
2. Start the Mail Merge Wizard.
3. At the third step, click the *Edit recipient list* hyperlink and then click the Edit button at the Mail Merge Recipients dialog box. Make the following changes to the records:
   a. Display the record for Ms. Theresa Dusek and then change the address from *12044 Ridgway Drive* to *1390 Fourth Avenue*.
   b. Display the record for Mr. Preston Miller and add *and Mrs.* in the title (so the title field displays as *Mr. and Mrs.*).
   c. Display and then delete the record for Mrs. Mary Arguello.
4. At the sixth step, click the *Edit individual letters* hyperlink. At the Merge to New Document dialog box, click OK.
5. Save the merged letters with the name SF Edited Letters.
6. Print and then close SF Edited Letters.
7. Save and then close SF Main Doc.

Assessment 5

1. Open Word Document 02.
2. Save the document with Save As and name it EWd C01 SA05.
3. Sort the names alphabetically by last name.
4. Save, print, and then close EWd C01 SA05.

Assessment 6

1. Open Word Tab 02.
2. Save the document with Save As and name it EWd C01 SA06.
3. Sort the columns of text alphabetically by last name in the first column. (Display the Sort Options dialog box and make sure Tabs is selected in the Separate fields at section.) *(Hint: Select the columns of text but not the title, subtitle, and headings.)*
4. Print EWd C01 SA06.
5. Sort the columns of text by the date of hire in the third column.
6. Print EWd C01 SA06.
7. Sort the columns of text alphabetically by the department name and then alphabetically by last name.
8. Save, print, and then close EWd C01 SA06.

Assessment 7

1. Open Word Table 02.
2. Save the document with Save As and name it EWd C01 SA07.
3. Sort the text alphabetically by State in the first column of the table. (Make sure no text displays in the Then by option box.)
4. Save and then print EWd C01 SA07.
5. Sort the text numerically by First Quarter in ascending order in the second column of the table.
6. Display the Table AutoFormat dialog box and apply a table style of your choosing to the table.
7. Save, print, and then close EWd C01 SA07.

Assessment 8

1. Open EWd C01 LFS Main Doc.
2. Save the document with Save As and name it EWd C01 SA08.
3. Display the Mail Merge Recipients dialog box and then select those clients living in the city of Baltimore.
4. Merge the selected records to the printer.
5. Save and then close EWd C01 SA08.

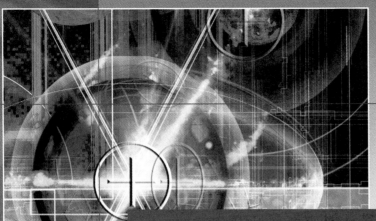

FORMATTING WITH SPECIAL FEATURES

PERFORMANCE OBJECTIVES

Upon successful completion of chapter 2, you will be able to:

- Save, insert, edit, and delete an AutoText entry
- Insert a nonbreaking space between words in a document
- Insert a manual line break
- Turn on/off the widow/orphan control feature
- Keep a paragraph or paragraphs of text together
- Reveal formatting
- Apply borders and shading to paragraphs and pages in a document
- Find and replace special formatting, characters, and nonprinting elements
- Create, view, edit, move, copy, and delete footnotes and endnotes
- Format the first page in a document differently than subsequent pages
- Format text into newspaper-style columns and create balanced columns
- Automatically summarize a document

Word Chapter 02E

In this chapter, you will learn to use a variety of Word features that can automate the creation of documents, add visual appeal, and automate formatting. Use Word's AutoText feature to simplify inserting commonly used words, names, or phrases in a document. Insert nonbreaking spaces between words that are to be kept together as a unit and insert a manual line break to move the insertion point down to the next line without the paragraph formatting. Control the location of page breaks with the widow/orphan control feature and identify specific text to be kept together on a page.

Add visual appeal to a page by adding a border, formatting text into newspaper-style columns and balancing columns, and formatting the first page of a document differently than subsequent pages. Create references in a document by inserting footnotes or endnotes and insert a cross-reference in a document to refer a reader to another location within the document. Identify the key points in a document automatically using the AutoSummarize feature.

Using AutoText

Word's AutoText feature is similar to the AutoCorrect feature. With AutoCorrect, the text is automatically inserted in a document when the spacebar is pressed. For example, if you assign the letters *HC* to *Hartland Corporation*, keying **HC** and then pressing the spacebar automatically inserts *Hartland Corporation* in the document. If you use text on a less frequent basis and do not want it automatically inserted in the document when you press the spacebar, use Word's AutoText feature. An AutoText entry is inserted in the document by pressing the Enter key or with the shortcut key, F3.

Saving an AutoText Entry

The AutoText feature is useful for items such as addresses, company logos, lists, standard text, and letter closing. To save an AutoText entry, key the desired text and apply any necessary formatting. Select the text, click Insert, point to AutoText, and then click New. At the Create AutoText dialog box shown in figure 2.1, key a short name for the text, and then click OK.

FIGURE

2.1 Create AutoText Dialog Box

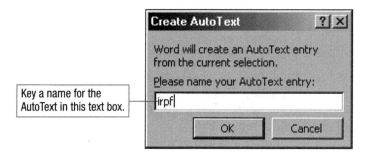

Key a name for the AutoText in this text box.

Show/Hide ¶

When you save selected text as an AutoText entry, the formatting applied to the text is also saved. If you are saving a paragraph or paragraphs of text that have paragraph formatting applied, make sure you include the paragraph mark with the selected text. To make sure the paragraph mark is included, turn on the display of nonprinting characters before selecting the text. Turn on the display of nonprinting characters by clicking the Show/Hide ¶ button on the Standard toolbar.

An AutoText entry name can contain a maximum of 32 characters and can include spaces. Try to give the AutoText a name that is short but also gives you an idea of the contents of the entry.

Inserting an AutoText Entry

Insert an AutoText entry in a document by keying the name of the AutoText and then pressing the Enter key or the shortcut key, F3. An AutoText entry name must be at least four characters in length to display the AutoText with the Enter key. Use the shortcut key, F3, on an AutoText entry name of any length. To insert an AutoText entry with the Enter key, key the name given (at least four characters) to the AutoText entry (the full entry displays in a yellow box above

WORD

the insertion point), and then press the Enter key. To insert an AutoText entry
with the shortcut key, key the name given the AutoText entry, and then press F3.

Editing an AutoText Entry

Edit an AutoText entry by inserting the entry in a document, making any
necessary changes, and then saving it again with the same AutoText entry name.
When a message displays asking if you want to redefine the AutoText entry, click
Yes.

Deleting an AutoText Entry

Delete an AutoText entry at the AutoCorrect dialog box with the AutoText tab
selected. Display this dialog box by clicking Insert, pointing to AutoText, and
then clicking AutoText. At the AutoCorrect dialog box, click the entry to be
deleted in the list box, and then click the Delete button.

(Note: Before completing computer exercises, delete the Word Chapter 01E *folder on
your disk. Next, copy to your disk the* Word Chapter 02E *subfolder from the* Word 2002
Expert *folder on the CD that accompanies this textbook.)*

exercise

CREATING AND DELETING AUTOTEXT ENTRIES

1. At a clear document screen, create an AutoText entry for Individual Retirement Pension
   Fund, by completing the following steps:
   a. Key **Individual Retirement Pension Fund**.
   b. Select *Individual Retirement Pension Fund*. (Be sure
      you do not include the paragraph symbol when
      selecting text. You may want to turn on the display
      of nonprinting characters.)
   c. Click Insert, point to AutoText, and then click
      New.
   d. At the Create AutoText dialog box, key **irpf**.
   e. Click OK.
   f. Deselect the text.
   g. Close the document without saving it.

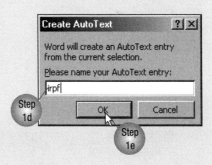

2. At a clear document screen, create an AutoText entry for
   the letter complimentary closing shown in figure 2.2 by completing the following steps:
   a. Key the text as shown in figure 2.2. (Insert your initials where you see the *XX*.)
   b. Select the text.
   c. Click Insert, point to AutoText, and then click New.
   d. At the Create AutoText dialog box, key **cc**.
   e. Click OK.
   f. Deselect the text.
   g. Close the document without saving it.
3. At a clear document screen, create the letter shown in figure 2.3 with the following
   specifications:
   a. While keying the letter, insert the *irpf* AutoText by keying **irpf** (this displays
      Individual Retirement Pension Fund in a yellow box above the insertion point), and then
      pressing the Enter key.

b. Insert the *cc* AutoText entry at the end of the letter by keying **cc** and then pressing F3.

4. When the letter is completed, save it and name it EWd C02 Ex01.

5. Print and then close EWd C02 Ex01.

6. At a clear document screen, delete the *irpf* AutoText entry by completing the following steps:

   a. Click Insert, point to AutoText, and then click AutoText.

   b. At the AutoCorrect dialog box with the AutoText tab selected, click *irpf* in the list box below the Enter AutoText entries here text box.

   c. Click the Delete button.

   d. Complete steps similar to those in 6b and 6c to delete the *cc* entry.

   e. Click OK to close the dialog box.

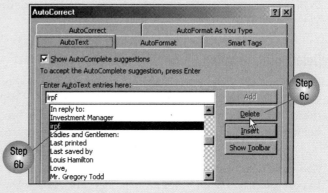

2.2 **Exercise 1**

Sincerely,

Chris Warren
Director of Financial Services

XX:

WORD

2.3 *Exercise 1*

November 7, 2002

Dear Investors:

Stradford Funds is offering the new irpf for investors. This new fund offers an excellent opportunity for self-employed individuals as well as those who want to supplement their existing retirement fund. The irpf will be available to investors beginning January 1.

If you would like more information on the irpf, please give me a call at 1-888-555-3455. I can send you a brochure explaining the fund along with a fact sheet prepared by Stradford Funds. The irpf is an exciting opportunity and I would like to schedule a private consultation with you to determine if it fits with your investment needs.

cc

Inserting a Nonbreaking Space

As you key text in a document, Word makes line-end decisions and automatically wraps text to the next line. In some situations, word wrap may break up words or phrases on separate lines that should remain together. For example, a name such as *Daniel C. Lagasa* can be broken after, but should not be broken before, the initial *C*. The phrase *World War II* can be broken between *World* and *War*, but should not be broken between *War* and *II*.

To control what text is wrapped to the next line, insert a nonbreaking space between words. When a nonbreaking space is inserted, Word considers the words as one unit and will not divide them. To insert a nonbreaking space between words, key the first word, press Ctrl + Shift + spacebar, and then key the second word.

If nonprinting characters are displayed, a normal space displays as a dot and a nonbreaking space displays as a degree symbol. To turn on the display of nonprinting characters, click the Show/Hide ¶ button on the Standard toolbar.

HINT

A nonbreaking space can be inserted at the Symbol dialog box with the (normal text) font selected.

 *exercise* 2

1. At a clear document screen, turn on the display of nonprinting characters (click Show/Hide ¶ button on the Standard toolbar), and then key the memo shown in figure 2.4. Insert nonbreaking spaces within the commands in the memo (for example, within *Ctrl + B* and *Ctrl + I*). Insert a nonbreaking space by pressing Ctrl + Shift + spacebar before and after the plus symbol in all of the shortcut commands.
2. Save the document and name it EWd C02 Ex02.
3. Turn off the display of nonprinting characters.
4. Print and then close EWd C02 Ex02.

F I G U R E

2.4 **Exercise 2**

DATE: January 16, 2003

TO: All Employees

FROM: Jolene Risse

SUBJECT: SHORTCUT COMMANDS

The transition to Office XP is almost complete. During the transition, I will continue to offer helpful hints to all employees. Word offers a variety of shortcut commands to quickly access features. For example, press Ctrl + B to bold selected text and press Ctrl + U to underline text. Italicize selected text with Ctrl + I.

In addition to the shortcut commands for applying character formatting, you can use shortcut commands to display certain dialog boxes. For example, use the command Ctrl + F to display the Find and Replace dialog box with the Find tab selected. Press Ctrl + O to display the Open dialog box.

XX:EWd C02 Ex02

W O R D

Inserting a Manual Line Break

When you press the Enter key, the insertion point is moved down to the next line and a paragraph mark is inserted in the document. Paragraph formatting is stored in this paragraph mark. For example, if your paragraph includes formatting such as spacing before and/or after the paragraph, pressing the Enter key continues this formatting to the next line. If you want to move the insertion point down to the next line without the before and/or after paragraph spacing, press Shift + Enter, which is the manual line break command. If you turn on the display of nonprinting symbols, a manual line break displays as the ↵ symbol.

exercise 3

INSERTING A MANUAL LINE BREAK IN A DOCUMENT

1. Open Word Document 05.
2. Save the document with Save As and name it EWd C02 Ex03.
3. Make the following changes to the document:
   a. Select the text from the beginning of the first paragraph to the end of the document.
   b. Display the Paragraph dialog box by clicking Format and then Paragraph.
   c. At the Paragraph dialog box with the Indents and Spacing tab selected, click the up-pointing triangle at the right side of the After text box until *12 pts* displays in the text box.
   d. Click OK to close the dialog box.
   e. Deselect the text.
4. Insert text and use the manual line break by completing the following steps:
   a. Click the Show/Hide ¶ button on the Standard toolbar. (This turns on the display of nonprinting symbols.)
   b. Move the insertion point to the end of the one-line second paragraph immediately left of the ¶ symbol (the line that begins *Research has centered...*)
   c. Press the Enter key.
   d. Press the Tab key and then key **Problem solving**.
   e. Press Shift + Enter. (This moves the insertion point down to the next line without including the space after formatting.)
   f. Press the Tab key and then key **Pattern recognition**.
   g. Press Shift + Enter.
   h. Press the Tab key and then key **Natural-language processing**.
   i. Press Shift + Enter.
   j. Press the Tab key and then key **Learning**.
   k. Press Shift + Enter.
   l. Press the Tab key and then key **Representation of real-world knowledge**.
   m. Click the Show/Hide ¶ button to turn off the display of nonprinting symbols.
5. Save, print, and then close EWd C02 Ex03.

ARTIFICIAL·INTELLIGENCE¶
¶
The·science·of·using·computers·to·simulate·intelligent·behavior
artificial·intelligence·from·one·of·its·early·practitioners,·John·M
years,·researchers·in·the·field·of·artificial·intelligence·have·mad
imitating,·on·computers,·many·behaviors·that·are·considered·int

Research·has·centered·on·imitation·of·such·human·abilities·as¶

→   Problem·solving↵
→   Pattern·recognition↵
→   Natural-language·processing↵
→   Learning↵
→   Representation·of·real-world·knowledge¶

Each·of·these·areas·of·research,·however,·has·proved·to·be·muc
early·researchers·expected.·Consider,·for·example,·the·problem·

Steps
4b-4l

Affecting Text Flow

Several options from the Paragraph dialog box with the Line and Page Breaks tab selected will affect the position of page breaks within a document. With the Line and Page Breaks tab selected, the Paragraph dialog box displays as shown in figure 2.5.

FIGURE

2.5 *Paragraph Dialog Box with Line and Page Breaks Tab Selected*

Use options in this section of the dialog box to control the location of page breaks in a document.

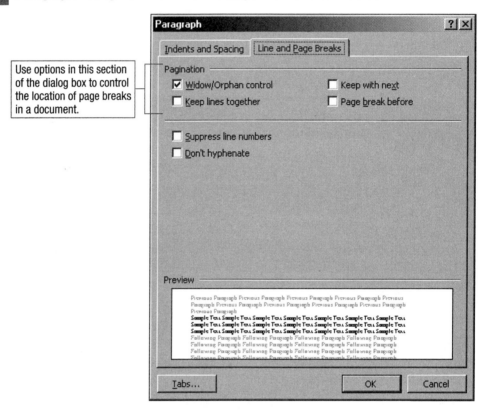

Turning On/Off Widow/Orphan Control

In a long document, you will want to avoid creating widows or orphans. A widow is the last line of a paragraph that appears at the top of a page. An orphan is the first line of a paragraph that appears at the bottom of a page.

In Word, widows and orphans are automatically prevented from appearing in text. Word accomplishes this by adjusting the page breaks in a document. Because of this, the last line of text on various pages will not always occur at the same line measurement or count. If you wish to turn off the widow and orphan control, display the Paragraph dialog box with the Line and Page Breaks tab selected, and then click Widow/Orphan control. This removes the check mark from the option.

Keeping a Paragraph or Paragraphs Together

Even with widow/orphan control on, Word may insert a page break between text in a paragraph or several paragraphs that should stay together as a unit. The Paragraph dialog box with the Line and Page Breaks tab selected contains options to keep a paragraph, a group of paragraphs, or a group of lines together.

To keep a paragraph together, you can instruct Word not to insert a page break within a paragraph. This format instruction is stored in the paragraph mark, so as the paragraph is moved within the document, the format instruction moves with it. To tell Word not to insert a page break within a paragraph, display the Paragraph dialog box with the Line and Page Breaks tab selected, and then click Keep lines together. The same steps can be used to keep a group of consecutive paragraphs together. To do this, select the paragraphs first, display the Paragraph dialog box, and then click Keep lines together.

With the Keep with next option at the Paragraph dialog box, you can tell Word to keep the paragraph where the insertion point is located together with the next paragraph (for example, to keep a heading together with the paragraph of text that follows it). If there is not enough room for the paragraph and the next paragraph, Word moves both paragraphs to the next page.

Use the Page break before option if you want a particular paragraph to print at the top of a page. Position the insertion point in the paragraph that you want to begin a new page, display the Paragraph dialog box with the Line and Page Breaks tab selected, and then click Page break before.

Revealing Formatting

Display formatting applied to specific text in a document in the Reveal Formatting Task Pane. Display this task pane, shown in figure 2.6, by clicking Format and then Reveal Formatting. You can also display the Reveal Formatting Task Pane by clicking Help, clicking What's This at the drop-down list, and then clicking the desired text. The Reveal Formatting Task Pane displays font, paragraph, and section formatting applied to text where the insertion point is positioned or selected text.

HINT

Click the plus symbol or minus symbol in the Formatting of selected text section of the Reveal Formatting Task Pane to display or hide information about formatting.

FIGURE

2.6 *Reveal Formatting Task Pane*

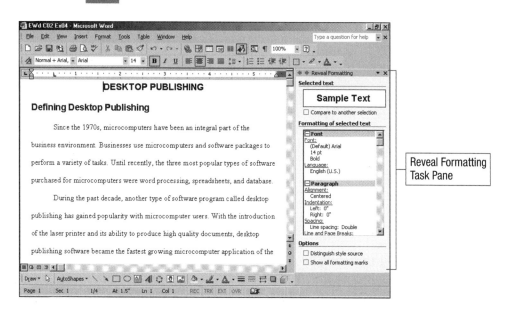

Reveal Formatting Task Pane

Generally, a minus symbol precedes *Font* and *Paragraph* and a plus symbol precedes *Section* in the Formatting of selected text section of the Reveal Formatting Task Pane. Click the minus symbol to hide any items below a heading and click the plus symbol to reveal items. For example, click the plus symbol preceding the *Section* heading and several items display below the heading including information on margins, layout, and paper.

Some items below headings in the Formatting of selected text section of the Reveal Formatting Task Pane are hyperlinks. For example, click the *Font* hyperlink and the Font dialog box displays. Click the *Alignment* or *Indentation* hyperlink in the Reveal Formatting Task Pane and the Paragraph dialog box displays. Use these hyperlinks to make changes to the document formatting.

exercise 4 — KEEPING TEXT TOGETHER AND REVEALING FORMATTING

(Note: Due to slight differences in how printers interpret line height, a page break may not display in the report after the heading Planning the Publication. *Before completing this exercise, check with your instructor to see if you need to make any minor changes to margins or font size for text and headings.)*

1. Open Word Report 01.
2. Save the document with Save As and name it EWd C02 Ex04.
3. Make the following changes to the document:
   a. Change the top, left, and right margins to 1.5 inches.
   b. Select the title *DESKTOP PUBLISHING* and then change the font to 14-point Arial bold.
   c. Select the heading *Defining Desktop Publishing* and then change the font to 14-point Arial bold.
   d. Use Format Painter to apply 14-point Arial bold to the remaining headings: *Initiating the Desktop Publishing Process*, *Planning the Publication*, and *Creating the Content*.
4. Tell Word to keep the heading *Planning the Publication* and the paragraph that follows it together on the same page and turn off the widow/orphan control by completing the following steps:
   a. Position the insertion point on any character in the heading *Planning the Publication* (located at the bottom of page 2).
   b. Click Format and then Paragraph.
   c. At the Paragraph dialog box, click the Line and Page Breaks tab.
   d. Click in the Keep with next check box to insert a check mark.
   e. Click the Widow/Orphan control option to remove the check mark.
   f. Click OK or press Enter.
5. Reveal formatting applied to the title by completing the following steps:
   a. Position the insertion point anywhere in the title *DESKTOP PUBLISHING*.
   b. Click Format and then Reveal Formatting. (This displays the Reveal Formatting Task Pane with information on the formatting applied to the title.)

c. Click anywhere in the heading *Defining Desktop Publishing*. (Notice the formatting applied to the paragraph.)

d. Click anywhere in the first paragraph of text below the *Defining Desktop Publishing* heading. (Notice the formatting applied to the paragraph.)

e. Click anywhere in the heading *Planning the Publication*.

f. In the Reveal Formatting Task Pane, scroll down the Formatting of selected text list box until the *Line and Page Breaks* hyperlink displays and then click the hyperlink. (This displays the Paragraph dialog box with the Line and Page Breaks tab selected.)

g. Click the Cancel button to close the dialog box.

h. Close the Reveal Formatting Task Pane by clicking the Close button located in the upper right corner of the task pane.

6. Save, print, and then close EWd C02 Ex04.

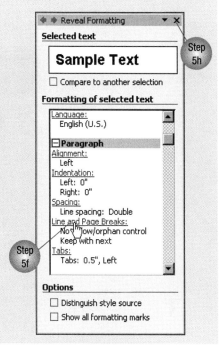

Step 5h

Step 5f

Adding Borders and Shading

Every paragraph you create in Word contains an invisible frame. A border that appears around this frame can be added to a paragraph. A border can be added to specific sides of the paragraph or to all sides. The type of border line and thickness of the line can be customized. In addition, you can add shading and fill within the border. When a border is added to a paragraph of text, the border expands and contracts as text is inserted or deleted from the paragraph. You can create a border around a single paragraph or a border around selected paragraphs.

One method for creating a border is to use options from the Border button on the Formatting toolbar. The name of the button changes depending on the border choice that was previously selected at the button drop-down palette. When Word is first opened, the button name displays as Outside Border. Click the down-pointing triangle at the right side of the button and a palette of border choices displays. At this palette, click the desired border.

Border

Another method for creating a border is to use options at the Borders and Shading dialog box with the Borders tab selected. Display this dialog box, shown in figure 2.7, by clicking Format and then Borders and Shading.

2.7 *Borders and Shading Dialog Box with the Borders Tab Selected*

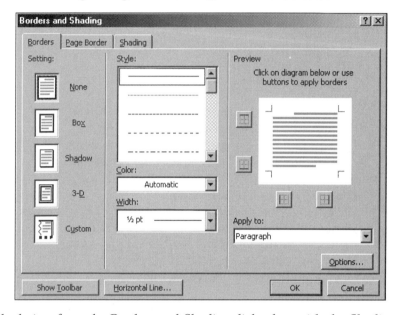

With choices from the Borders and Shading dialog box with the Shading tab selected, shown in figure 2.8, you can add shading to the border around text. Fill color choices display in the upper left corner of the dialog box. To add a fill, click the desired color in this section. If you want to add a pattern, click the down-pointing triangle at the right side of the Style text box and then click the desired pattern at the drop-down list. If a pattern is added inside a border, the color of the pattern can be changed with the Color option. Click the down-pointing triangle at the right side of the Color text box and then click the desired color at the drop-down list. The Preview area of the Borders and Shading dialog box with the Shading tab selected displays how the border shading and/or pattern will display.

HINT

Use graphic elements such as borders and shading to break the monotony of regular text, emphasize text, and draw the reader's attention.

2.8 *Borders and Shading Dialog Box with Shading Tab Selected*

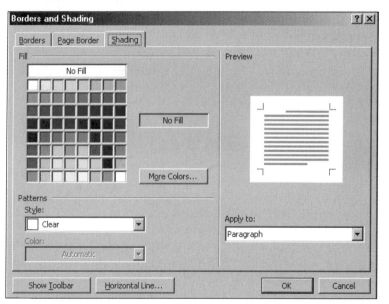

WORD

1. Open Word Document 03.
2. Save the document with Save As and name it EWd C02 Ex05.
3. Create a border around all of the paragraphs in the document that is 3 points thick and contains 25% shading by completing the following steps:
   a. Select all paragraphs in the document.
   b. Click Format and then Borders and Shading.
   c. At the Borders and Shading dialog box with the Borders tab selected, click the Box button located at the left side of the dialog box.
   d. Click the down-pointing triangle at the right side of the Width text box and then click *3 pt* at the pop-up list.
   e. Make sure that *Automatic* is selected in the Color text box. If not, click the down-pointing triangle at the right side of the Color text box and then click *Automatic* at the drop-down list. (This option is located at the beginning of the list.)
   f. Click the Shading tab.
   g. Click the light turquoise color in the Fill section of the dialog box.
   h. Click the down-pointing triangle at the right side of the Style list box and then click *5%* at the drop-down list.
   i. Click OK to close the dialog box.
4. Deselect the text.
5. Save, print, and then close EWd C02 Ex05.

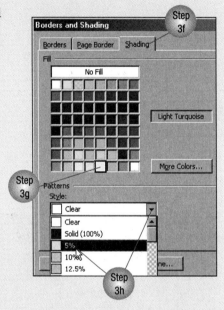

Inserting Horizontal Lines

Word includes a horizontal line feature that inserts a graphic horizontal line in a document. To display the Horizontal Line dialog box shown in figure 2.9, display the Borders and Shading dialog box with any tab selected, and then click the Horizontal Line button located at the bottom of the dialog box. Insert a horizontal line into a document by clicking the desired line option and then clicking the OK button.

HINT
The first time you try to insert a horizontal line, Word may need to install the feature.

2.9 *Horizontal Line Dialog Box*

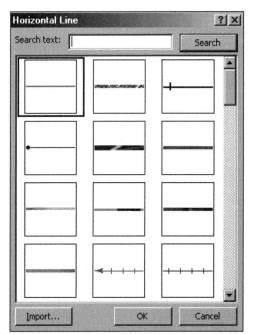

exercise 6

INSERTING HORIZONTAL LINES IN A DOCUMENT

1. Open Word Notice 01.
2. Save the document with Save As and name it EWd C02 Ex06.
3. Make the following changes to the document:
   a. Select the entire document, change the font to 14-point Goudy Old Style bold, and then deselect the document.
   b. Move the insertion point to the beginning of the document and then press Enter three times.
   c. Move the insertion point back to the beginning of the document and then insert a graphic horizontal line by completing the following steps:
      1) Click Format and then click Borders and Shading.
      2) At the Borders and Shading dialog box, click the Horizontal Line button located at the bottom of the dialog box.
      3) At the Horizontal Line dialog box, click the second horizontal line option in the second row.
      4) Click the OK button.
   d. Move the insertion point a triple space below the last line of text in the document and then insert the same graphic horizontal line as the one inserted in step 3c.
4. Save, print, and then close EWd C02 Ex06.

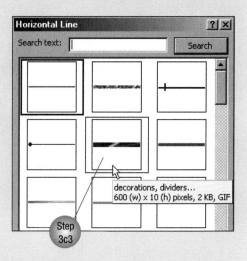

decorations, dividers...
600 (w) x 10 (h) pixels, 2 KB, GIF

Step 3c3

Adding Page Borders

The border you created in exercise 5 was inserted around selected paragraphs of text. Word also includes a page border feature that will insert a border around an entire page rather than just a paragraph. To insert a page border in a document, display the Borders and Shading dialog box and then click the Page Border tab. This displays the dialog box as shown in figure 2.10. The options at the Borders and Shading dialog box with the Page Border tab selected are basically the same as those for paragraph borders. The difference is that the border is inserted around the page rather than the paragraph of text.

FIGURE

2.10 *Borders and Shading Dialog Box with Page Border Tab Selected*

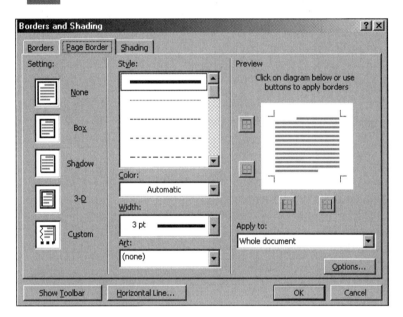

---

exercise 7

INSERTING A PAGE BORDER IN A DOCUMENT

1. Open Word Report 02.
2. Save the document with Save As and name it EWd C02 Ex07.
3. Make the following changes to the document:
   a. Select the entire document and then change the font to 12-point Garamond (or a similar serif typeface).
   b. Bold the following title and headings in the document:
      DESKTOP PUBLISHING DESIGN
      Designing a Document
      Creating Focus
4. Add a border to each page in the document by completing the following steps:
   a. With the insertion point positioned at the beginning of the document, click Format and then Borders and Shading.
   b. At the Borders and Shading dialog box, click the Page Border tab.
   c. Click the Box button in the Setting section.

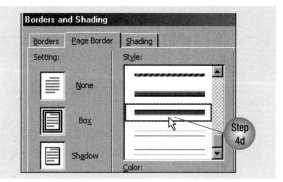

d. Scroll down the list of line styles in the Style list box until the end of the list displays and then click the third line from the end.
e. Click OK to close the dialog box.
5. Save, print, and then close EWd C02 Ex07.

HINT

The first time you try to insert a page border containing an image, Word may need to install the feature.

The Borders and Shading dialog box with the Page Border tab selected offers an option for inserting on the page a border containing an image. To display the images available, click the down-pointing triangle at the right side of the Art text box and then scroll down the list. Click the desired image. This image is used to create the border around the page.

exercise 8

INSERTING A PAGE BORDER CONTAINING BALLOONS

1. Open Word Notice 02.
2. Save the document with Save As and name it EWd C02 Ex08.
3. Make the following changes to the document:
   a. Select the entire document and then change to a decorative font of your choosing.
   b. Center the text vertically on the page by completing the following steps:
      1) Click File and then Page Setup.
      2) At the Page Setup dialog box, click the Layout tab.
      3) At the Page Setup dialog box with the Layout tab selected, click the down-pointing triangle at the right side of the Vertical alignment text box, and then click *Center* at the drop-down list.
      4) Click OK to close the Page Setup dialog box.
4. Add a decorative border to the document by completing the following steps:
   a. Display the Borders and Shading dialog box.
   b. At the Borders and Shading dialog box, click the Page Border tab.
   c. Click the Box button in the Setting section.
   d. Click the down-pointing triangle at the right side of the Art text box, scroll down the drop-down until balloons display, and then click the balloons.
   e. Click the up-pointing triangle at the right side of the Width text box until *25 pt* displays.
   f. Click OK to close the dialog box.
5. Save, print, and then close EWd C02 Ex08.

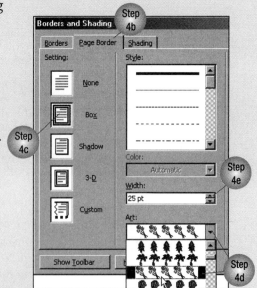

Finding and Replacing Special Formatting and Characters

You can use the find and replace feature to find special text and replace with other text. You can also use this feature to find special formatting, characters, or nonprinting elements in a document. Special formatting, characters, or nonprinting elements can then be removed from the document or replaced with other formatting or characters.

Finding and Replacing Formatting

With Word's Find and Replace feature, you can search for specific formatting or characters containing specific formatting and replace it with other characters or formatting. For example, you can search for the text *Type Size* set in 14-point Arial and replace it with the text *Type Size* set in 18-point Times New Roman.

HINT

Press Ctrl + H to display the Find and Replace dialog box.

exercise 9

FINDING AND REPLACING FONTS

1. Open Word Survey.
2. Save the document with Save As and name it EWd C02 Ex09.
3. Make the following changes to the document:
   a. Change the top and bottom margins to 0.75 inch and the left and right margins to 1 inch.
   b. Change the font for the entire document to 12-point Garamond (or a similar serif typeface such as Century Schoolbook or Bookman Old Style).
   c. Select the title *TEACHER DEVELOPMENT TOPICS* and the subtitle *Activities within Your Classroom*, and then change the font to 16-point Arial bold.
   d. Select *Directions:* (be sure to include the colon) in the first paragraph and then change the font to 14-point Arial bold. Use Format Painter to change the font to 14-point Arial bold for the following:
      Classroom Presentations:
      Expertise in Your Discipline:
      Information Technology:
      Thinking Skills:
      Active Listening:
4. Save and then print EWd C02 Ex09.
5. With EWd C02 Ex09 still open, find text set in 16-point Arial bold and replace it with text set in 14-point Garamond bold (or the typeface you chose in step 3b) by completing the following steps:
   a. Move the insertion point to the beginning of the document, click Edit, and then click Replace.
   b. At the Find and Replace dialog box, click the More button.
   c. With the insertion point positioned in the Find what text box (make sure there is no text in the text box), click the Format button located at the bottom of the dialog box and then click *Font* at the pop-up list.

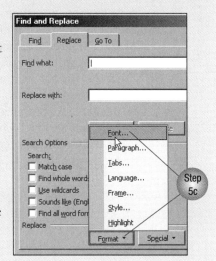

Step 5c

d. At the Find Font dialog box, click *Arial* in the Font list box, click *Bold* in the Font style list box, and then click *16* in the Size list box.

e. Click OK or press Enter to close the Find Font dialog box.

f. At the Find and Replace dialog box, click inside the Replace with text box. (Make sure there is no text in the text box.)

g. Click the Format button located at the bottom of the dialog box and then click *Font* at the pop-up list.

h. At the Replace Font dialog box, click *Garamond* in the Font list box (or the typeface you chose in step 3b), click *Bold* in the Font style list box, and then click *14* in the Size list box.

i. Click OK or press Enter to close the Find Font dialog box.

j. At the Find and Replace dialog box, click the Replace All button.

k. At the message telling you that Word has completed the search, click OK.

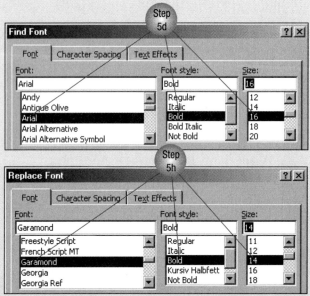

Step 5d

Step 5h

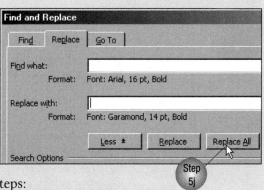

Step 5j

6. With the Find and Replace dialog box still open, find all text set in 14-point Arial bold and replace it with text set in 12-point Garamond bold by completing the following steps:

a. Click inside the Find what text box at the Find and Replace dialog box.

b. Click the No Formatting button located at the bottom of the dialog box.

c. With the insertion point still positioned in the Find what text box, click the Format button located at the bottom of the dialog box and then click *Font* at the pop-up list.

d. At the Find Font dialog box, click *Arial* in the Font list box, click *Bold* in the Font style list box, and then click *14* in the Size list box.

e. Click OK or press Enter to close the Find Font dialog box.

f. At the Find and Replace dialog box, click inside the Replace with text box.

g. Click the No Formatting button located at the bottom of the dialog box.

h. Click the Format button located at the bottom of the dialog box and then click *Font* at the pop-up list.

i. At the Replace Font dialog box, click *Garamond* in the Font list box, click *Bold* in the Font style list box (or the typeface you chose in step 3b), and then click *12* in the Size list box.

j. Click OK or press Enter to close the dialog box.

k. At the Find and Replace dialog box, click the Replace All button.

l. At the message telling you that Word has completed the search, click OK.

m. At the Find and Replace dialog box, click the Less button to turn off the display of the additional options.

n. Close the Find and Replace dialog box.

7. Save, print, and then close EWd C02 Ex09.

Finding and Replacing Special Characters

In addition to finding and replacing text and formatting, you can use the find and replace feature to search for special characters such as an en dash or an em dash and search for nonprinting elements such as a paragraph mark, tab character, or nonbreaking space. To display a list of special characters and nonprinting elements, display the Find and Replace dialog box with the Replace tab selected, expand the dialog box, and then click the Special button. This displays a pop-up menu as shown in figure 2.11.

FIGURE

2.11   *Special Button Pop-Up Menu*

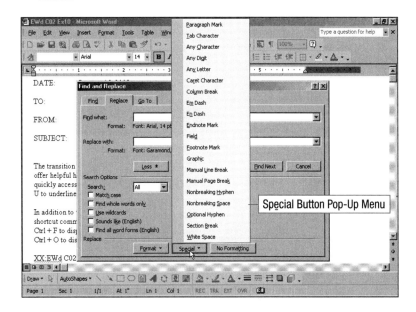

exercise 10

FINDING AND REPLACING A NONPRINTING ELEMENT

1. Open EWd C02 Ex02. (You created this document in exercise 2.)
2. Save the document with Save As and name it EWd C02 Ex10.
3. Find all occurrences of the nonbreaking space and replace with a regular space by completing the following steps:
   a. Click Edit and then Replace.
   b. At the Find and Replace dialog box with the Replace tab selected, click the More button.
   c. With the insertion point positioned in the Find what text box (make sure there is no text in the text box), click the No Formatting button that displays toward the bottom of the dialog box. (This removes any formatting that was inserted in a previous exercise.)

d. With the insertion point still positioned in the Fi_nd what text box, click the Sp_ecial button that displays toward the bottom of the dialog box.

e. At the pop-up menu that displays, click *Nonbreaking Space*. (This inserts ^s in the Fi_nd what text box.

f. Click in the Replace with text box (make sure there is no text in the text box) and then click the No Formatting button located toward the bottom of the dialog box. (This removes any formatting that was inserted in a previous exercise.)

g. With the insertion point still positioned in the Replace with text box, press the spacebar once. (This tells the Find and Replace feature to find a nonbreaking space and replace it with a regular space.)

h. Click the Replace A_ll button.

i. At the message telling you that Word has completed the search, click OK.

j. When the replacements are made, click the L_ess button.

k. Click the Close button to close the Find and Replace dialog box.

4. Save, print, and then close EWd C02 Ex10.

Find and Replace dialog box:

Find | Replace | Go To

Find what:
Format: Font: Arial, 14 pt

Replace with:
Format: Font: Garamond,

Less ±

Search Options
Search: All
☐ Match case
☐ Find whole words only
☐ Use wildcards
☐ Sounds like (English)
☐ Find all word forms (English)

Replace

Format ▾ | Special ▾ | No Formatting

Pop-up menu:
Column Break
Em Dash
En Dash
Endnote Mark
Field
Footnote Mark
Graphic
Manual Line Break
Manual Page Break
Nonbreaking Hyphen
Nonbreaking Space
Optional Hyphen
Section Break
White Space

Step 3e

Step 3d

Creating Footnotes and Endnotes

A research paper or report contains information from a variety of sources. To give credit to those sources, a footnote can be inserted in the document. A *footnote* is an explanatory note or reference that is printed at the bottom of the page where it is referenced. An *endnote* is also an explanatory note or reference, but it prints at the end of the document.

Two steps are involved when creating a footnote or endnote. First, the note reference number is inserted in the document at the location where the note is referred. The second step for creating a footnote or endnote is to key the note entry text. Footnotes and endnotes are created in a similar manner. To create a footnote in a document, you would complete the following steps:

1. Position the insertion point at the location in the document where the reference number is to appear.
2. Click I_nsert, point to Refere_nce, and then click Foot_note.
3. At the Footnote and Endnote dialog box shown in figure 2.12, make sure F_ootnotes is selected, and then click the I_nsert button.
4. At the footnote pane shown in figure 2.13, key the footnote entry text.
5. Click the C_lose button.

2.12 *Footnote and Endnote Dialog Box*

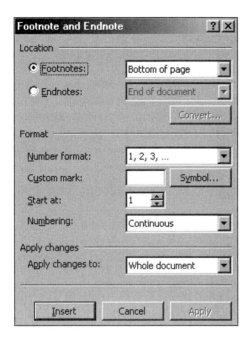

2.13 *Footnote Pane*

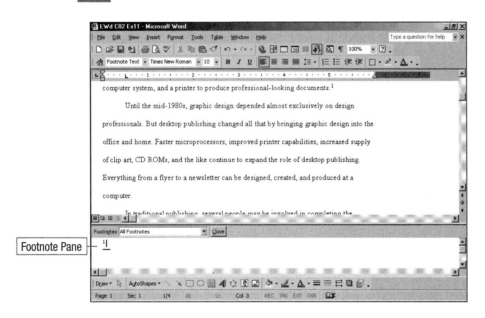

When creating footnotes, Word numbers footnotes with Arabic numbers (1, 2, 3, etc.). If you press the Enter key after keying the footnote entry text, footnotes will be separated by a blank line (double space).

1. Open Word Report 01.
2. Save the document with Save As and name it EWd C02 Ex11.
3. Make the following changes to the document:
    a. Select the title *DESKTOP PUBLISHING* and then change the font to 14-point Arial bold.
    b. Select the heading *Defining Desktop Publishing* and then change the font to 14-point Arial bold.
    c. Use Format Painter to apply 14-point Arial bold to the remaining headings: *Initiating the Desktop Publishing Process*, *Planning the Publication*, and *Creating the Content*.
4. Create the first footnote shown in figure 2.14 at the end of the second paragraph in the Defining Desktop Publishing section by completing the following steps:
    a. Position the insertion point at the end of the second paragraph in the Defining Desktop Publishing section.
    b. Click Insert, point to Reference, and then click Footnote.
    c. At the Footnote and Endnote dialog box, make sure Footnotes is selected, and then click the Insert button.
    d. At the footnote pane, key the first footnote shown in figure 2.14. Press the Enter key once after keying the footnote text (this will separate the first footnote from the second footnote by a blank line).

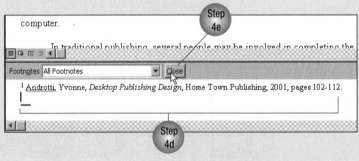

    e. Click the Close button to close the footnote pane.
5. Move the insertion point to the end of the fourth paragraph in the Defining Desktop Publishing section and then create the second footnote shown in figure 2.14 by completing steps similar to those in 4.
6. Move the insertion point to the end of the only paragraph in the Initiating the Desktop Publishing Process section and then create the third footnote shown in figure 2.14 by completing steps similar to those in 4.
7. Move the insertion point to the end of the last paragraph in the Planning the Publication section and then create the fourth footnote shown in figure 2.14.
8. Move the insertion point to the end of the last paragraph in the Creating the Content section (the last paragraph in the document) and then create the fifth footnote shown in figure 2.14.
9. Check page breaks in the document and, if necessary, adjust the page breaks.
10. Save, print, and then close EWd C02 Ex11.

Androtti, Yvonne, *Desktop Publishing Design,* Home Town Publishing, 2001, pages 102-112.

Bolle, Lynette and Jonathon Steadman, "Designing with Style," *Design Technologies,* January/February 2000, pages 22-24.

Doucette, Wayne, "Beginning the DTP Process," *Desktop Designs,* November 2000, pages 31-34.

Elstrom, Lisa, *Desktop Publishing Technologies,* Lilly-Harris Publishers, 2001, pages 88-94.

Busching, Wallace, "Designing a Newsletter," *Business Computing,* April 2000, pages 15-22.

Create an endnote in a similar manner as a footnote. At the Footnote and Endnote dialog box, click Endnotes, and then click the Insert button. At the endnote pane, key the endnote entry text, and then click the Close button. When creating endnotes, Word numbers endnotes with lowercase Roman numerals (i, ii, iii, etc.). The endnote numbering method will display after AutoNumber at the Footnote and Endnote dialog box. Later in this chapter, you will learn how to change the numbering method. Press the Enter key after keying the endnote entry text if you want the endnote separated from the next endnote by a blank line (double space).

You can format footnotes and endnotes in the normal manner. The note reference number and the note entry number print in the default font at 8-point size. The note entry text prints in the default font size. You can format the note reference and the note entry text, if desired, to match the formatting of the document text.

> **HINT**
> Press Ctrl + Alt + D to display the endnote pane.

Printing Footnotes and Endnotes

When a document containing footnotes is printed, Word automatically reduces the number of text lines on a page by the number of lines in the footnote plus two lines for spacing between the text and the footnote. If the page does not contain enough space, the footnote number and footnote entry text are taken to the next page. Word separates the footnotes from the text with a 2-inch separator line that begins at the left margin. When endnotes are created in a document, Word prints all endnote references at the end of the document separated from the text by a 2-inch separator line.

> **HINT**
> Specify where you want footnotes or endnotes printed with options at the Footnote and Endnote dialog box.

1. Open Word Report 02.
2. Save the document with Save As and name it EWd C02 Ex12.
3. Make the following changes to the document:
   a. Select the entire document and then change the font to 12-point Century Schoolbook (or a similar serif typeface).
   b. Select the title *DESKTOP PUBLISHING DESIGN* and then change the font to 14-point Century Schoolbook bold.
   c. Apply 14-point Century Schoolbook bold to the headings *Designing a Document* and *Creating Focus*.
4. Create the first endnote shown in figure 2.15 at the end of the last paragraph in the Designing a Document section by completing the following steps:
   a. Position the insertion point at the end of the last paragraph in the Designing a Document section.
   b. Click Insert, point to Reference, and then click Footnote.
   c. At the Footnote and Endnote dialog box, click Endnotes.
   d. Click the Insert button.
   e. At the endnote pane, key the first endnote shown in figure 2.15. Press the Enter key once after keying the endnote text.

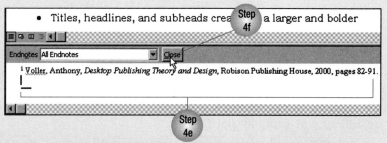

   f. Click the Close button to close the endnote pane.
5. Move the insertion point to the end of the first paragraph below the two bulleted paragraphs in the Creating Focus section and then create the second endnote shown in figure 2.15 by completing steps similar to those in 4.
6. Move the insertion point to the last paragraph in the document and then create the third endnote shown in figure 2.15 by completing steps similar to those in 4.
7. Check page breaks in the document and, if necessary, adjust the page breaks.
8. Save, print, and then close EWd C02 Ex12. (You may want to preview the document before printing.)

FIGURE

2.15 **Exercise 12**

Voller, Anthony, *Desktop Publishing Theory and Design,* Robison Publishing House, 2000, pages 82-91.

Rubiano, Lee and Eleanor Bolton, "Choosing the Right Typeface," *Designing Publications,* December 2002, pages 20-23.

Klein, Leland, "Focusing in on Your Document," *System Technologies,* March/April 2001, pages 9-12.

Viewing and Editing Footnotes and Endnotes

To edit existing footnote or endnote entry text, display the footnote or endnote text or the pane. In the Normal view, the footnote or endnote text does not display. To display footnotes or endnotes, change to the Print Layout view. Footnotes will display at the bottom of the page where they are referenced and endnotes will display at the end of the document. Footnotes or endnotes can be edited in the normal manner in the Print Layout view.

Another method for displaying a footnote or endnote pane is to click <u>V</u>iew and then <u>F</u>ootnotes. (The <u>F</u>ootnotes option is dimmed unless an open document contains footnotes or endnotes.) If the document contains footnotes, the footnote pane is opened. If the document contains endnotes, the endnote pane is opened. If the document contains both footnotes and endnotes, you can switch between the panes by choosing All Footnotes or All Endnotes from the Notes option at the top of the footnote or endnote pane. To do this, click the down-pointing triangle at the right side of the option box at the top of the pane, and then click *All Footnotes* or *All Endnotes*. With the footnote or endnote pane visible, you can move the insertion point between the pane and the document by clicking in the document text or clicking in the footnote or endnote pane.

If you insert or delete footnotes or endnotes in a document, check the page breaks to determine if they are in a desirable position. You can adjust the soft page breaks in the document using the widow/orphan control, using options in the Pagination section of the Paragraph dialog box with the Line and <u>P</u>age Breaks tab selected, or by inserting a hard page break by pressing Ctrl + Enter.

exercise **13**

EDITING FOOTNOTES

1. Open EWd C02 Ex11.
2. Save the document with Save As and name it EWd C02 Ex13.
3. Edit the footnotes by completing the following steps:
   a. Change to the Print Layout view.
   b. Move the insertion point to the bottom of the second page until the second footnote is visible.
   c. Make the following changes to the second footnote:
      1) Change *January/February* to *May/June*.
      2) Change *22-24* to *31-33*.
   d. Move the insertion point to the bottom of the third page until the fourth footnote is visible and then make the following changes to the fourth footnote:
      1) Change *Lilly-Harris Publishers* to *Gray Mountain Press*.
      2) Change *2001* to *2002*.
   e. Change back to the Normal view.
4. Check page breaks in the document and, if necessary, adjust the page breaks.
5. Save, print, and then close EWd C02 Ex13.

Moving, Copying, or Deleting Footnotes or Endnotes

Cut

Paste

Copy

You can move, copy, or delete footnote or endnote reference numbers. If a footnote or endnote reference number is moved, copied, or deleted, all footnotes or endnotes remaining in the document are automatically renumbered. To move a footnote or endnote in a document, select the reference mark of the footnote or endnote you want moved, and then click the Cut button on the Standard toolbar. Position the insertion point at the location where you want the footnote or endnote reference inserted and then click the Paste button on the Standard toolbar. You can also move a reference number to a different location in the document by selecting the reference number and then dragging it to the desired location.

To copy a reference number, complete similar steps, except click the Copy button on the Standard toolbar. A reference number can also be copied to a different location in the document by selecting the reference number, holding down the Ctrl key, dragging the reference number to the desired location, then releasing the mouse key and then the Ctrl key.

To delete a footnote or endnote from a document, select the reference number, and then press the Delete key. When the reference number is deleted, the entry text is also deleted.

exercise 14

EDITING AND DELETING FOOTNOTES

1. Open EWd C02 Ex11.
2. Save the document with Save As and name it EWd C02 Ex14.
3. Select the entire document and then change the font to Century Schoolbook (or a similar serif typeface such as Bookman Old Style or Garamond).
4. Change the font for the footnotes by completing the following steps:
   a. Click View and then Footnotes.
   b. At the footnote pane, press Ctrl + A to select all the footnote entry text and footnote numbers.
   c. Change the font to 12-point Century Schoolbook (or the typeface you chose in step 3).
   d. Click the Close button to close the footnote pane.
5. Delete the fourth footnote by completing the following steps:
   a. Move the insertion point to the fourth footnote reference number in the document text.
   b. Select the fourth footnote reference number and then press the Delete key.
6. Move the third footnote reference number from the end of the only paragraph in Initiating the Desktop Publishing Process section to the end of the second paragraph in the Planning the Publication section by completing the following steps:
   a. Move the insertion point to the third footnote reference number.
   b. Select the third footnote reference number.
   c. Click the Cut button on the Standard toolbar.

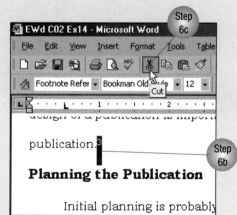

d. Position the insertion point at the end of the second paragraph in the Planning the Publication section.
e. Click the Paste button on the Standard toolbar.
7. Check page breaks in the document and, if necessary, adjust the page breaks.
8. Save, print, and then close EWd C02 Ex14.

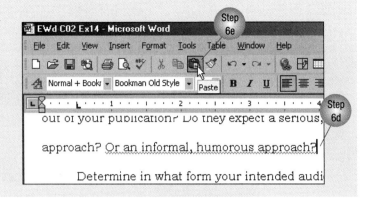

Formatting Pages in a Document

You have created and formatted a variety of multiple-paged documents. Formatting in a multiple-paged document can affect all pages in a document, or you can format the first page of a document differently than subsequent pages. For example, you can insert a page border on only the first page of a document or on every other page in the document except the first page. You can number all pages in a document or number second and subsequent pages and not the first page. Additionally, you can create a header or footer for the first page in a document and then change the header or footer for subsequent pages.

Inserting a Page Border on Specific Pages in a Document

As you learned earlier in this chapter, you can insert a page border in a document with options at the Borders and Shading dialog box with the Page Border tab selected. To insert a page border on only the first page of a multiple-paged document, click the down-pointing triangle at the right side of the Apply to option at the Borders and Shading dialog box with the Page Border tab selected, and then click *This Section – First page only*. Click *This Section – All except first page* if you want the page border to print on all pages except the first page.

exercise 15

INSERTING A PAGE BORDER ON THE FIRST PAGE OF A DOCUMENT

1. Open Word Report 02.
2. Save the document with Save As and name it EWd C02 Ex15.
3. Make the following changes to the document:
   a. Select the entire document, change to a serif typeface other than Times New Roman (you determine the typeface), and then deselect the text.
   b. Bold the title *DESKTOP PUBLISHING DESIGN* and the two headings *Designing a Document* and *Creating Focus*.
4. Insert a page border that prints only on the first page by completing the following steps:
   a. Click Format and then Borders and Shading.
   b. At the Borders and Shading dialog box, click the Page Border tab.
   c. At the Borders and Shading dialog box with the Page Border tab selected, choose a page border. (You determine the type of page border. Choose a border from the Style list box or choose a graphic border from the Art list box.)

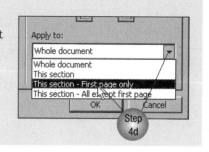

d. With the Borders and Shading dialog box still displayed, click the down-pointing triangle at the right side of the Apply to option and then click *This Section – First page only* at the drop-down list.

e. Click OK to close the dialog box.

5. Save the document again and then print pages 1 and 2.

6. Close EWd C02 Ex15.

Inserting Page Numbers on Specific Pages

Consider inserting page numbering in multiple-paged documents. Page numbers can appear on every page of the document, in specific sections of a document, or on all pages except the first page. To insert page numbering in a document, display the Page Numbers dialog box shown in figure 2.16, specify the position and alignment of the page numbers, and then close the Page Numbers dialog box. To print page numbers on all pages except the first page, remove the check mark from the Show number on first page option at the Page Numbers dialog box.

FIGURE

2.16 *Page Numbers Dialog Box*

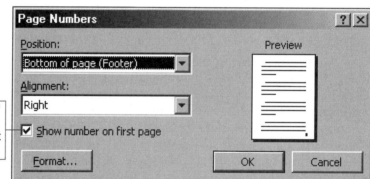

Inserting a Header/Footer on Specific Pages

You can insert a header and/or footer in a document that prints on all pages, only on odd pages, or only on even pages. Additionally, a header or footer can be created on the first page of a document that is different than a header or footer on second and subsequent pages. The first page header or footer can be a blank header or footer. Create a different first page header or footer with the Different first page option at the Page Setup dialog box with the Layout tab selected as shown in figure 2.17.

WORD

FIGURE

2.17 *Page Setup Dialog Box with Layout Tab Selected*

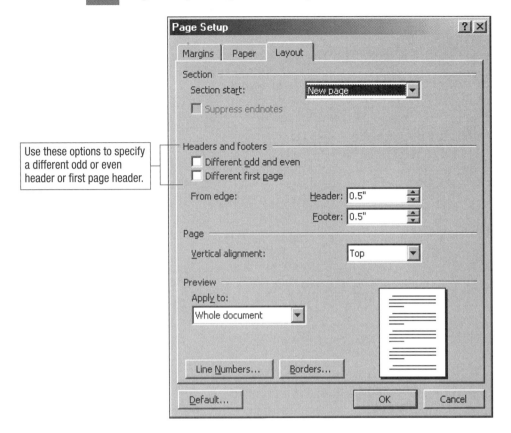

Use these options to specify a different odd or even header or first page header.

exercise

FORMATTING THE FIRST PAGE OF A DOCUMENT DIFFERENTLY THAN SUBSEQUENT PAGES

1. Open Word Report 03.
2. Save the document with Save As and name it EWd C02 Ex16.
3. Make the following changes to the document:
   a. Select the entire document, change the font size to 13 points (leave the typeface at Times New Roman), and then deselect the text.
   b. Change the top, left, and right margins to 1.5 inches.
4. Create a header that prints on second and subsequent pages by completing the following steps:
   a. Make sure the insertion point is positioned at the beginning of the document.
   b. Click View and then Header and Footer.
   c. Click the Page Setup button on the Header and Footer toolbar.
   d. At the Page Setup dialog box, make sure the Layout tab is selected.
   e. Click the Different first page option. (This inserts a check mark.)
   f. Click OK or press Enter.

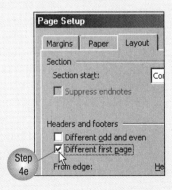

Step 4e

g. With the header pane displayed, click the Show Next button on the Header and Footer toolbar. (This opens another header pane.)

h. Click the Align Right button on the Formatting toolbar, turn on bold, and then key **Desktop Publishing Technology**.

i. Click the <u>C</u>lose button on the Header and Footer toolbar.

5. Insert page numbering on all pages except the first page by completing the following steps:

a. Click <u>I</u>nsert and then Page <u>N</u>umbers.

b. At the Page Numbers dialog box, click the down-pointing triangle at the right side of the <u>A</u>lignment option, and then click *Center* at the drop-down list.

c. Make sure the <u>S</u>how number on first page option does not contain a check mark. (If it does, click the option to remove the check mark.)

d. Click OK to close the dialog box.

6. Save, print, and then close EWd C02 Ex16. (The header and page number should not print on the first page.)

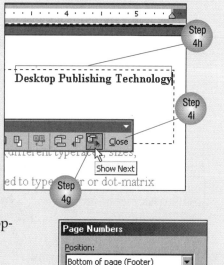

Step 4h

Desktop Publishing Technology

Step 4i

Close

Show Next

ed to type Step 4g

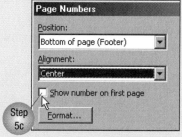

Page Numbers

Position:
Bottom of page (Footer)

Alignment:
Center

Show number on first page

Step 5c

Format...

Creating and Balancing Columns

Columns

Create newspaper-style columns using the Columns button on the Standard toolbar or with options at the Columns dialog box. To create columns with the Columns button, click the button. At the grid that displays, drag down and to the right until the desired number of columns displays with a black background, and then click the left mouse button.

Create and customize columns with options at the Columns dialog box. Display this dialog box by clicking F<u>o</u>rmat and then <u>C</u>olumns. At the Columns dialog box, you can choose preset columns, specify the number of columns, specify the width of columns, and insert a line between columns.

Balancing Columns on a Page

In a document containing text formatted into columns, Word automatically lines up (balances) the last line of text at the bottom of each column, except the last page. Text in the first column of the last page may flow to the end of the page, while the text in the second column may end far short of the end of the page. Columns can be balanced by inserting a section break at the end of the text. To do this, position the insertion point at the end of the text in the last column of the section you want to balance, click <u>I</u>nsert, and then click <u>B</u>reak. At the Break dialog box, click Con<u>t</u>inuous, and then click OK. Figure 2.18 shows the last page of a document containing unbalanced columns and a page where the columns have been balanced.

2.18 *Unbalanced and Balanced Columns*

UNBALANCED COLUMNS

BALANCED COLUMNS

Inserting a Column Break

Inserting a continuous break at the end of a document will balance the columns on the last page. At the Break dialog box, you can also insert a column break. When formatting text into columns, Word automatically breaks the columns to fit the page. At times, column breaks may appear in an undesirable location. For example, a heading may appear at the bottom of the column, while the text after the heading begins at the top of the next column. You can insert a column break into a document to control where columns end and begin on the page.

To insert a column break, position the insertion point where you want the new column to begin, display the Break dialog box, click the Column break option, and then click OK. You can also insert a column break by positioning the insertion point where you want the break to appear and then pressing Ctrl + Shift + Enter.

If you insert a column break in the last column on a page, the column begins on the next page. If you want a column that is not the last column on the page to begin on the next page, insert a page break. To do this, press Ctrl + Enter. You can also insert a page break by positioning the insertion point at the location in the text where you want the new page to begin, clicking Insert, and then clicking Break. At the Break dialog box, click Page Break, and then click OK or press Enter.

exercise 17

CREATING COLUMNS, INSERTING A COLUMN BREAK, AND BALANCING COLUMNS

1. Open Word Report 07.
2. Save the document with Save As and name it EWd C02 Ex17.
3. Make the following changes to the report:
   a. Select the entire document, change the line spacing to single, and then deselect the document.
   b. Bold the three headings *Early Painting and Drawing Programs*, *Developments in Painting and Drawing Programs*, and *Painting and Drawing Programs Today*.
   c. Move the insertion point to the beginning of the first paragraph (begins with *Graphics are pictures, still and moving...*) and press the Enter key.

d. Move the insertion point to the beginning of the heading *Early Painting and Drawing Programs* and press the Enter key.

e. Move the insertion point to the beginning of the heading *Developments in Painting and Drawing Programs* and press the Enter key.

f. Move the insertion point to the beginning of the heading *Painting and Drawing Programs Today* and press the Enter key.

4. Format the document into two columns by completing the following steps:

a. Position the insertion point at the beginning of the first paragraph (begins with *Graphics are pictures, still and moving...*).

b. Click Format and then Columns.

c. At the Columns dialog box, click Two in the Presets section of the dialog box.

d. Click the down-pointing triangle at the right side of the Apply to option and then click *This point forward* at the drop-down list.

e. Click OK to close the dialog box.

5. Insert a column break at the beginning of the heading *Developments in Painting and Drawings Programs* by completing the following steps:

a. Position the insertion point at the beginning of the heading *Developments in Painting and Drawing Programs*.

b. Click Insert and then Break.

c. At the Break dialog box, click Column break.

d. Click OK to close the dialog box.

6. Balance the columns on the second page by completing the following steps:

a. Move the insertion point to the end of the document.

b. Click Insert and then Break.

c. At the Break dialog box, click Continuous.

d. Click OK to close the dialog box.

7. Save, print, and then close EWd C02 Ex17.

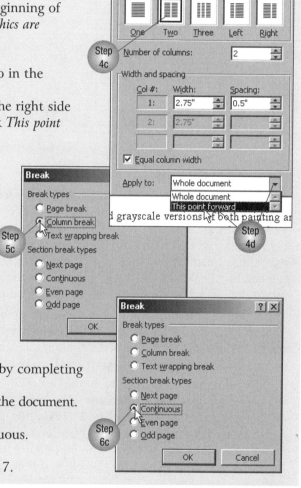

Automatically Summarizing a Document

Use the AutoSummarize feature to identify the key points in a document. AutoSummarize identifies key points by analyzing the text in the document and then assigning a score to each sentence. Sentences containing frequently used words in the document are assigned a higher score. By default, AutoSummarize chooses 25% of the highest scoring sentences. You can increase or decrease this default number. AutoSummarize operates most efficiently on well-structured documents such as reports and articles.

When using the AutoSummarize feature, you can choose to highlight key points, insert an executive summary or abstract at the top of the document, create a new document containing the summary, or hide everything but the summary. To use AutoSummarize, open the desired document, click Tools and then click AutoSummarize. This displays the AutoSummarize dialog box shown in figure 2.19. At the AutoSummarize dialog box, specify the type of summary desired, the length of the summary (by number of sentences or percentage), and specify whether or not you want the document statistics updated. After making the desired selections, click OK.

FIGURE

2.19 *AutoSummarize Dialog Box*

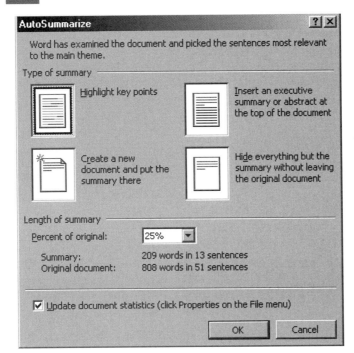

exercise 18

SUMMARIZING A DOCUMENT WITH AUTOSUMMARIZE

1. Open Word Report 02
2. Save the document with Save As and name it EWd C02 Ex18.
3. Summarize the document automatically by completing the following steps:
   a. Click Tools and then AutoSummarize.
   b. At the AutoSummarize dialog box, make sure Highlight key points is selected in the Type of summary section, and then click OK.
   c. At the document with the AutoSummarize toolbar displayed, click the left-pointing triangle on the Percent of Original button until *15%* displays.

Step 3b

d. Click the Close button (Close AutoSummarize) on the AutoSummarize toolbar.

4. Summarize the document and insert the summary in a separate document by completing the following steps:
   a. Click Tools and then AutoSummarize.
   b. At the AutoSummarize dialog box, click the Create a new document and put the summary there option.
   c. Click the down-pointing triangle at the right side of the Percent of original option and then click *10%* at the drop-down list.
   d. Click OK to close the dialog box.
5. Save the summary document and name it EWd C02 Summary.
6. Print and then close EWd C02 Summary.
7. Close EWd C02 Ex18 without saving the changes.

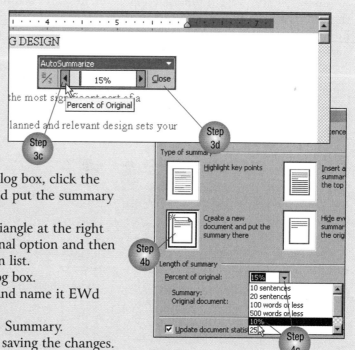

CHAPTER summary

➤ Text that is used frequently can be saved as an AutoText entry and then inserted in a document. An AutoText entry is inserted in the document with the Enter key or the shortcut key, F3.

➤ When a nonbreaking space is inserted between words, Word considers these words as one unit and will not divide them. Insert a nonbreaking space with the shortcut command, Ctrl + Shift + spacebar.

➤ Press Shift + Enter to move the insertion point down to the next line without applying paragraph formatting.

➤ In Word, widows and orphans are automatically prevented from appearing in text. Turn off this feature at the Paragraph dialog box with the Line and Page Breaks tab selected.

➤ The Paragraph dialog box with the Line and Page Breaks tab selected contains options to keep a paragraph, a group of paragraphs, or a group of lines together.

➤ Every paragraph created in Word contains an invisible frame. A border that appears around this frame can be added to a paragraph.

➤ Display formatting applied to specific text in a document at the Reveal Formatting Task Pane. Display this task pane by clicking Format and then Reveal Formatting.

➤ Use options at the Borders and Shading dialog box with the Borders tab selected to add a customized border to a paragraph or selected paragraphs.

➤ Use options at the Borders and Shading dialog box with the Shading tab selected to add shading or a pattern to a paragraph of text or selected paragraphs.

➤ Add a page border to a document at the Borders and Shading dialog box with the <u>P</u>age Border tab selected.

➤ Use the find and replace feature to find special formatting, characters, or nonprinting elements, and replace with other special text.

➤ Footnotes and endnotes are explanatory notes or references. Footnotes are printed at the bottom of the page and endnotes are printed at the end of the document. Key footnote/endnote text at the footnote or endnote pane.

➤ By default, footnotes are numbered with Arabic numbers and endnotes are numbered with lowercase Roman numerals.

➤ Move and/or copy a reference number in a document and all other footnotes/endnotes are automatically renumbered.

➤ Delete a footnote or endnote by selecting the reference number and then pressing the Delete key.

➤ Formatting in a multiple-paged document can affect all pages in a document or you can format the first page differently than subsequent pages.

➤ Use the Appl<u>y</u> to option at the Borders and Shading dialog box with the <u>P</u>age Border tab selected to specify whether the page border is to print on all pages, the first page only, or on all pages except the first page.

➤ Insert page numbering in a document with options at the Page Numbers dialog box. To print page numbers on all pages except the first page, remove the check mark from the <u>S</u>how number on first page option.

➤ You can create a header or footer on the first page of a document that is different than a header or footer on second and subsequent pages. Create a different first page header or footer with the Different first <u>p</u>age option at the Page Setup dialog box with the Layout tab selected.

➤ Create newspaper-style columns using the Columns button on the Standard toolbar or with options at the Columns dialog box.

➤ Balance columns on a page by inserting a continuous section break.

➤ Insert a column break to control where one column ends and the next begins.

➤ Use the AutoSummarize feature to identify the key points in a document. AutoSummarize identifies key points by analyzing the text in the document and then assigning a score to each sentence.

COMMANDS review

Command	Mouse/Keyboard
Display Create AutoText dialog box	Click <u>I</u>nsert, point to <u>A</u>utoText, then click <u>N</u>ew
Insert a nonbreaking space	Press Ctrl + Shift + spacebar
Insert a manual line break	Press Shift + Enter
Display Paragraph dialog box	Click F<u>o</u>rmat and then <u>P</u>aragraph
Display Reveal Formatting Task Pane	Click F<u>o</u>rmat and then Re<u>v</u>eal Formatting
Display Borders and Shading dialog box	Click F<u>o</u>rmat and then <u>B</u>orders and Shading
Display Find and Replace dialog box	Click <u>E</u>dit and then <u>R</u>eplace

Display the Footnote and Endnote dialog box	Click Insert, point to Reference, click Footnote
Edit a footnote/endnote	Click View and then Footnotes
Display Page Numbers dialog box	Click Insert and then Page Numbers
Display Columns dialog box	Click Format and then Columns
Display AutoSummarize dialog box	Click Tools and then AutoSummarize

CONCEPTS check

Completion: On a blank sheet of paper, indicate the correct term, command, or number for each item.

1. If an AutoText entry name is less than four characters in length, key the AutoText entry name and then press this key on the keyboard to insert the full text.
2. This is the keyboard shortcut command to insert a nonbreaking space.
3. Turn on/off the widow/orphan control at the Paragraph dialog box with this tab selected.
4. Click the Page Border tab at this dialog box to display options for adding a page border to a document.
5. Click this button at the expanded Find and Replace dialog box to display a pop-up menu containing special characters and nonprinting elements.
6. To display the Footnote and Endnote dialog box, first click this option on the Menu bar.
7. The footnote entry text is keyed here.
8. Word numbers footnotes with this type of number.
9. Word numbers endnotes with this type of number.
10. To print a page border only on the first page of the document, change this option at the Page Borders dialog box to *This Section – First page only*.
11. Create a different first page header or footer with the *Different first page* option at the Page Setup dialog box with this tab selected.
12. To balance all columns on the last page of a document, insert this at the end of the text.
13. Use this feature to identify the key points in a document.
14. Write the steps you would complete to create an AutoText entry for *Kellerman Manufacturing Corporation* with the name *kmc*.

SKILLS check

Assessment 1

1. Create an AutoText entry for *Stradford Annuity Mutual Funds* and use the initials *samf*.
2. Key the document shown in figure 2.20 using the AutoText entry you created.
3. Save the document and name it EWd C02 SA01.
4. Print and then close EWd C02 SA01.
5. At a clear document screen, delete the *samf* AutoText entry.

FIGURE

2.20 *Assessment 1*

STRADFORD ANNUITY ASSOCIATION

The *samf* complement your traditional retirement savings by putting your after-tax dollars to work. The *samf* offer some very important advantages that can make your retirement dreams a reality including:

- No-loads
- Exceptionally low operating costs
- A low $250 initial investment
- Easy access to your money
- No marketing or distribution fees

The *samf* are backed by the investment expertise that has made Stradford Annuity Association one of the most respected companies in the financial industry.

Assessment 2

1. At a clear document screen, create the memo shown in figure 2.21.
   Insert nonbreaking spaces within the shortcut commands.
2. Save the document and name it EWd C02 SA02.
3. Print and then close EWd C02 SA02.

DATE: (current date)

TO: All Employees

FROM: Cynthia Stophel

SUBJECT: SHORTCUT COMMANDS

Shortcut commands can be used to format text, display dialog boxes, and insert special characters. For example, insert a nonbreaking space in text with the command Ctrl + Shift + spacebar. You can also insert symbols in a document with shortcut commands. For example, insert a copyright symbol in a document by pressing Alt + Ctrl + C and insert a registered trademark symbol with the shortcut command Alt + Ctrl + R.

A Microsoft Word training session has been scheduled for next month. At this training, additional shortcut commands will be introduced.

XX:EWd C02 SA02

Assessment 3

1. Open Word Report 02.
2. Save the document with Save As and name it EWd C02 SA03.
3. Make the following changes to the document:
    a. Change the top, left, and right margins to 1.5 inches.
    b. Select the entire document and then change the font size to 13 points. (To change the size to 13 points, you will need to select the current size, and then key **13**.)
    c. Select the title *DESKTOP PUBLISHING DESIGN* and then change the font size to 16 points and turn on bold.
    d. Change the font size to 16 points and turn on bold for the headings *Designing a Document* and *Creating Focus*.
    e. Select the last two bulleted paragraphs in the first list of bulleted items. (These last two bulleted paragraphs should display at the bottom of the first page and the top of the second page.)
    f. Display the Paragraph dialog box with the Line and <u>P</u>age Breaks tab selected, click Keep with ne<u>x</u>t, and then close the dialog box.
4. Check page breaks and, if necessary, make adjustments to page breaks.
5. Save, print, and then close EWd C02 SA03.

Assessment 4

1. Open Word Notice 01.
2. Save the document with Save As and name it EWd C02 SA04.
3. Make the following changes to the document:
   a. Set the text in the document in a decorative font of your choosing. (You also determine the font size and font color.)
   b. Center the text vertically on the page.
   c. Insert a page border using one of the images available in the Art drop-down list.
4. Save, print, and then close EWd C02 SA04.

Assessment 5

1. Open Word Report 05.
2. Save the document with Save As and name it EWd C02 SA05.
3. Make the following changes to the report:
   a. Insert a section break that begins a new page at the line containing the title *MODULE 4: CREATING A NEWSLETTER LAYOUT.*
   b. Create the first footnote shown in figure 2.22 at the end of the first paragraph in the Applying Desktop Publishing Guidelines section of the report.
   c. Create the second footnote shown in figure 2.22 at the end of the third paragraph in the Applying Desktop Publishing Guidelines section of the report.
   d. Create the third footnote shown in figure 2.22 at the end of the last paragraph in the Applying Desktop Publishing Guidelines section of the report.
   e. Create the fourth footnote shown in figure 2.22 at the end of the only paragraph in the Choosing Paper Size and Type section of the report.
   f. Create the fifth footnote shown in figure 2.22 at the end of the only paragraph in the Choosing Paper Weight section of the report.
4. Check page breaks in the document and, if necessary, adjust the page breaks.
5. Save, print, and then close EWd C02 SA05.

FIGURE

2.22 *Assessment 5*

Habermann, James, "Designing a Newsletter," *Desktop Designs,* January/February 2002, pages 23-29.

Pilante, Shirley G., "Adding Pizzazz to Your Newsletter," *Desktop Publisher,* September 2001, pages 32-39.

Maddock, Arlita G., "Guidelines for a Better Newsletter," *Business Computing,* June 2001, pages 9-14.

Alverso, Monica, "Paper Styles for Newsletters," *Design Technologies,* March 14, 2000, pages 45-51.

Alverso, Monica, "Paper Styles for Newsletters," *Design Technologies,* March 14, 2000, pages 52-53.

Assessment 6

1. Open EWd C02 SA05.
2. Save the document with Save As and name it EWd C02 SA06.
3. Make the following changes to the report:
   a. Select the entire document and then change the font to 12-point Century Schoolbook (or a similar serif typeface).
   b. Display the footnote pane, select all of the footnotes, and then change the font to 12-point Century Schoolbook (or the serif typeface you chose in step 3a).
   c. Move the first footnote (the one after the first paragraph in the Applying Desktop Publishing Guidelines section) to the end of the fourth paragraph in the Applying Desktop Publishing Guidelines section.
   d. Delete the third footnote.
4. Check page breaks in the document and, if necessary, adjust the page breaks.
5. Save, print, and then close EWd C02 SA06.

Assessment 7

1. Open Word Report 01.
2. Save the document with Save As and name it EWd C02 SA07.
3. Make the following changes to the document:
   a. Select the entire document, change the line spacing to 1.5, and then deselect the document.
   b. Set the title *DESKTOP PUBLISHING* in 16-point Arial bold.
   c. Set the headings *Defining Desktop Publishing*, *Initiating the Desktop Publishing Process*, *Planning the Publication*, and *Creating the Content* in 14-point Arial bold.
   d. Format the text from the beginning of the heading *Defining Desktop Publishing* to the end of the document into two evenly spaced columns.
   e. Balance the columns on the last page in the document.
4. Save and then print EWd C02 SA07.
5. With EWd C02 SA07 still open, make the following changes:
   a. Search for all 14-point Arial bold formatting and replace with 12-point Times New Roman bold formatting. (Use the find and replace feature to do this.)
   b. Insert page numbering in the upper right corner on all pages except the first page.
   c. Insert a page border of your choosing that prints only on the first page of the document.
6. Save, print, and then close EWd C02 SA07.

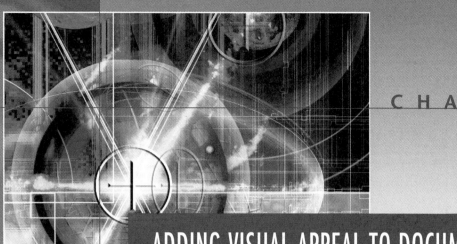

ADDING VISUAL APPEAL TO DOCUMENTS

PERFORMANCE OBJECTIVES

Upon completion of chapter 3, you will be able to:
- Insert, size, move, and format clip art images in a document
- Precisely size and position a clip art image
- Apply advanced text wrapping and layout options to images
- Align and distribute graphic elements
- Create a watermark
- Download images from the Microsoft Design Gallery Live Web site
- Create shapes, autoshapes, and text boxes using buttons on the Drawing toolbar
- Format and customize drawn objects
- Create and modify text using WordArt
- Size and move a WordArt text box
- Create a drop cap in a document
- Add buttons to and remove buttons from a toolbar
- Create custom menus

Word Chapter 03E

Microsoft Word contains a variety of features that help you enhance the visual appeal of a document. Some methods for adding visual appeal that you will learn in this chapter include inserting and modifying images, inserting a watermark in a document, drawing and aligning shapes, inserting WordArt, and creating dropped caps. You will also learn how to customize toolbars and create custom menus.

Inserting and Customizing Images

Word includes a gallery of media images you can insert in a document such as clip art images, photographs, and movie images, as well as sound clips. Insert images in a document using options at the Insert Clip Art Task Pane shown in figure 3.1. Display this task pane by clicking Insert, pointing to Picture, and then clicking Clip Art; or by clicking the Insert Clip Art button on the Drawing toolbar. To display the Drawing toolbar, click the Drawing button on the Standard toolbar. If you are searching for specific images, click in the Search text text box, key the desired topic, and then click the Search button.

Insert
Clip Art

3.1 *Insert Clip Art Task Pane*

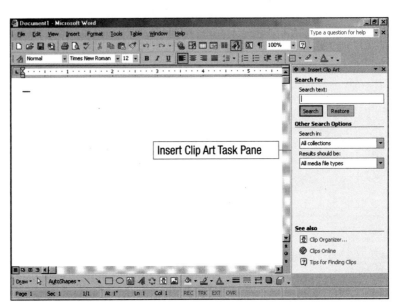

Insert Clip Art Task Pane

Sizing and Moving an Image

Text Wrapping

Click an image in a document to select it and then use the sizing handles that display around the image to change the size. To move an image in a document you must first choose a text wrapping option. To do this, select the image, click the Text Wrapping button on the Picture toolbar, and then click a wrapping option. This changes the sizing handles that display around the selected image from squares to white circles and also inserts a green rotation handle. To move the image, position the mouse pointer inside the image until the pointer turns into a four-headed arrow. Hold down the left mouse button, drag the image to the desired position, and then release the mouse button. Rotate the image by positioning the mouse pointer on the round, green rotation handle until the pointer displays as a circular arrow. Hold down the left mouse button, drag in the desired direction, and then release the mouse button.

HINT

Move an image up, down, left, or right in small increments by clicking the D<u>r</u>aw button, pointing to <u>N</u>udge, and then clicking the desired direction option.

Formatting an Image with Buttons on the Picture Toolbar

The Picture toolbar, shown in figure 3.2, offers a number of buttons you can use to format a selected image. Display this toolbar by clicking an image in a document. If the Picture toolbar does not display, position the mouse pointer on the image, click the *right* mouse button, and then click Show Picture Toolbar.

3.2 *Picture Toolbar Buttons*

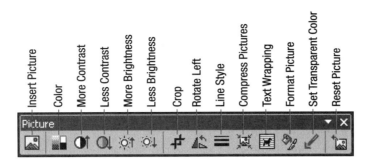

(Note: Before completing computer exercises, delete the Word Chapter 02E *folder on your disk. Next, copy to your disk the* Word Chapter 03E *subfolder from the* Word 2002 Expert *folder on the CD that accompanies this textbook.)*

exercise 1

INSERTING AND FORMATTING AN IMAGE

1. At a clear document screen, create the text and image shown in figure 3.3 by completing the following steps:
   a. Change to the Print Layout view.
   b. Change font to 36-point Curlz MT bold (or a similar decorative typeface).
   c. Key **Party Planners** and then press Enter.
   d. Key **1-888-555-4444**.
   e. Click Insert, point to Picture, and then click Clip Art.
   f. Click in the Search text text box, key **balloons**, and then press Enter.
   g. Click the balloon image shown at the right. (If this image is not available, choose another image containing a balloon, a party hat, or party supplies.)
   h. Close the Insert Clip Art Task Pane.
   i. Move the insertion point to the beginning of the document.
   j. Crop the image so just the party hat displays by completing the following steps:
      1) Click the image to select it. (Make sure the Picture toolbar displays.)
      2) Click the Crop button on the Picture toolbar.
      3) Position the mouse pointer on the upper left sizing handle (the mouse pointer turns into a crop tool, which is a

black square with overlapping lines), hold down the left mouse button, drag into the image to isolate the party hat as shown at the bottom of the previous page, and then release the mouse button.

    4) Drag the bottom middle sizing and the right middle sizing handle until the image displays as shown in figure 3.3. (If you are not satisfied with the result, click the Reset Picture button on the Picture toolbar and then try again.)

    5) With the party hat isolated, click the Crop button on the Picture toolbar to turn it off.

k. Change the wrapping style by clicking the Text Wrapping button on the Picture toolbar and then clicking Tight at the drop-down list.

l. Rotate the image as shown in figure 3.3 by completing the following steps:

    1) Position the mouse pointer on the round, green sizing handle until the pointer turns into a circular arrow.

    2) Hold down the left mouse button, drag to the left until the image is rotated as shown in figure 3.3, and then release the mouse button.

    3) Increase the size of the image and drag it to the approximate location shown in figure 3.3.

m. Click outside the image to deselect it.

2. Save the image and name it EWd C03 Ex01.

3. Print and then close EWd C03 Ex01.

FIGURE

3.3 **Exercise 1**

WORD

Formatting an Image at the Format Picture Dialog Box

With buttons on the Picture toolbar you can customize an image. The same options on the Picture toolbar are also available at the Format Picture dialog box along with some additional options. To display the Format Picture dialog box, select an image, and then click the Format Picture button on the Picture toolbar. You can also display the Format Picture dialog box by selecting an image, then clicking Format on the Menu bar and then clicking Picture.

Format Picture

The Format Picture dialog box displays with a variety of tabs. Click the Colors and Lines tab and options are available for choosing fill color; line color, style, and weight; and arrows. Click the Size tab and display options for specifying the height, width, and rotation degree of the image. Options at the Format Picture dialog box with the Layout tab selected include wrapping style and horizontal alignment. Click the Picture tab to display options for cropping the image and changing the Color.

Applying Advanced Layout and Text Wrapping Options

Use options at the Advanced Layout dialog box to specify horizontal and vertical layout options as well as text wrapping options. Display the Advanced Layout dialog box by displaying the Format Picture dialog box with the Layout tab selected and then clicking the Advanced button. Choose options at the Advanced Layout dialog box with the Picture Position tab selected, as shown in figure 3.4, to specify the horizontal and vertical position of the image.

In the Horizontal section, choose the Alignment option to specify whether you want the image horizontally left, center, or right aligned relative to the margin, page, column, or character. Choose the Book Layout option if you want to align the image with inside or outside margins on the page. Use the Absolute position option to align the image horizontally with the specified amount of space between the left edge of the image and the left edge of the page, column, left margin, or character. In the Vertical section of the dialog box, use the Alignment option to align the image at the top, bottom, center, inside, or outside relative to the page, margin, or line.

In the Options section, you can attach (anchor) the image to a paragraph so that the image and paragraph move together. Choose the Move object with text option if you want the image to move up or down on the page with the paragraph to which it is anchored. Keep the image anchored in the same place on the page by choosing the Lock anchor option. Choose the Allow overlap option if you want images with the same wrapping style to overlap.

3.4 **Advanced Layout Dialog Box with Picture Position Tab Selected**

Use options in this section to specify the horizontal position of the image.

Use options in this section to specify the vertical position of the image.

Use options in this section to specify how you want the image anchored.

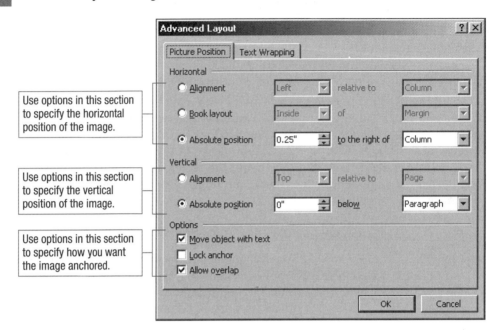

Use options at the Advanced Layout dialog box with the Text Wrapping tab selected, as shown in figure 3.5, to specify the wrapping style for the image as well as the sides around which you want text to wrap, and the amount of space you want between the text and the top, bottom, left, and right edges of the image.

3.5 **Advanced Layout Dialog Box with Text Wrapping Tab Selected**

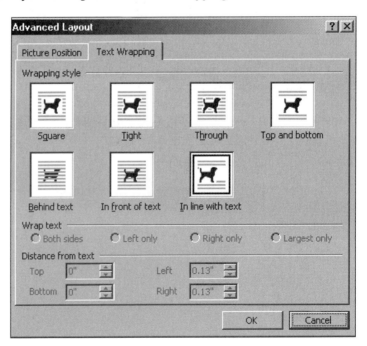

WORD

1. Open Word Report 01.
2. Save the document with Save As and name it EWd C03 Ex02.
3. Make the following changes to the document:
   a. Delete the text from the heading *Initiating the Desktop Publishing Process* to the end of the document.
   b. Select the entire document, change the line spacing to single, change the font to Bookman Old Style (or a similar serif typeface), and then deselect the document.
   c. Insert 12 points of space before the heading *Defining Desktop Publishing* and 6 points of space after the heading.
   d. Bold the title *DESKTOP PUBLISHING* and the heading *Defining Desktop Publishing* in the document.
4. Insert an image of a computer in the document as shown in figure 3.6 by completing the following steps:
   a. Change to the Print Layout view.
   b. Click the Insert Clip Art button on the Drawing toolbar. (If the Drawing toolbar is not visible, click the Drawing button on the Standard toolbar.)
   c. At the Insert Clip Art Task Pane, click in the Search text text box, key **computer**, and then press Enter.
   d. Click once on the computer image shown in figure 3.6 (and at the right). (If this image is not available, choose another computer image.)
   e. Close the Insert Clip Art Task Pane.

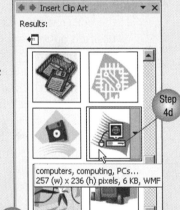

5. Change the size, position, and wrapping style of the image by completing the following steps:
   a. Click once on the image to select it.
   b. Click the Format Picture button on the Picture toolbar.
   c. At the Format Picture dialog box, click the Size tab.
   d. Select the current measurement in the Height text box and then key **2.5**.
   e. Click the Layout tab.
   f. Click the Advanced button located in the lower right corner of the dialog box.
   g. Click the Text Wrapping tab.
   h. Click the Tight option in the Wrapping style section.
   i. Click the up-pointing triangle at the right side of the Left option until *0.3″* displays in the text box.
   j. Click the up-pointing triangle at the right side of the Right option until *0.3″* displays in the text box.

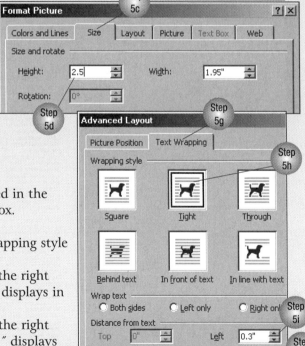

k. Click the Picture Position tab.
l. Click the Alignment option in the Horizontal section.
m. Click the down-pointing triangle at the right side of the Alignment box (in the Horizontal section) and then click *Centered* at the drop-down list.
n. Click the down-pointing triangle at the right side of the relative to box and then click *Page* at the drop-down list.
o. Click the Absolute position in the Vertical section.
p. Select the current measurement in the box to the right of the Absolute position option and then key **4**.

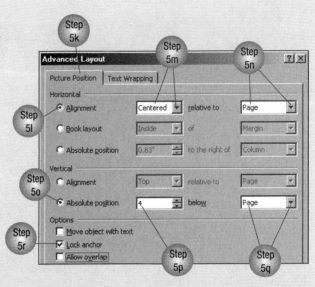

q. Click the down-pointing triangle at the right side of the below option and then click *Page* at the drop-down list.
r. Click in the Lock anchor check box to insert a check mark.
s. Remove the check marks from the other two options in the Options section.
t. Click OK to close the Advanced Layout dialog box.
u. Click OK to close the Format Picture dialog box.
6. At the document screen, click outside the image to deselect it.
7. Save, print, and then close EWd C03 Ex02.

FIGURE

3.6 *Exercise 2*

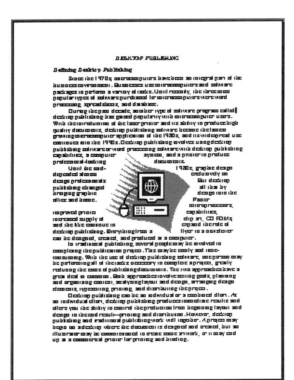

Creating a Watermark

An interesting effect can be created in a document with a watermark. A *watermark* is a lightened image that displays in a document. Text can be inserted in front of the watermark creating a document with a foreground and a background. The foreground is the text and the background is the watermark image. Figure 3.8 shows an example of a watermark you will be creating in exercise 3. The image of the computer is the watermark and creates the background and the text of the notice displays in front of the watermark and creates the foreground. Create a watermark with options from the Printed Watermark dialog box or with buttons on the Picture toolbar.

HINT

Use a watermark to add visual appeal to a document.

With options at the Printed Watermark dialog box shown in figure 3.7, you can create a picture watermark or a text watermark. Display the Printed Watermark dialog box by clicking Format, pointing to Background, and then clicking Printed Watermark. If you are creating a picture watermark, click Picture watermark, and then click the Select Picture button. This displays the Insert Picture dialog box. At this dialog box, specify the drive or folder where the picture is located, and then double-click the desired picture image. To create a text watermark, click the Text watermark option and then customize the watermark by choosing the font, size, color, and layout of the watermark.

FIGURE

3.7 *Printed Watermark Dialog Box*

Click this option to create a picture watermark.

Click this option to create a text watermark.

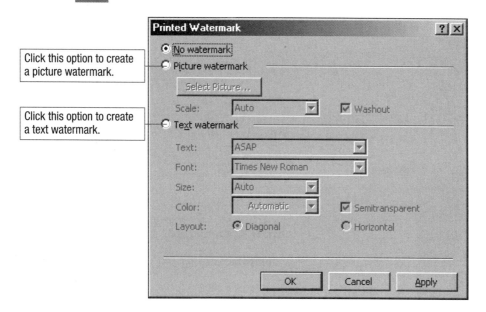

1. Insert the CD that accompanies this textbook in the CD drive.
2. Open Word Notice 03 from the *Word Chapter 03E* folder on your disk in drive A.
3. Save the document with Save As and name it EWd C03 Ex03.
4. Insert from the CD an image of a computer by completing the following steps:

   a. Click Format, point to Background, and then click Printed Watermark.
   b. At the Printed Watermark dialog box, click the Picture watermark option button.
   c. Click the Select Picture button.
   d. At the Insert Picture dialog box, click the down-pointing triangle at the right side of the Look in option.

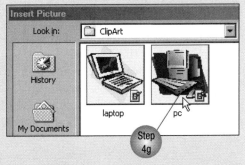

   e. At the drop-down list, click the drive where the CD is located.
   f. Scroll down the list of folders on the CD until *ClipArt* is visible and then double-click *ClipArt*.
   g. Double-click the document named *pc* in the list box.
   h. At the Printed Watermark dialog box, click OK.
5. Save, print, and then close EWd C03 Ex03.

FIGURE

3.8 *Exercise 3*

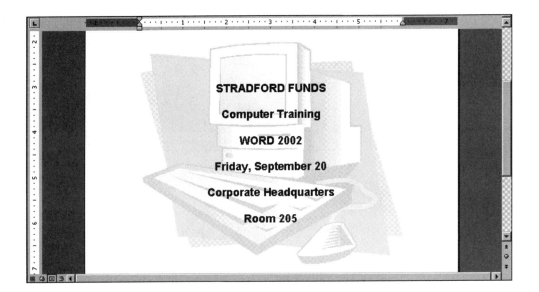

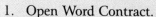

1. Open Word Contract.
2. Save the document with Save As and name it EWd C03 Ex04.
3. Insert a text watermark by completing the following steps:
   a. Click Format, point to Background, and then click Printed Watermark.
   b. At the Printed Watermark dialog box, click Text watermark.
   c. Select the text *ASAP* in the Text box and then key **Sample Agreement**.
   d. Change the Font option to Arial.
   e. Click OK to close the Printed Watermark dialog box.
4. Save, print, and then close EWd C03 Ex04.

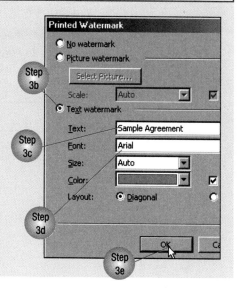

Step 3b

Step 3c

Step 3d

Step 3e

Downloading Images

(Note: The steps in exercise 5 assume that Microsoft Internet Explorer is your default browser. If this is not your default browser, steps may need to be modified. Please check with your instructor.)

The Microsoft Design Gallery Live Web site offers a gallery with hundreds of images you can download. To display the Design Gallery, you must have access to the Internet. To download an image, display the Insert Clip Art Task Pane, and then click the *Clips Online* hyperlink located toward the bottom of the Insert Clip Art Task Pane. At the Microsoft Design Gallery Live Web site shown in figure 3.9 (this Web site may vary), click in the Search for text box, key the desired category, and then click the Go button. Download the desired image by clicking the download button that displays below the image.

You can also copy an image from the Design Gallery and paste it into a Word document. To do this, download the image. At the Microsoft Clip Gallery 5.0 dialog box, right-click the image and then click Copy at the shortcut menu. Close the Microsoft Clip Gallery 5.0 dialog box and Internet Explorer. Make the Word document active and then click the Paste button on the Standard toolbar.

3.9 *Microsoft Design Gallery Live Web Site*

Deleting Images

Delete an image in the Insert Clip Art Task Pane by right-clicking the image and then clicking <u>D</u>elete from Clip Organizer at the shortcut menu. At the message that displays, click the OK button.

exercise 5

DOWNLOADING AN IMAGE FROM THE MICROSOFT DESIGN GALLERY LIVE WEB SITE

(Note: Check with your instructor before completing this exercise to determine if you have Internet access.)

1. Open Word Notice 01.
2. Save the document with Save As and name it EWd C03 Ex05.
3. Select the entire document, change the font to 14-point Arial bold, click the Align Left button on the Formatting toolbar, and then deselect the document.
4. Download a stock image from the Microsoft Design Gallery Live Web site by completing the following steps:
   a. Make sure you are connected to the Internet.
   b. Display the Insert Clip Art Task Pane.
   c. At the Insert ClipArt dialog box, click the *Clips Online* hyperlink.
   d. At the Microsoft Design Gallery Live Web site, click in the Search for text box and then key **stocks**.
   e. Click the Go button that displays at the right side of the Search for text box.

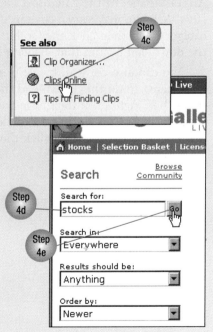

f. Scroll through the images related to *stocks* until you see an image that interests you (and fits the text in the document).

g. Click the download button that displays immediately below the image (contains a small down-pointing red arrow).

h. When the Microsoft Clip Gallery 5.0 dialog box displays, right-click the stock image, and then click <u>C</u>opy at the shortcut menu.

i. Close the dialog box by clicking the Close button (displays with an *X*) located in the upper right corner of the dialog box.

j. Click <u>F</u>ile and then <u>C</u>lose to close the Microsoft Internet Explorer.

5. Insert the stock image into the document by completing the following steps:

a. At the EWd C03 Ex05 document, click the Paste button. (This pastes the stock image into the document.)

b. Click the stock image to select it. (Make sure the Picture toolbar displays.)

c. Click the Text Wrapping button on the Picture toolbar and then click the <u>T</u>ight option.

d. Move and/or size the image so it is positioned at the right side of the text.

e. Deselect the image.

6. Save, print, and then close EWd C03 Ex05.

Drawing Shapes, Lines, and AutoShapes

With buttons on the Drawing toolbar, you can draw a variety of shapes such as circles, squares, rectangles, ovals, straight lines, freeform lines, lines with arrowheads, and much more. To display the Drawing toolbar, shown in figure 3.10, click the Drawing button on the Standard toolbar. When you click a button on the Drawing toolbar, Word switches to the Print Layout view and inserts a drawing canvas. You can draw objects inside the drawing canvas or delete the canvas and draw directly in the document. Using the drawing canvas, you can create objects with an absolute position and also protect objects from being split by a page break.

FIGURE

3.10 *Drawing Toolbar*

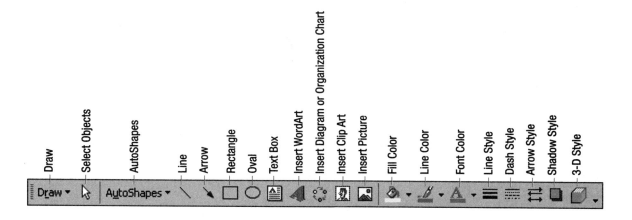

Line

Arrow

Rectangle

Oval

With some of the buttons on the Drawing toolbar, you can draw a shape. If you draw a shape with the Line button or the Arrow button, the shape you draw is considered a *line drawing*. If you draw a shape with the Rectangle or Oval button, the shape you draw is considered an *enclosed object*. If you want to draw the same shape more than once, double-click the shape button on the Drawing toolbar. After drawing the shapes, click the button again to deactivate it.

Use the Rectangle button on the Drawing toolbar to draw a square or rectangle in a document. If you want to draw a square, hold down the Shift key while drawing the shape. The Shift key keeps all sides of the drawn object equal. Use the Oval button to draw a circle or an oval object. To draw a circle, hold down the Shift key while drawing the object.

exercise **6**

DRAWING A CIRCLE AND SQUARE

1. At a clear document screen, draw a circle and a square by completing the following steps:
   a. Display the Drawing toolbar by clicking the Drawing button on the Standard toolbar. (Skip this step if the Drawing toolbar is already displayed.)
   b. Click the Oval button on the Drawing toolbar. (This inserts a drawing canvas on the document screen.)
   c. Position the crosshairs in the drawing canvas toward the left side.
   d. Hold down the Shift key and the left mouse button, drag the mouse down and to the right until the outline image displays as approximately a 2-inch circle, release the mouse button, and then the Shift key.
   e. Click the Rectangle button on the Drawing toolbar.
   f. Position the crosshairs in the drawing canvas toward the right side.
   g. Hold down the Shift key and the left mouse button, drag the mouse down and to the right until the outline image displays as approximately a 2-inch square, release the mouse button, and then the Shift key.
2. Save the document and name it EWd C03 Ex06.
3. Print and then close EWd C03 Ex06.

With the Line button, you can draw a line in the drawing canvas. To do this, click the Line button on the Drawing toolbar. Position the crosshairs where you want to begin the line, hold down the left mouse button, drag the line to the location where you want the line to end, and then release the mouse button.

You can add as many lines as desired on the document screen by repeating the steps above. For example, you can draw a triangle by drawing three lines. If you want to draw more than one line, double-click the Line button. This makes the button active. After drawing all of the necessary lines, click the Line button again to deactivate it.

WORD

1. At a clear document screen, create the document shown in figure 3.11 by completing the following steps:
   a. Make sure the Drawing toolbar is displayed.
   b. Change the font to 24-point Copperplate Gothic Bold (or a similar decorative typeface).
   c. Click the Center button on the Formatting toolbar.
   d. Key **Mainline Manufacturing**. (The Copperplate Gothic Bold typeface uses small caps for lowercase letters.)
   e. Press the Enter key.
   f. Click the Arrow button on the Drawing toolbar.
   g. Delete the drawing canvas by pressing the Delete key. (You will be drawing the arrow in the document, rather than the drawing canvas.)
   h. Hold down the Shift key and then draw the line in the document as shown in figure 3.11. (The line will display with an arrow on one end. This will be changed in the next step.)
   i. With the line still selected (a white sizing handle displays at each end), click the Arrow Style button on the Drawing toolbar.
   j. At the pop-up list that displays, click the second option from the bottom of the list (Arrow Style 10).
   k. Click outside the line to deselect it and display the arrow style.
2. Save the completed document and name it EWd C03 Ex07.
3. Print and then close EWd C03 Ex07.

FIGURE

3.11 *Exercise 7*

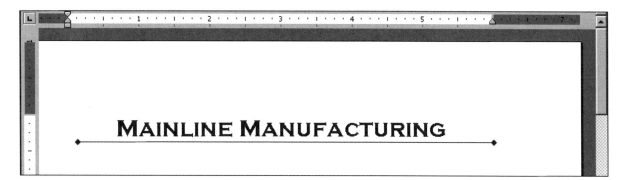

Text Box

Creating a Text Box

Use the Text Box button on the Drawing toolbar to create a box and then insert text inside the box. Text inside a box can be formatted in the normal manner. For example, you can change the font, alignment, or indent of the text. To create a text box, click the Text Box button, position the crosshairs in the drawing canvas or on the document screen where you want the text to appear, hold down the left mouse button, drag to create the box, and then release the mouse button. This inserts a text box in the document in which you can key text. If the text you key fills more than the first line in the box, the text wraps to the next line. (The box, however, will not increase in size. If you need more room in the text box, select the box, and then use the sizing handles to make it bigger.)

AutoShapes

Creating AutoShapes

Draw a variety of shapes with options from the AutoShapes button. Click the AutoShapes button and a pop-up menu displays. Point to the desired menu option and a side menu displays. This side menu offers autoshape choices for the selected option. For example, if you point to the Basic Shapes option, a number of shapes display at the right side of the pop-up menu such as a circle, square, triangle, box, stop sign, and so on. Click the desired shape and the mouse pointer turns into crosshairs. Position the crosshairs in the drawing canvas or on the document screen, hold down the left mouse button, drag to create the shape, and then release the button.

HINT

Choose an autoshape and then click in the drawing canvas or document (rather than dragging to create the image) and Word inserts a standard-sized object.

Fill Color

Adding Fill Color

Use the Fill Color button on the Drawing toolbar to add color to an enclosed object such as a shape. To add color, select the object, and then click the Fill Color button. This fills the object with the fill color displayed on the Fill Color button. To choose a different color, select the object, click the down-pointing triangle at the right side of the Fill Color button, and then click the desired color at the palette that displays.

HINT

Add a 3-D effect to a selected image by clicking the 3-D Style button on the Drawing toolbar and then clicking the desired effect.

Line Color

Changing Line Color

A line, shape, or text box is drawn with a black line. Change the color of this line with the Line Color button on the Drawing toolbar. To change the color, click the object, and then click the Line Color button. The line color of the selected object changes to the color displayed on the button. To change to a different color, click the down-pointing triangle at the right side of the button, and then click the desired color at the color palette.

HINT

Select at least two objects to make alignment options available and at least three objects to make distribution options available.

Aligning Graphic Elements

Graphic elements such as clip art images, autoshapes, text boxes, and shapes can be aligned and distributed in a document. Distribute and align graphic elements with the Draw button on the Drawing toolbar. To align and distribute graphic elements, select the elements, click the Draw button on the Drawing toolbar, and then point to Align or Distribute. This causes a side menu to display with alignment and distribution options. Choose the desired alignment and distribution option from this list.

Draw

To identify the graphic elements you want to align and/or distribute, click the Select Objects button on the Drawing toolbar and then draw a border around the elements. Another method for selecting elements is to click the first element, hold down the Shift key, and then click any other elements you want aligned.

Select Objects

CREATING A CERTIFICATE WITH ALIGNED AUTOSHAPES

1. Create the certificate shown in figure 3.12 by completing the following steps:
   a. At a clear document screen, change margins and page orientation by completing the following steps:
      1) Click File and then Page Setup.
      2) At the Page Setup dialog box with the Margins tab selected, change the top, bottom, left, and right margins to 0.75˝.
      3) Click Landscape in the Orientation section.
      4) Click OK.

   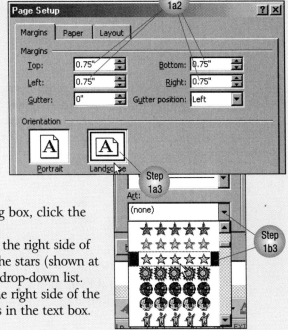

   b. Insert the page borders shown in figure 3.12 by completing the following steps:
      1) Click Format and then Borders and Shading.
      2) At the Borders and Shading dialog box, click the Page Border tab.
      3) Click the down-pointing triangle at the right side of the Art option box and then click the stars (shown at the right and in figure 3.12) at the drop-down list.
      4) Click the up-pointing triangle at the right side of the Width text box until *20 pt* displays in the text box.
      5) Click OK to close the dialog box.
   c. Create the text in the certificate as shown in figure 3.12 with the following specifications:
      1) Set *Gold Star Service Award* in 42-point Lucida Calligraphy bold with a Shadow effect. (Add the shadow effect by clicking the Shadow check box at the Font dialog box. If the Lucida Calligraphy typeface is not available, choose a similar decorative typeface.)
      2) Set *Awarded to* in 18-point Lucida Calligraphy bold.
      3) Set *Presented by* in 18-point Lucida Calligraphy bold.
      4) Set *King County Outreach* in 22-point Lucida Calligraphy bold.
      5) Set *June 2002* in 18-point Lucida Calligraphy bold.
   d. Create the star in the middle of the certificate by completing the following steps:
      1) Click the AutoShapes button on the Drawing toolbar, point to Stars and

   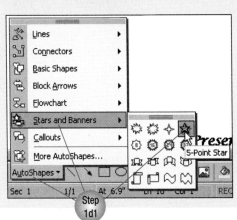

Banners, and then click 5-Point Star in the side menu (last option from the left in the top row).

2) Press the Delete key to delete the drawing canvas.

3) Draw the star in the middle of the certificate as shown in figure 3.12.

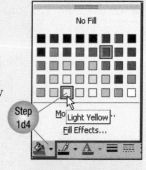

4) Add light yellow fill to the star by clicking the down-pointing triangle at the right side of the Fill Color button on the Drawing toolbar, and then clicking the Light Yellow color (third color option from the left in the bottom row of the color palette).

5) Click the Text Box button on the Drawing toolbar and then draw a text box inside the star.

6) Key **Chad Jeffries** inside the text box. Set *Chad Jeffries* in 22-point Lucida Calligraphy bold.

7) Click the Fill Color button to add light yellow fill to the text box.

8) Remove the line around the text box by clicking the down-pointing triangle at the right side of the Line Color button and then clicking *No Line* at the pop-up menu.

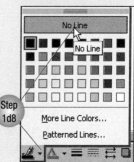

e. Create and align the small stars toward the bottom of the certificate by completing the following steps:

1) Click the AutoShapes button on the Drawing toolbar, point to Stars and Banners, and then click 5-Point Star at the side menu.

2) Press the Delete key to delete the drawing canvas.

3) Hold down the Shift key and then drag to create the first star. (If you are not happy with the size of the star, delete it, and then draw it again.)

4) Add light yellow fill to the star.

5) Copy the star by holding down the Ctrl key, dragging to the right, then releasing the Ctrl key and then the mouse button.

6) Copy the star four more times so the six stars are positioned as shown in figure 3.12.

7) Align the stars at the bottom by completing the following steps:
   a) Click the Select Objects button on the Drawing toolbar.
   b) Draw a border around all six stars.
   c) Click the Draw button on the Drawing toolbar, point to Align and Distribute, and then click Align Bottom.

8) Select the three stars at the left side of the certificate and then distribute the stars horizontally. (To do this, click the Draw button, point to Align and Distribute, and then click Distribute Horizontally.)

9) Select the three stars at the right side of the certificate and then align and distribute the stars horizontally.

2. Save the completed certificate and name it EWd C03 Ex08.

3. Print and then close EWd C03 Ex08.

FIGURE

3.12 **Exercise 8**

Flipping and Rotating an Object

A selected object can be rotated and flipped horizontally or vertically. To rotate or flip an object, select the object, click the Draw button on the Drawing toolbar, point to Rotate or Flip, and then click the desired rotation or flip option at the side menu that displays. A drawn object can be rotated but a text box cannot.

exercise 9

CREATING A LETTERHEAD AND ROTATING AN ARROW

1. At a clear document screen, create the letterhead shown in figure 3.13 by completing the following steps:
    a. Press Enter four times.
    b. Click the Center button on the Formatting toolbar.
    c. Change the font to 36-point Impact. (If Impact is not available, choose a similar typeface.)
    d. Key **Quick Time Printing**.
    e. Create the yellow arrow at the left side of the text by completing the following steps:
        1) Click the AutoShapes button on the Drawing toolbar.
        2) Point to Block Arrows. (This displays a side menu.)
        3) Click the first arrow from the left in the third row (the Bent Arrow).

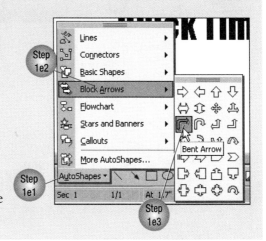

4) Press the Delete key to delete the drawing canvas.
5) Draw the arrow at the left side of the text as shown in figure 3.13. If you are not satisfied with the location of the arrow, drag it to the desired location. If you are not satisfied with the size of the arrow, use the sizing handles to increase or decrease the size.

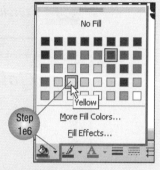

6) With the arrow still selected, add yellow fill. To do this, click the down-pointing triangle at the right side of the Fill Color button on the Drawing toolbar. At the palette of color choices that displays, click the Yellow color (third color from the left in the fourth row).

f. With the yellow arrow still selected, copy it to the right side of the text. To do this, position the mouse pointer inside the arrow (displays with a four-headed arrow attached), hold down the Ctrl key, and then the left mouse button. Drag the arrow to the right side of the text, release the mouse button, and then release the Ctrl key.

g. Flip the arrow horizontally by completing the following steps:
1) With the arrow at the right side of the text still selected, click the Draw button on the Drawing toolbar.
2) At the pop-up menu that displays, point to Rotate or Flip.
3) At the side menu that displays, click Flip Horizontal.

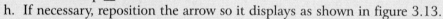

h. If necessary, reposition the arrow so it displays as shown in figure 3.13.

2. Save the document and name it EWd C03 Ex09.
3. Print and then close EWd C03 Ex09.

FIGURE

3.13 *Exercise 9*

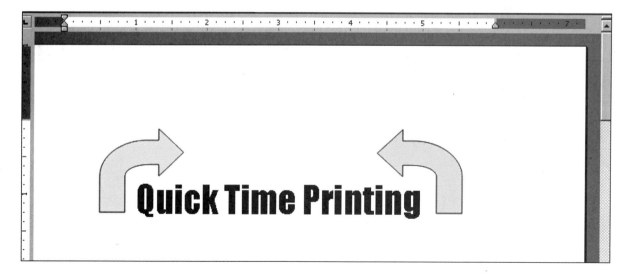

Quick Time Printing

WORD

Using WordArt

With the WordArt application, you can distort or modify text to conform to a variety of shapes. This is useful for creating company logos and headings. With WordArt, you can change the font, style, and alignment of text. You can also use different fill patterns and colors, customize border lines, and add shadow and three-dimensional effects. Display the WordArt Gallery shown in figure 3.14 by clicking the Insert WordArt button on the Drawing toolbar. Double-click a WordArt style at the WordArt Gallery and the Edit WordArt Text dialog box displays. At this dialog box, key the desired WordArt text, and then click the OK button.

Insert
WordArt

FIGURE

3.14 *WordArt Gallery*

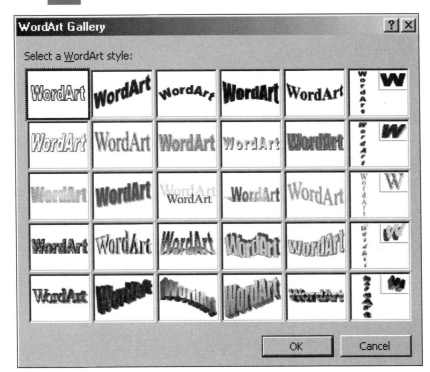

exercise 10

CREATING A HEADING WITH WORDART

1. At a clear document screen, create the heading shown in figure 3.15 using WordArt by completing the following steps:
    a. Press Enter seven times, and then move the insertion point back up to the first line.
    b. Display the Drawing toolbar.
    c. Click the Insert WordArt button on the Drawing toolbar.

d. At the WordArt Gallery, double-click the second option from the left in the fourth row.

e. At the Edit WordArt Text dialog box, key **Retirement Investment Funds**.

f. Click OK to close the dialog box.

g. Create the line below the company name by completing the following steps:

1) Click the Arrow button on the Drawing toolbar.

2) Press the Delete key to delete the drawing canvas.

3) Draw a horizontal line as shown in figure 3.15.

4) With the horizontal line selected, change the arrow style by clicking the Arrow Style button on the Drawing toolbar, and then clicking the second option from the bottom (Arrow Style 10).

5) Increase the width of the line by clicking the Line Style button on the Drawing toolbar and then clicking the *3 pt* line at the pop-up menu.

6) Change the color of the horizontal line by clicking the down-pointing triangle at the right side of the Line Color button and then clicking the Blue-Gray color (second color option from the *right* in the second row from the top).

2. Deselect the line.

3. Save the document and name it EWd C03 Ex10.

4. Print and then close EWd C03 Ex10.

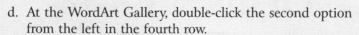

FIGURE

3.15 *Exercise 10*

Sizing and Moving WordArt

WordArt text displays in the document with the formatting you selected at the WordArt Gallery. Click the WordArt text to select it and black, square sizing handles display around the text. Use these handles to increase or decrease the WordArt size.

If you want to move and/or format the WordArt text, choose a wrapping style and the sizing handles change to white circles along with a green rotation handle and a yellow adjustment diamond. Use the green rotation handle to rotate the WordArt text and use the yellow adjustment diamond to change the slant of the text.

To move WordArt text, position the mouse pointer on any letter of the text until the mouse pointer displays with a four-headed arrow attached. Hold down the left mouse button, drag the outline of the WordArt text box to the desired position, and then release the mouse button. When all changes have been made to the WordArt text, click outside the WordArt text box to remove the sizing handles.

exercise 11

CREATING, MOVING, AND SIZING WORDART TEXT

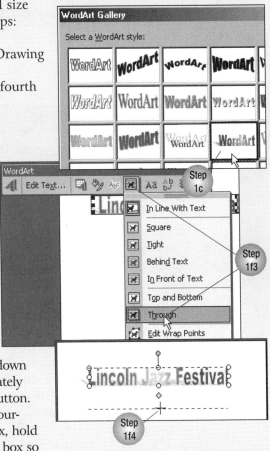

1. At a clear document screen, create, move, and size WordArt text by completing the following steps:
   a. Change to the Print Layout view.
   b. Click the Insert WordArt button on the Drawing toolbar.
   c. At the WordArt Gallery, double-click the fourth option from the left in the third row.
   d. At the Edit WordArt Text dialog box, key **Lincoln Jazz Festival**.
   e. Click OK to close the dialog box.
   f. Increase the size of the WordArt text by completing the following steps:
      1) Click the Zoom button on the Standard toolbar and then click *Whole Page* at the drop-down list.
      2) Click the WordArt text to select it.
      3) Click the Text Wrapping button on the WordArt toolbar and then click Through at the drop-down list.
      4) Make the WordArt text twice as big by positioning the mouse pointer on the middle sizing handle at the bottom of the WordArt text box, drag down until the height of the box is approximately doubled, and then release the mouse button.
   g. Position the mouse pointer (turns into a four-headed arrow) inside the WordArt text box, hold down the left mouse button, drag the text box so it is centered horizontally and vertically on the page, and then release the mouse button.
2. Click outside the WordArt text box to deselect it.
3. Save the document and name it EWd C03 Ex11.
4. Print and then close EWd C03 Ex11.

Customizing WordArt

The WordArt toolbar, shown in figure 3.16, contains buttons for customizing WordArt text. Using buttons on the WordArt toolbar, you can perform such actions as changing size and shape, rotating WordArt text, changing wrapping style, changing the letter height and alignment of text, and changing character spacing.

FIGURE

3.16 *WordArt Toolbar Buttons*

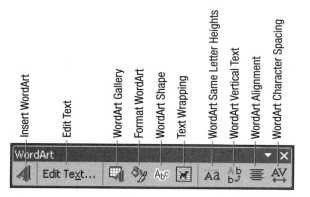

exercise 12

CREATING AND THEN CUSTOMIZING WORDART TEXT

1. At a clear document screen, create WordArt text, and then change the font, shape, and size of the text by completing the following steps:
    a. Change to the Print Layout view.
    b. Click the Insert WordArt button on the Drawing toolbar.
    c. At the WordArt Gallery, double-click the second option from the left in the second row.
    d. At the Edit WordArt Text dialog box, make the following changes:
        1) Key **Now is the time**.
        2) Press Enter and then key **to get out and**.
        3) Press Enter and then key **vote!**.
        4) Change the font to Braggadocio. To do this, click the down-pointing triangle at the right side of the Font option box, and then click *Braggadocio* at the drop-down list. (You will need to scroll up the list to display *Braggadocio*.)
        5) Click the OK button to close the dialog box.
    e. Change the alignment, size, and position of the WordArt text by completing the following steps:
        1) Click the WordArt text to select it.
        2) Click the Text Wrapping button on the WordArt toolbar and then click Through at the drop-down list.

3) Click the WordArt Alignment button on the WordArt toolbar and then click Letter Justify at the drop-down list.

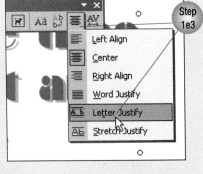

Step 1e3

Left Align
Center
Right Align
Word Justify
Letter Justify
Stretch Justify

4) Change the size and position of the WordArt by completing the following steps:
   a) Click the Format WordArt button on the WordArt toolbar.
   b) At the Format WordArt dialog box, click the Size tab.
   c) At the Format WordArt dialog box with the Size tab selected, select the current measurement in the Height text box (in the Size and rotate section), and then key **2.5**.
   d) Select the current measurement in the Width text box (in the Size and rotate section), and then key **5**.
   e) Click the Layout tab.
   f) At the Format WordArt dialog box with the Layout tab selected, click the Advanced button (located at the bottom of the dialog box).

Step 1e4b

Format WordArt   ? | X |

Colors and Lines | Size | Layout | Picture | Text Box | Web

Size and rotate

Height: 2.5   Width: 5

Rotation: 0°

Step 1e4c

Step 1e4d

   g) At the Advanced Layout dialog box, click the Picture Position tab.
   h) At the Advanced Layout dialog box with the Picture Position tab selected, click the down-pointing triangle at the right side of the *to the right of* option box (in the Horizontal section—contains the word *Column*) and then click *Margin* at the drop-down list.
   i) Select the current measurement in the Absolute position text box in the Horizontal section and then key **0.5**. (Be sure to key a zero and not the letter *O*.)
   j) Select the current measurement in the Absolute position text box in the Vertical section and then key **3**.

Step 1e4g

Advanced Layout   ? | X |

Picture Position | Text Wrapping

Horizontal

○ Alignment   Left   relative to   Column

○ Book layout   Inside   of   Margin

● Absolute position   0.5   to the right of   Margin

Vertical

○ Alignment   Top   relative to   Page

● Absolute position   3   below   Paragraph

Step 1e4i

Step 1e4h

Step 1e4j

   k) Click OK to close the Advanced Layout dialog box.
   l) Click OK to close the Format WordArt dialog box.
   f. Click outside the WordArt text box to deselect it.
2. Save the document and name it EWd C03 Ex12.
3. Print and then close EWd C03 Ex12.

Customizing WordArt with Buttons on the Drawing Toolbar

In a previous section of this chapter, you learned about the buttons on the Drawing toolbar. Buttons on this toolbar can also be used to customize WordArt text. For example, with buttons on the Drawing toolbar, you can change the letter color, line color, and line style, add a shadow, and add a three-dimensional effect.

exercise 13

CREATING AND THEN APPLYING PATTERN, COLOR, AND SHADING TO WORDART TEXT

1. Create the WordArt text shown in figure 3.17 by completing the following steps:
   a. Change to the Print Layout view.
   b. Click the Insert WordArt button on the Drawing toolbar.
   c. At the WordArt Gallery, double-click the third option from the left in the top row.
   d. At the Edit WordArt Text dialog box, key **Exploring Office XP**, and then click OK to close the dialog box.

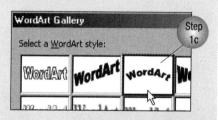

   e. Click the WordArt text to select it.
   f. Click the Text Wrapping button on the WordArt toolbar and then click Through at the drop-down list.
   g. Click the WordArt Shape button on the WordArt toolbar and then click the second shape from the left in the fourth row (Deflate).

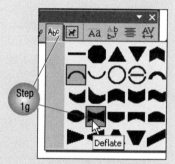

   h. Change the size and position of the WordArt by completing the following steps:
      1) Click the Format WordArt button on the WordArt toolbar.
      2) At the Format WordArt dialog box, click the Size tab.
      3) At the Format WordArt dialog box with the Size tab selected, select the current measurement in the Height text box (in the Size and rotate section), and then key **2**.
      4) Select the current measurement in Width text box (in the Size and rotate section) and then key **6**.
      5) Click the Layout tab.
      6) At the Format WordArt dialog box with the Layout tab selected, click the Advanced button (located at the bottom of the dialog box).
      7) At the Advanced Layout dialog box, click the Picture Position tab.
      8) Select the current measurement in the Absolute position text box (in the Vertical section of the dialog box) and then key **3.5**.
      9) Click OK to close the Advanced Layout dialog box.
      10) Click OK to close the Format WordArt dialog box.

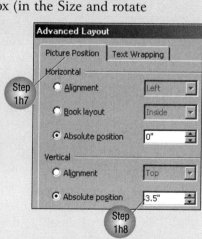

   i. Add a pattern and change colors by completing the following steps:

1) Click the down-pointing triangle at the right side of the Fill Color button on the Drawing toolbar.
2) At the palette of color choices that displays, click Fill Effects located at the bottom of the palette.
3) At the Fill Effects dialog box, click the Pattern tab.
4) At the Fill Effects dialog box with the Pattern tab selected, make the following changes:
   a) Click the fourth pattern option from the left in the second row (Light horizontal).
   b) Click the down-pointing triangle at the right side of the Foreground box.
   c) At the color palette that displays, click the Turquoise color (fifth color from the left in the fourth row).
   d) Click the down-pointing triangle at the right side of the Background box.
   e) At the color palette that displays, click the Pink color (first color from the left in the fourth row).
5) Click OK to close the Fill Effects dialog box.
   j. Add a shadow to the text by clicking the Shadow Style button on the Drawing toolbar and then clicking the second shadow option from the left in the fourth row (Shadow Style 14).

Step 1j

No Shadow

Shadow Style 14

Shadow Settings...

   k. Click outside the WordArt text to deselect the WordArt box.
2. Save the document and name it EWd C03 Ex13.
3. Print and then close EWd C03 Ex13.

FIGURE

3.17 *Exercise 13*

Creating a Dropped Capital Letter

In publications such as magazines, newsletters, brochures, and so on, a graphic feature called *dropped caps* can be used to enhance the appearance of text. A drop cap is the first letter of the first word of a paragraph that is set into a paragraph. Drop caps identify the beginning of major sections or parts of a document.

Drop caps look best when set in a paragraph containing text set in a proportional font. The drop cap can be set in the same font as the paragraph text or it can be set in a complementary font. For example, a drop cap can be set in a sans serif font while the paragraph text is set in a serif font.

Drop caps in Word are created through the Drop Cap dialog box shown in figure 3.18. To display this dialog box, click Format and then Drop Cap. At the Drop Cap dialog box, click the desired drop cap option, and then click OK or press Enter. When you create a drop cap, Word automatically changes to the Page Layout view.

FIGURE

3.18 *Drop Cap Dialog Box*

HINT

Remove a drop cap from text by choosing the None option at the Drop Cap dialog box.

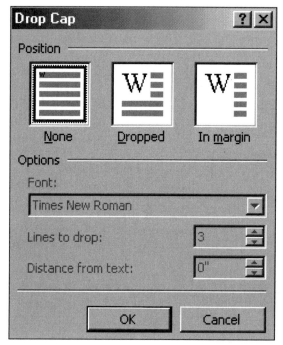

CREATING DROP CAPS

1. Open Word Document 04.
2. Save the document with Save As and name it EWd C03 Ex14.
3. Create a drop cap for the first paragraph by completing the following steps:
   a. Position the insertion point anywhere in the first paragraph.
   b. Click Format and then Drop Cap.
   c. At the Drop Cap dialog box, click Dropped in the Position section.
   d. Click OK or press Enter.
   e. Deselect the drop cap.
4. Complete steps similar to those in 3 to create a drop cap for the second paragraph.
5. Complete steps similar to those in 3 to create a drop cap for the third paragraph.
6. Save, print, and then close EWd C03 Ex14.

If you want more than the first letter of a paragraph to be set in drop caps, you must select the word before displaying the Drop Cap dialog box.

1. Open Word Document 04.
2. Save the document with Save As and name it EWd C03 Ex15.
3. Create a drop cap for the first word of the first paragraph and change the font of the word by completing the following steps:
   a. Select the first word *(The)* of the first paragraph.
   b. Click F**o**rmat and then **D**rop Cap.
   c. At the Drop Cap dialog box, click **D**ropped in the Position section.
   d. Click the down-pointing triangle at the right of the **F**ont option box and then click *Desdemona* at the drop-down menu. (If Desdemona is not available, choose a similar decorative typeface.)
   e. Click OK or press Enter.
   f. Deselect the drop cap.
4. Save, print, and then close EWd C03 Ex15.

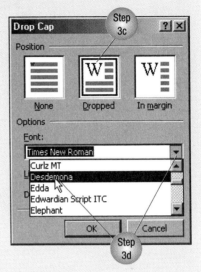

To remove drop caps from a paragraph, position the insertion point in the paragraph, click F**o**rmat and then **D**rop Cap. At the Drop Cap dialog box, click **N**one in the Position section of the dialog box, and then click OK or press Enter.

Customizing Toolbars

Word 2002 contains customizable toolbars. For example, you can add to a toolbar buttons representing features you use on a consistent basis or remove buttons you do not need. You can also move buttons on a toolbar or reset the position of buttons.

To add a button to or remove a button from a toolbar, click the Toolbar Options button located at the right side of the toolbar, point to **A**dd or Remove Buttons, and then click the name of the toolbar at the side menu. For example, click the Toolbar Options button at the right side of the Standard toolbar, point to **A**dd or Remove Buttons, and then point to Standard and a drop-down list of button options displays as shown in figure 3.19.

HINT
Increase the size of toolbar buttons by choosing the **L**arge icons option at the Customize dialog box with the **O**ptions tab selected.

3.19 *Standard Toolbar Buttons Drop-Down List*

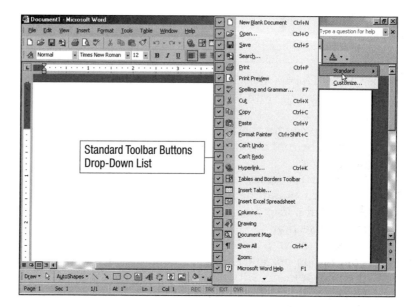

Standard Toolbar Buttons
Drop-Down List

HINT

If you add buttons to a
full toolbar, some of the
buttons may be hidden.

HINT

Move a toolbar by
positioning the arrow
pointer at the left edge
of the toolbar until the
pointer turns into a
four-headed arrow, hold
down the left mouse
button, and then drag
the toolbar to the
desired location.

To add a button to the toolbar, click the desired option at the drop-down list. This inserts the button at the right side of the toolbar. To remove a button, click the desired option to remove the check mark. Another method for removing a button from a toolbar is to display the Customize dialog box and then drag the button off the toolbar.

Buttons you add to a toolbar are inserted at the right side of the toolbar. You may want to move buttons to different locations on a toolbar. To do this, click Tools and then Customize. With the Customize dialog box displayed, drag a button to the desired position. You can also move a button from one toolbar to another.

You can reset buttons on a toolbar back to their original positions. To do this, display the Customize dialog box with the Toolbars tab selected, and then click the Reset button. At the Reset Toolbar dialog box, click OK.

exercise **16**

ADDING/REMOVING BUTTONS FROM THE STANDARD TOOLBAR

1. Add a Close button to the Standard toolbar and remove the Document Map button by completing the following steps:
   a. At a clear document screen, click the Toolbar Options button located at the right side of the Standard toolbar.
   b. Point to Add or Remove Buttons option and then point to Standard.
   c. At the drop-down list that displays, click Document Map. (This removes the check mark from the option.)

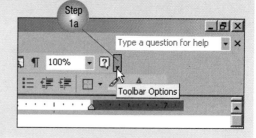

Step 1a

d. Scroll down the drop-down list until the <u>C</u>lose button is visible and then click <u>C</u>lose. (This inserts a check mark before the option.)

e. Click outside the drop-down list to remove it from the screen. (Check the Standard toolbar and notice the Close button that displays at the right side of the toolbar.)

2. Drag the Close button on the Standard toolbar so it is positioned between the Open button and the Save button by completing the following steps:

a. Click <u>T</u>ools and then <u>C</u>ustomize.

b. With the Customize dialog box displayed, position the mouse pointer on the Close button, hold down the left mouse button, drag the icon representing the button so it is positioned between the Open button and Save button, and then release the mouse button.

c. Close the Customize dialog box by clicking the Close button in the dialog box.

3. Move the Insert Clip Art button from the Drawing toolbar to the Standard toolbar by completing the following steps:

a. Display the Drawing toolbar by clicking the Drawing button on the Standard toolbar.

b. Display the Customize dialog box by clicking <u>T</u>ools and then <u>C</u>ustomize.

c. Position the arrow pointer on the Insert Clip Art button on the Drawing toolbar, hold down the left mouse button, drag up so the button icon displays between the Spelling and Grammar button and the Cut button on the Standard toolbar, and then release the mouse button.

d. Close the Customize dialog box by clicking the Close button in the dialog box.

4. Open Word Document 04.

5. Save the document with Save As and name it EWd C03 Ex16.

6. Make the following changes to the document:

a. Click the Insert Clip Art button on the Standard toolbar (you moved this button to the Standard toolbar).

b. At the Insert Clip Art Task Pane, search for a computer clip art image and then insert the image in the document.

c. Size and/or move the image to a desirable location in the document (you choose the size and location). Make sure text wraps around the image.

7. Save and then print EWd C03 Ex16.

8. Close the document by clicking the Close button on the Standard toolbar. (You added this button to the Standard toolbar.)

9. Reset the Standard toolbar (removing the Close button, Insert Clip Art button, and adding the Document Map button) by completing the following steps:

a. At a clear document screen, click <u>T</u>ools and then <u>C</u>ustomize.

b. At the Customize dialog box, click the Tool<u>b</u>ars tab.

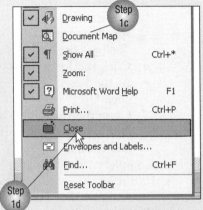

Step 1c

Step 1d

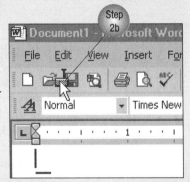

Step 2b

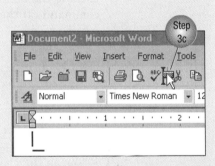

Step 3c

c. At the Customize dialog box with the Toolbars tab selected, make sure *Standard* is selected in the Toolbars list box.
d. Click the Reset button.
e. At the Reset Toolbar dialog box, click OK.
f. Close the Customize dialog box by clicking the Close button in the dialog box.

10. Complete steps similar to those in step 9 to reset the Drawing toolbar. (At the Customize dialog box, click *Drawing* in the Toolbars list box.)

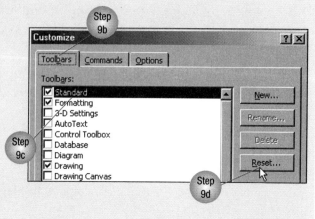

Customizing Menus

Menus, like toolbars, can be customized. For example, you can add or remove commands from a menu and also create a custom menu. Customize an existing menu by displaying the Customize dialog box with the Commands tab selected and then clicking the desired menu category. In the Commands list box, drag and then drop the desired command to the specific menu option on the Menu bar. Remove a command from a menu by displaying the Customize dialog box, clicking the desired menu option on the Menu bar, and then dragging the command off the menu.

exercise **17**

1. Add two commands to the Format menu by completing the following steps:
   a. Click Tools and then Customize.
   b. At the Customize dialog box, click the Commands tab.
   c. Click *Format* in the Categories list box.
   d. Scroll down the Commands list box until the *Grow Font 1 Pt* and *Shrink Font 1 Pt* commands display.
   e. Position the mouse pointer on the *Grow Font 1 Pt* command, hold down the left mouse button, drag to the Format menu option on the Menu bar, drag down below the Font option until a black line displays below Font, and then release the mouse button. (The *Grow Font 1 Pt* command now displays below Font on the Format drop-down menu.)
   f. Drag the *Shrink Font 1 Pt* command below the *Grow Font 1 Pt* command on the Format drop-down menu.

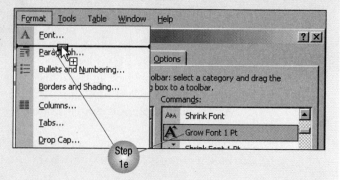

WORD

g. Click the Close button in the Customize dialog box.
2. Open Word Notice 01.
3. Save the document with Save As and name it EWd C03 Ex17.
4. Make the following changes to the document:
   a. Select the entire document and then change the font to 14-point Bookman Old Style bold (or a similar serif typeface).
   b. Increase the font size for specific text by completing the following steps:
      1) Select *McCORMACK FUNDS* and *Annual Stockholders' Meeting*.
      2) Click Format and then Grow Font 1 Pt at the drop-down list.
      3) Click Format and then Grow Font 1 Pt. (The size of the selected text should now be 16 points.)
   c. Reduce the font size for specific text by completing the following steps:
      1) Select *King Auditorium, Wednesday, September 18, 2002,* and *6:30 p.m.*
      2) Click Format and then Shrink Font 1 Pt.
      3) Click Format and then Shrink Font 1 Pt again. (The size of the selected text should now be 12 points.)
5. Save, print, and then close EWd C03 Ex17.
6. Remove the two font commands from the Format drop-down menu by completing the following steps:
   a. Click Tools and then Customize.
   b. Make sure the Commands tab is selected.
   c. Click Format on the Menu bar.
   d. Position the mouse pointer on *Grow Font 1 Pt*, hold down the left mouse button, drag onto the document screen, and then release the mouse button.
   e. Drag *Shrink Font 1 Pt* onto the document screen.
   f. Click the Close button in the Customize dialog box.

Along with customizing existing menu, you can create your own menu and then include it on the Menu bar. To create a custom menu, display the Customize dialog box with the Commands tab selected. Click *New Menu* in the Categories list box and then drag the New Menu command to the Menu bar. Rename the menu and then add commands to the menu.

exercise 18

CREATING A CUSTOM MENU

1. Create a custom menu named Go To that contains commands for moving to specific locations in a document by completing the following steps:
   a. Click Tools and then Customize.
   b. At the Customize dialog box, make sure the Commands tab is selected.
   c. Scroll down the Categories list box until *New Menu* is visible and then click *New Menu*.

d. Position the mouse pointer on *New Menu* in the Commands list box, hold down the left mouse button, drag to the right of the <u>V</u>iew option on the Menu bar, and then release the mouse button. (This inserts *New Menu* between <u>V</u>iew and <u>I</u>nsert.)

e. Rename *New Menu* to *Go To* by completing the following steps:
   1) Right-click *New Menu* on the Menu bar.
   2) At the drop-down list that displays, select the text *New Menu* that displays in the <u>N</u>ame text box, and then key **Go To**.
   3) Press Enter.

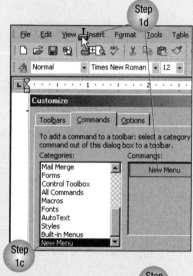

f. At the Customize dialog box, click *Edit* in the Categories list box. (You will need to scroll up this list box to display *Edit*.)

g. Scroll down the Comman<u>d</u>s list box until *Go To Next Page* is visible.

h. Drag *Go To Next Page* in the Comman<u>d</u>s list box to the Go To menu option on the Menu bar. (This displays a square, gray box below the Go To menu option.)

i. Drag down to the square, gray box below Go To and then release the mouse button.

j. Drag *Go To Previous Page* from the Comman<u>d</u>s list box in the Customize dialog box so it is positioned below the <u>G</u>o To Next Page command on the Go To menu.

k. Click the Close button in the Customize dialog box.

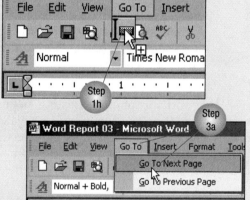

2. Open Word Report 03.
3. Use options on the Go To menu by completing the following steps:
   a. Move the insertion point to page 2 by clicking Go To on the Menu bar and then clicking <u>G</u>o To Next Page at the drop-down list.
   b. Move the insertion point to page 3 by clicking Go To and then <u>G</u>o To Next Page.
   c. Move the insertion point to page 2 by clicking Go To and then <u>G</u>o To Previous Page.
4. Remove the Go To menu option from the Menu bar by completing the following steps:
   a. Click <u>T</u>ools and then <u>C</u>ustomize.
   b. With the Customize dialog box displayed, drag the Go To menu option onto the document screen.
   c. Close the Customize dialog box.
5. Close Word Report 03.

CHAPTER summary

➤ Insert clip art images, photographs, movie images, and sound clips with options at the Insert Clip Art Task Pane.

➤ Click an image in the Insert Clip Art Task Pane and the image is inserted in the current document.

➤ Click an image in the document to select it and sizing handles display around the image. Use these handles to increase or decrease the image size.

➤ To move a selected image, choose a text wrapping option, and then drag the image to the desired location.

➤ Format a selected image using buttons on the Picture toolbar. This toolbar displays when an image is selected.

➤ Format a selected image with options at the Format Picture dialog box. Display this dialog box by clicking the Format Picture button on the Picture toolbar.

➤ With options at the Advanced Layout dialog box, you can specify the horizontal and vertical position of an image, choose a text wrapping style, and specify where the image is anchored. Display the Advanced Layout dialog box by clicking the Advanced button at the Format Picture dialog box with the Layout tab selected.

➤ A watermark is a lightened image that displays in a document. Create a watermark with an image or with text using options at the Printed Watermark dialog box.

➤ If you are connected to the Internet, clicking the _Clips Online_ hyperlink at the Insert Clip Art Task Pane will display the Microsoft Design Gallery Live Web site. This site offers a gallery with hundreds of images you can download.

➤ Use buttons on the Drawing toolbar to draw a variety of shapes and lines as well as a text box. A shape drawn with the Line or Arrow button is considered a line drawing and a shape drawn with the Rectangle or Oval button is considered an enclosed drawing.

➤ When you click a button on the Drawing toolbar, the drawing canvas displays. Draw the shape in the drawing canvas or delete the drawing canvas and draw in the document.

➤ Customize a drawn shape by adding fill color or changing line color.

➤ Distribute and align graphic elements such as a clip art image, shape, autoshape, or text box with the Draw button on the Drawing toolbar.

➤ Rotate and/or flip a selected object by clicking the Draw button on the Drawing toolbar, pointing to Rotate or Flip, and then clicking the desired rotation or flip option.

➤ Use the WordArt application to distort or modify text to conform to a variety of shapes. Create WordArt text using the WordArt Gallery. Click the Insert WordArt button on the Drawing toolbar to display the WordArt Gallery.

➤ Click WordArt text and sizing handles display around the text. Use these sizing handles to increase or decrease the size of the WordArt text.

➤ To move selected WordArt text, choose a text wrapping style, and then drag the text to the desired location.

➤ Customize WordArt text using buttons on the WordArt toolbar or with buttons on the Drawing toolbar.

➤ A drop cap is the first letter of the first word of a paragraph that is set into the paragraph. Create a drop cap with options at the Drop Cap dialog box.

➤ Customize toolbars by adding, removing, and/or moving buttons. Return toolbars to the default buttons with the <u>R</u>eset button at the Customize dialog box.

➤ Customize menus by adding and/or removing commands or create a custom menu.

COMMANDS review

Command	Mouse/Keyboard
Insert Clip Art Task Pane	<u>I</u>nsert, <u>P</u>icture, <u>C</u>lip Art; or click Insert Clip Art button on Drawing toolbar
Display Drawing toolbar	Click Drawing button on Standard toolbar
Display Picture toolbar	Click image; or right-click image and then click Show Picture Toolbar
Display Format Picture dialog box	Click Format Picture button on Picture toolbar
Display Advanced Layout dialog box	Click <u>A</u>dvanced button at Format Picture dialog box with Layout tab selected
Display Printed Watermark dialog box	F<u>o</u>rmat, <u>B</u>ackground, Printed <u>W</u>atermark
Display Microsoft Design Gallery Live Web site	Click *Clips Online* hyperlink at Insert Clip Art Task Pane
Display WordArt Gallery	Click Insert WordArt button on Drawing toolbar
Display Drop Cap dialog box	F<u>o</u>rmat, <u>D</u>rop Cap
Display Customize dialog box	<u>T</u>ools, <u>C</u>ustomize

CONCEPTS check

Completion: On a blank sheet of paper, indicate the correct term, command, or number for each item.

1. Insert images in a document with options at this task pane.
2. Use buttons on this toolbar to format a selected image.
3. Display the Advanced Layout dialog box by clicking the <u>A</u>dvanced button at this dialog box with the Layout tab selected.
4. Create a picture or text watermark with options at this dialog box.
5. Click this hyperlink at the Insert Clip Art Task Pane and the Microsoft Design Gallery Live Web site displays.
6. Use buttons on this toolbar to draw a variety of shapes and lines as well as a text box.
7. Display the WordArt Gallery by clicking this button on the Drawing toolbar.
8. Display the Drop Cap dialog box by clicking this option on the Menu bar and then clicking <u>D</u>rop Cap at the drop-down menu.

9. To add a button to or remove a button from a toolbar, begin by clicking this button located at the right side of the toolbar.
10. Reset buttons on a toolbar back to their original positions by displaying this dialog box and then clicking the Reset button.
11. Customize an existing menu by displaying the Customize dialog box with this tab selected.

SKILLS check

Assessment 1

1. Open Word Report 07.
2. Save the document with Save As and name it EWd C03 SA01.
3. Make the following changes to the document:
   a. Change the line spacing for the entire document to single spacing.
   b. Delete the text in the document from the heading *Painting and Drawing Programs Today* to the end of the document.
   c. Bold the headings *Early Painting and Drawing Programs* and *Developments in Painting and Drawing Programs*.
   d. Insert a clip art image with the following specifications:
      1) Insert a clip art image related to "software." (If no matches are found for "software," look for images related to "computers.")
      2) Change the height of the image to 2.5 inches.
      3) Change the wrapping style to Tight.
      4) Change the horizontal alignment of the image to *Centered* relative to the *Margin*.
      5) Change the vertical alignment of the image to *Centered* relative to *Page*.
4. Save, print, and then close EWd C03 SA01.

Assessment 2

1. Open Word Notice 04.
2. Save the document with Save As and name it EWd C03 SA02.
3. Insert as a watermark the image named *laptop* that is located in the *ClipArt* folder on the CD that accompanies this textbook. *(Hint: Use the Printed Watermark dialog box to insert the image as a watermark.)*
4. Save, print, and then close EWd C03 SA02.

Assessment 3

1. At a clear document screen, draw the square, circle, and rectangle shown in figure 3.20. After drawing the shapes, make the following changes:
   a. Select each shape, click the Line Style button on the Drawing toolbar, and then click the $2^{1}/_{4}$ *pt* option. (This makes the line thicker.)
   b. Add red fill to the square, yellow fill to the circle, and blue fill to the rectangle.
2. Save the document and name it EWd C03 SA03.
3. Print and then close EWd C03 SA03.

3.20 *Assessment 3*

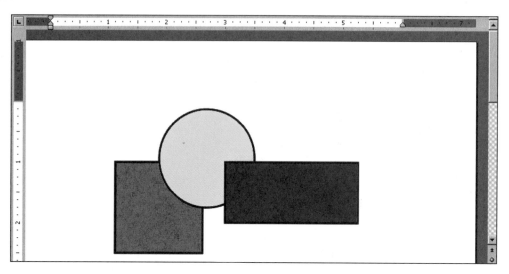

Assessment 4

1. At a clear document screen, create the letterhead shown in figure 3.21 with the following specifications:
    a. Change the paragraph alignment to center.
    b. Set **FRONT STREET** in 16-point Arial bold and set **Moving Company** in 14-point Arial bold.
    c. Draw the arrow at the left using the Striped Right Arrow autoshape. (Display this autoshape by clicking A<u>u</u>toShapes, pointing to Block <u>A</u>rrows, and then clicking Striped Right Arrow.)
    d. Add red fill to the arrow.
    e. Copy the arrow to the right and then flip the arrow as shown in figure 3.21.
2. Save the completed document and name it EWd C03 SA04.
3. Print and then close EWd C03 SA04.

3.21 *Assessment 4*

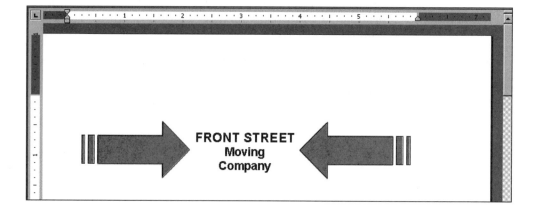

Assessment 5

1. At a clear document screen, create the WordArt text and border line shown in figure 3.22 by completing the following steps:
   a. Display the WordArt Gallery.
   b. Double-click the third option from the left in the top row.
   c. At the Edit WordArt Text dialog box, key **Mountain**, press Enter, key **Ski Resort**, and then close the dialog box.
   d. Click the WordArt text to select it and then change the text wrapping to Through.
   e. Change the shape of the text to Triangle Up. *(Hint: Click the WordArt Shape button on the WordArt toolbar.)*
   f. Display the Format WordArt dialog box with the Size tab selected, change the height to *1.2* and the width to *2*, and then close the dialog box.
   g. Display the Format WordArt dialog box with the Layout tab selected, click Left in the Horizontal alignment section, and then close the dialog box.
   h. Change the fill color and line color to Blue. *(Hint: Do this with the Fill Color and Line Color buttons on the Drawing toolbar.)*
   i. Deselect the WordArt text.
   j. Create the line below the company name with the following specifications:
      1) Use the Arrow button on the Drawing toolbar to draw the line. *(Hint: After clicking the Arrow button, press the Delete key to delete the drawing canvas.)*
      2) With the horizontal line selected, change the arrow style by clicking the Arrow Style and then clicking the second option from the bottom (Arrow Style 10).
      3) Increase the width of the line by clicking the Line Style button on the Drawing toolbar and then clicking the *4½ pt* line at the pop-up menu.
      4) Change the color of the horizontal line to Blue.
2. Save the document and name it EWd C03 SA05.
3. Print and then close EWd C03 SA05.

FIGURE

3.22 *Assessment 5*

Assessment 6

1. At a clear document screen, create the WordArt text shown in figure 3.23 with the following specifications. (Figure 3.23 displays the WordArt on the full page. Your text will appear much larger than what you see in the figure.)
   a. Change to the Print Layout view.
   b. Display the WordArt Gallery.
   c. Double-click the fifth option from the left in the top row.
   d. At the Edit WordArt Text dialog box, complete the following steps:
      1) Key **Coleman Development Corporation** and then press Enter.
      2) Key **Forest Renovation** and then press Enter.
      3) Key **and Revitalization Project**.
      4) Close the Edit WordArt Text dialog box.
   e. Click the WordArt text to select it and then change the text wrapping to Through.
   f. Change the shape of the text to a Button (Curve). *(Hint: Click the WordArt Shape button on the WordArt toolbar and then click the fourth option from the left in the second row.)*
   g. Display the Format WordArt dialog box with the Size tab selected, change the height and width to 6 inches, and then close the dialog box.
   h. Change the Fill Color to Green.
   i. Change the Zoom to Whole Page and then drag the WordArt text so it is centered horizontally and vertically on the page.
2. Save the document and name it EWd C03 SA06.
3. Print and then close EWd C03 SA06.

FIGURE

3.23 *Assessment 6*

Assessment 7

1. Open Word Document 06.
2. Save the document with Save As and name it EWd C03 SA07.
3. Create a drop cap with the first letter of each of the three paragraphs of text in the document.
4. Save, print, and then close EWd C03 SA07.

WORD

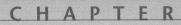

4

FORMATTING WITH MACROS AND STYLES

P E R F O R M A N C E   O B J E C T I V E S

Upon successful completion of chapter 4, you will be able to:
- **Record, run, edit, and delete macros**
- **Assign a macro to a keyboard command and a toolbar**
- **Format a document with the AutoFormat feature**
- **Format text with style templates at the Style Gallery**
- **Create, apply, modify, remove, and delete styles**
- **Assign a shortcut key combination to a style**
- **Create a cross-reference**
- **Navigate in documents**

Word Chapter 04E

In chapter 2, you learned about the AutoText feature that simplifies inserting commonly used words, names, or phrases in a document. Word includes other time-saving features such as macros and styles. With macros, you can automate the formatting of a document. Apply formatting and maintain formatting consistency in a document with styles. In this chapter, you will also learn techniques for navigating in lengthy documents.

Creating Macros

The word *macro* was coined by computer programmers for a collection of commands used to make a large programming job easier and save time. Like a macro created for a programming job, a Word macro is a document containing recorded commands that can accomplish a task automatically and save time.

In Word, creating a macro is referred to as *recording*. As a macro is being recorded, all of the keys pressed and the menus and dialog boxes displayed are recorded and become part of the macro. For example, you can record a macro to change the left or right margins or insert page numbering in a document. Two steps are involved in working with macros: recording a macro and running a macro. Word's macro feature can also be used to write macros. For more information on writing macros, please refer to Microsoft Word documentation.

Recording a Macro

Recording a macro involves turning on the macro recorder, performing the steps to be recorded, and then turning off the recorder. To record a macro, click Tools, point to Macro, and then click Record New Macro. You can also double-click the REC button that displays on the Status bar. This displays the Record Macro dialog box shown in figure 4.1.

4.1 *Record Macro Dialog Box*

HINT

Some reasons for recording a macro:
- Speed up formatting and editing
- Combine multiple commands
- Make an option in a dialog box more accessible
- Automate a series of tasks

Key a name for the macro in this text box.

Specify where the macro is to be stored with this option.

Key a description for the macro in this text box.

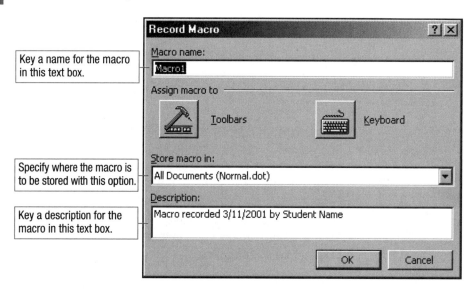

HINT

Before recording a macro, plan the steps and commands.

HINT

When recording a macro, you can use the mouse to click commands and options, but the macro recorder does not record mouse movements on the document screen.

Stop Recording

At the Record Macro dialog box, key a name for the macro in the Macro name text box. A macro name must begin with a letter and can contain only letters and numbers. Key a description for the macro in the Description text box located at the bottom of the dialog box. A macro description can contain a maximum of 255 characters and may include spaces.

By default, Word stores a macro in the Normal template document. Macros stored in this template are available for any document based on the Normal template. In a company or school setting where computers may be networked, consider storing macros in personalized documents or templates. Specify the location for macros with the Store macro in option at the Record Macro dialog box (refer to figure 4.1).

After keying the macro name, specifying where the macro is to be stored, and keying a description, click OK or press Enter to close the Record Macro dialog box. This displays the document screen with the Macro Record toolbar displayed as shown in figure 4.2. At this screen, perform the actions to be recorded. After all steps to be recorded have been performed, stop the recording of the macro by clicking the Stop Recording button on the Macro Record toolbar, or by double-clicking the REC button on the Status bar.

4.2 *Macro Record Toolbar*

Stop Recording | Pause Recording

When you record macros in exercises in this chapter, you will be instructed to name the macros beginning with your initials. An exercise step may instruct you, for example, to "record a macro named XXXInd01." Insert your initials in the macro name instead of the *XXX*. Recorded macros are stored in the Normal template document by default and display at the Macros dialog box. If the computer you are using is networked, macros recorded by other students will also display at the Macros dialog box. Naming a macro with your initials will enable you to distinguish your macros from the macros of other users.

(Note: Before completing computer exercises, delete the Word Chapter 03E *folder on your disk. Next, copy to your disk the* Word Chapter 04E *subfolder from the* Word 2002 Expert *folder on the CD that accompanies this textbook.)*

RECORDING MACROS

1. Record a macro named XXXInd01 (where your initials are used instead of *XXX*) that indents text in a paragraph 0.5 inch and hang indents second and subsequent lines of the paragraph by completing the following steps:
    a. At a clear document screen, double-click the REC button on the Status bar.
    b. At the Record Macro dialog box, key **XXXInd01** in the Macro name text box.
    c. Click inside the Description text box and then key **Indent and hang text in paragraph**. (If the Description text box contains any text, select the text first, and then key **Indent and hang text in paragraph**.)
    d. Click OK.
    e. At the document screen with the Macro Record toolbar displayed, complete the following steps:
        1) Click Format and then Paragraph.
        2) At the Paragraph dialog box, click the up-pointing triangle at the right side of the Left option until *0.5˝* displays in the Left text box.
        3) Click the down-pointing triangle at the right side of the Special text box and then click *Hanging* at the drop-down list.
        4) Click OK or press Enter.

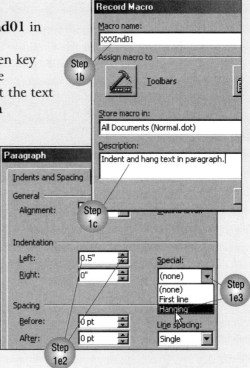

f. Double-click the REC button on the Status bar.
2. Complete steps similar to those in 1 to create a macro named *XXXInd02* that indents text in a paragraph 1 inch and hang indents second and subsequent lines of the paragraph.
3. Record a macro named XXXFormat01 that changes the top margin to 1.5 inches and the left and right margins to 1 inch by completing the following steps:
   a. At a clear document screen, click <u>T</u>ools, point to <u>M</u>acro, and then click <u>R</u>ecord New Macro.
   b. At the Record Macro dialog box, key **XXXFormat01** in the <u>M</u>acro name text box.
   c. Click in the <u>D</u>escription text box (or select existing text in the <u>D</u>escription text box) and then key **Change top, left, and right margins**.
   d. Click OK.
   e. At the document screen with the Macro Record toolbar displayed, change the top margin to 1.5 inches and the left and right margins to 1 inch. (Do this at the Page Setup dialog box with the Margins tab selected.)
   f. Click the Stop Recording button on the Macro Record toolbar.
4. Close the document without saving it.

Running a Macro

After a macro has been recorded, it can be run in a document. To run a macro, click <u>T</u>ools, point to <u>M</u>acro, and then click <u>M</u>acros. At the Macros dialog box, click the desired macro name in the list box, and then click the <u>R</u>un button. You can also just double-click the desired macro name in the list box.

exercise 2

1. Open Word Survey.
2. Save the document with Save As and name it EWd C04 Ex02.
3. Run the XXXFormat01 macro by completing the following steps:
   a. Click <u>T</u>ools, point to <u>M</u>acro, and then click <u>M</u>acros.
   b. At the Macros dialog box, click *XXXFormat01* in the <u>M</u>acro name list box, and then click the <u>R</u>un button.

4. Run the XXXInd01 macro for the first numbered paragraph by completing the following steps:
   a. Position the insertion point anywhere in the paragraph that begins with *1*.
   b. Click <u>T</u>ools, point to <u>M</u>acro, and then click <u>M</u>acros.
   c. At the Macros dialog box, double-click *XXXInd01* in the list box.
5. Complete steps similar to those in 4 to run the macro for each of the numbered paragraphs (just the numbered paragraphs, not the lettered paragraphs).
6. Run the XXXInd02 macro for the lettered paragraph (a through d) after the first numbered paragraph by completing the following steps:

WORD

a. Select paragraphs a through d below the first numbered paragraph.
b. Click Tools, point to Macro, and then click Macros.
c. At the Macros dialog box, double-click *XXXInd02* in the list box.

7. Complete steps similar to those in 6a through 6c to run the macro for the lettered paragraphs below each of the numbered paragraphs.

8. Save, print, and then close EWd C04 Ex02.

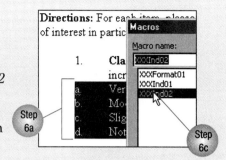

Pausing and Then Resuming a Macro

When recording a macro, you can temporarily suspend the recording, perform actions that are not recorded, and then resume recording the macro. To pause the recording of a macro, click the Pause Recording button on the Macro Record toolbar. To resume recording the macro, click the Resume Recorder button (previously the Pause Recording button).

Pause
Recording

Deleting a Macro

If you no longer need a macro, delete it at the Macros dialog box. At the Macros dialog box, click the macro name in the list box, and then click the Delete button. At the message asking if you want to delete the macro, click Yes. Click the Close button to close the Macros dialog box.

DELETING MACROS

1. At a clear document screen, delete the XXXFormat01 (where your initials display instead of the *XXX*) macro by completing the following steps:
   a. Click Tools, point to Macro, and then click Macros.
   b. At the Macros dialog box, click *XXXFormat01* in the list box.
   c. Click the Delete button.
   d. At the message asking if you want to delete XXXFormat01, click Yes.
   e. Click the Close button to close the Macros dialog box.
2. Close the document.

Assigning a Macro a Keyboard Command

If you use a macro on a regular basis, you may want to assign it a keyboard command. To run a macro that has been assigned a keyboard command, all you do is press the keys assigned to the macro. A macro can be assigned a keyboard command with a letter plus Alt + Ctrl, Ctrl + Shift, or Alt + Shift. Word has already used many combinations for Word functions. For example, pressing Ctrl + Shift + A changes selected text to all capital letters.

HINT

If you use a macro on a consistent basis, assign it to a toolbar or assign shortcut keys to the macro.

Assign a keyboard command to a macro at the Record Macro dialog box. In exercise 4 you will record a macro and then assign the macro to a keyboard command. If you delete the macro, the keyboard command is also deleted. This allows you to use the key combination again.

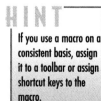

1. Record a macro named XXXLtrhd01 (where your initials are used instead of the *XXX*) that contains the letterhead text shown in figure 4.3 and assign it the keyboard command, Alt + Shift + S by completing the following steps:
   a. At a clear document screen, double-click the REC button on the Status bar.
   b. At the Record Macro dialog box, key **XXXLtrhd01** in the Macro name text box.
   c. Click in the Description text box (or select existing text in the Description text box) and then key **St. Francis Letterhead**.
   d. Click the Keyboard button.
   e. At the Customize Keyboard dialog box with the insertion point positioned in the Press new shortcut key text box, press Alt + Shift + S.
   f. Click the Assign button.
   g. Click the Close button.

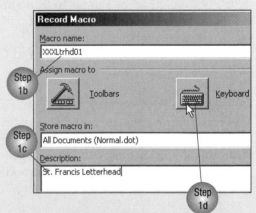

   h. At the document screen with the Macro Record toolbar displayed, create the letterhead shown in figure 4.3 by completing the following steps:
      1) Press Ctrl + E.
      2) Key **ST. FRANCIS MEDICAL CENTER**.
      3) Press Enter and then key **300 Blue Ridge Boulevard**.
      4) Press Enter and then key **Kansas City, MO 63009**.
      5) Press Enter and then key **(816) 555-2000**.
      6) Press Enter.
      7) Press Ctrl + L to return the paragraph alignment to left.
      8) Press Enter.
      9) Select (using the keyboard) the hospital name, address, and telephone number and then change the font to 18-point Goudy Old Style bold (or a similar serif typeface).
      10) Deselect the text (using the keyboard).
      11) Move the insertion point to the end of the document.

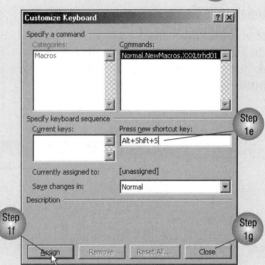

   i. Click the Stop Recording button on the Macro Record toolbar.
2. Close the document without saving changes.
3. At a clear document screen, run the XXXLtrhd01 macro by pressing Alt + Shift + S.
4. With the insertion point a double space below the letterhead, insert the document named Word Letter 01 by completing the following steps:
   a. Click Insert and then File.
   b. At the Insert File dialog box, navigate to the *Word Chapter 04E* folder on your disk and then double-click *Word Letter 01*.

5. Make the following changes to the document:
   a. Change the left and right margins to 1 inch.
   b. Run the XXXInd01 macro for the numbered paragraphs.
   c. Run the XXXInd02 macro for the lettered paragraphs.
6. Save the document and name it EWd C04 Ex04.
7. Print and then close EWd C04 Ex04.

FIGURE

4.3 *Exercise 4*

ST. FRANCIS MEDICAL CENTER
300 Blue Ridge Boulevard
Kansas City, MO 63009
(816) 555-2000

Assigning a Macro to the Toolbar

Add a macro that you use on a regular basis to a toolbar. To run a macro from a toolbar, just click the button. In exercise 5, you will assign a macro to the Standard toolbar. A macro can be assigned to any toolbar that is displayed. For example, a macro can be assigned to the Formatting toolbar if that toolbar is displayed on the document screen.

An existing macro can also be assigned to a toolbar. To do this, display the Customize dialog box with the Commands tab selected as shown in figure 4.4. Display this dialog box by clicking the Toolbars button at the Record Macro dialog box. You can also display this dialog box by clicking Tools, then Customize, and then clicking the Commands tab.

At the Customize dialog box with the Commands tab selected, click *Macros* in the Categories list box. Position the arrow pointer on the desired macro in the Commands list box, hold down the left mouse button, drag the outline of the button to the desired location on the desired toolbar, and then release the mouse button. Click the Close button to close the Customize dialog box.

A macro button can be removed from a toolbar with the Customize dialog box open. To do this, display the Customize dialog box. Position the arrow pointer on the button to be removed, hold down the left mouse button, drag the outline of the button off the toolbar, and then release the mouse button. Click Close to close the Customize dialog box. When a macro button is removed from a toolbar, the macro is not deleted. Delete the macro at the Macros dialog box.

4.4 *Customize Dialog Box with Commands Tab Selected*

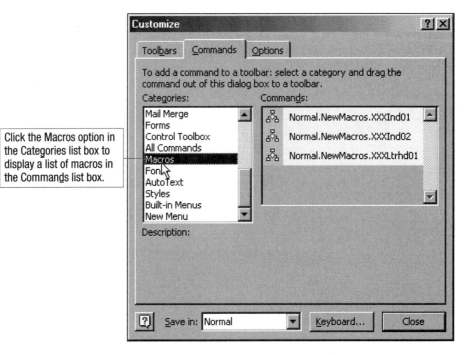

Click the Macros option in the Categories list box to display a list of macros in the Commands list box.

exercise **5**

ASSIGNING A MACRO TO THE STANDARD TOOLBAR

1. At a clear document screen, create a macro named XXXTab01 (where your initials are used instead of the *XXX*) and assign it to the Standard toolbar by completing the following steps:

   a. Double-click the REC button on the Status bar.
   b. At the Record Macro dialog box, key **XXXTab01** in the Macro name text box.
   c. Click inside the Description text box (or select text) and then key **Set left tab at 0.5 and right tab with leaders at 5.5.**
   d. Click the Toolbars button.
   e. At the Customize dialog box with the Commands tab selected, position the arrow pointer on the XXXTab01 macro in the Commands list box. (This macro name may display as

   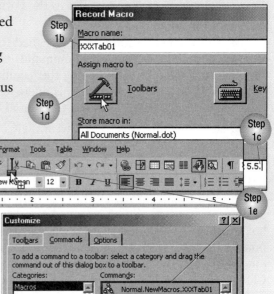

   Normal.NewMacros.XXXTab01.) Hold down the left mouse button, drag the mouse pointer with the button attached between the Spelling and Grammar button and the Cut button on the Standard toolbar, and then release the mouse button.
   f. Shorten the name of the macro by completing the following steps:

1) With the Customize dialog box still displayed, position the arrow pointer on the XXXTab01 button on the Standard toolbar, and then click the *right* mouse button.

2) At the drop-down list that displays, click <u>N</u>ame.

3) Key **T01** in the <u>N</u>ame text box, and then press Enter.

g. Click the Close button to close the Customize dialog box.

h. At the document screen with the Macro Record toolbar displayed, complete the necessary steps to set a left tab at the 0.5-inch mark and a right tab with preceding dot leaders at the 5.5-inch mark. (You must do this at the Tabs dialog box, not on the Ruler.)

i. After setting the tabs, click the Stop Recording button on the Macro Record toolbar.

2. Close the document without saving it.

3. At a clear document screen, create the document shown in figure 4.5 by completing the following steps:

a. Click the T01 button on the Standard toolbar.

b. Key the text as shown in figure 4.5. (Key the first column of text at the first tab stop, not the left margin.)

4. Save the document and name it EWd C04 Ex05.

5. Print and then close EWd C04 Ex05.

6. Remove the T01 button from the Standard toolbar by completing the following steps:

a. At a clear document screen, click <u>T</u>ools and then <u>C</u>ustomize.

b. At the Customize dialog box, position the arrow pointer on the T01 button on the Standard toolbar, hold down the left mouse button, drag the outline of the button off the toolbar, and then release the mouse button.

c. Click the Close button to close the Customize dialog box.

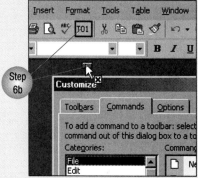

FIGURE

4.5 *Exercise 5*

STRADFORD FUNDS CORPORATION

Kelly Millerton ....Chief Executive Officer

Lyle Harmstead ....President

Alicia Wyatt ....Vice President

Alexander Li ....Vice President

Danielle Cohen ....Vice President

Recording a Macro with Fill-In Fields

In chapter 1, you inserted a Fill-in field in a document that prompted the operator to insert information at the keyboard during a merge. A Fill-in field can also be inserted in a macro that requires input from the keyboard. To insert a Fill-in field in a macro, begin the recording of the macro. At the point where the Fill-in field is to be inserted, click Insert and then Field. At the Field dialog box with *(All)* selected in the Categories list box as shown in figure 4.6, scroll down the Field names list box until *Fill-in* is visible and then click it. Add information telling the operator what text to enter at the keyboard by clicking in the Description text box and then keying the prompt message surrounded by parentheses. When the macro is run, key the desired text specified by the prompt message.

FIGURE

4.6 *Field Dialog Box*

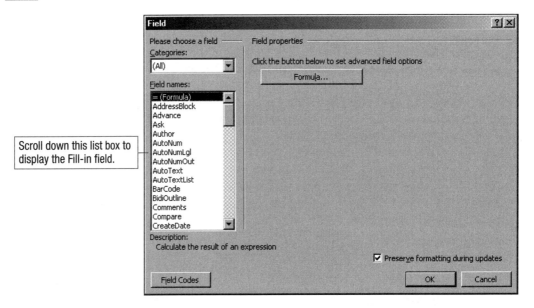

Scroll down this list box to display the Fill-in field.

exercise 6

RECORDING A MACRO WITH FILL-IN FIELDS

1. At a clear document screen, record a macro for inserting notary signature information by completing the following steps:
   a. Double-click the REC button on the Status bar.
   b. At the Record Macro dialog box, key **XXXNotary** (where your initials are used instead of the *XXX*) in the Macro name text box.
   c. Click in the Description text box (or select existing text in the Description text box) and then key **Notary signature information**.
   d. Click the Keyboard button.
   e. At the Customize Keyboard dialog box with the insertion point positioned in the Press new shortcut key text box, press Alt + Ctrl + A.
   f. Click the Assign button.
   g. Click the Close button.

WORD

h. At the document screen with the Macro Record toolbar displayed, key the text shown in figure 4.7 up to the text *(name of person)*. (Do not key the text *(name of person)*.)

i. Insert a Fill-in field by completing the following steps:
   1) Click Insert and then Field.
   2) At the Field dialog box with *(All)* selected in the Categories list box, scroll down the Field names list box until *Fill-in* is visible and then click it.
   3) Click in the Prompt: text box (below Field properties) and then key **Key name of person signing**.
   4) Click the OK button.
   5) At the Microsoft Word dialog box, key **(name of person)** in the text box, and then click OK.

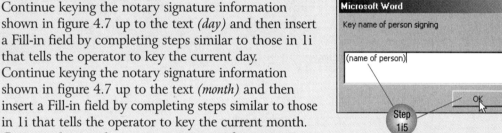

j. Continue keying the notary signature information shown in figure 4.7 up to the text *(day)* and then insert a Fill-in field by completing steps similar to those in 1i that tells the operator to key the current day.

k. Continue keying the notary signature information shown in figure 4.7 up to the text *(month)* and then insert a Fill-in field by completing steps similar to those in 1i that tells the operator to key the current month.

l. Continue keying the notary signature information shown in figure 4.7 up to the text *(expiration date)* and then insert a Fill-in field by completing steps similar to those in 1i that tells the operator to key the expiration date.

m. When all of the notary signature information is keyed, end the recording of the macro by double-clicking the REC button on the Status bar.

2. Close the document without saving it.

FIGURE

4.7 *Exercise 6*

STATE OF CALIFORNIA   )
) ss.
COUNTY OF LOS ANGELES   )

On this day personally appeared before me (name of person), known to me to be the individual described in and who executed the aforesaid instrument, and acknowledged that he/she signed as his/her free and voluntary act and deed for the uses and purposes therein mentioned.

Given under my hand and official seal this (day) of (month), 2003.

_____
NOTARY PUBLIC in and for the State of California
My appointment expires (expiration date)

1. Open Word Legal 01.
2. Save the document with Save As and name it EWd C04 Ex07.
3. Complete the following find and replaces:
   a. Find all occurrences of *NAME* and replace with *LOREN HOUSTON*. (Be sure to replace only the occurrences of *NAME* in all uppercase letters. *Hint: Expand the Find and Replace dialog box and insert a check mark in the Match case option.*)
   b. Find the one occurrence of *ADDRESS* and replace with *102 Marine Drive, Los Angeles, CA.* (Be sure to replace only the occurrence of *ADDRESS* in all uppercase letters and not the occurrence of *address* in all lowercase letters.)
4. Run the following macros:
   a. Run the XXXInd01 macro for the numbered paragraphs and the XXXInd02 macro for the lettered paragraphs.
   b. Move the insertion point to the end of the document a double space below the text and then run the XXXNotary macro by completing the following steps:
      1) Press Alt + Ctrl + A.
      2) When the macro stops and prompts you for the name of person signing, key **SYLVIA WHITT**, and then click OK.
      3) When the macro stops and prompts you for the day, key **12th**, and then click OK.
      4) When the macro stops and prompts you for the month, key **March**, and then click OK.
      5) When the macro stops and prompts you for the expiration date, key **12/31/05**, and then click OK.
5. Save, print, and then close EWd C04 Ex07.

Step 4b2

HINT

Editing a Macro

In Word, a macro is created with Visual Basic and can be edited using the Visual Basic Editor. To edit a macro, display the Macros dialog box, select the macro to be edited, and then click the Edit button. This displays the macro in the Visual Basic Editor as shown in figure 4.8. (The macro displayed in figure 4.8 is the one you will be creating and then editing in exercise 8.)

4.8 *Visual Basic Editor*

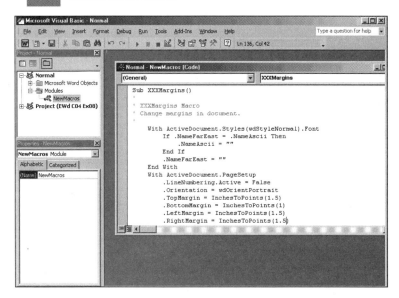

To edit the macro, remove unwanted steps from the list box, add steps, or change existing steps. When all changes are made, click the Save Normal button on the Visual Basic Editor Standard toolbar (third button from the left) or click File and then Save Normal. Close the Visual Basic Editor by clicking File and then Close and Return to Microsoft Word.

HINT

If you make a mistake while recording a macro, the corrections you make will also be recorded.

exercise 8

RECORDING, RUNNING, AND EDITING A MACRO

1. At a clear document screen, record a macro that changes the top, left, and right margins by completing the following steps:
   a. Double-click the REC button on the Status bar.
   b. At the Record Macro dialog box, key **XXXMargins** (where your initials are used instead of the *XXX*) in the Macro name text box.
   c. Click inside the Description text box and then key **Change margins in document**. (If any text is located in the Description text box, select the text first, and then key **Change margins in document**.)
   d. Click OK.
   e. At the document screen with the Macro Record toolbar displayed, complete the following steps:
      1) Click File and then Page Setup.
      2) At the Page Setup dialog box with the Margins tab selected, change the top, left, and right margins to 1.5 inches.
      3) Click OK to close the dialog box.
   f. Turn off recording by double-clicking the REC button on the Status bar.
2. Close the document without saving it.
3. Open Word Report 03.
4. Save the document with Save As and name it EWd C04 Ex08.

5. Run the XXXMargins macro by completing the following steps:
   a. Display the Macros dialog box.
   b. At the Macros dialog box, double-click *XXXMargins* in the list box.
6. Save and then print EWd C04 Ex08.
7. With EWd C04 Ex08 still open, edit the XXXMargins macro so it changes the left and right margins to 1 inch by completing the following steps:
   a. Display the Macros dialog box.
   b. At the Macros dialog box, click *XXXMargins* in the list box, and then click the Edit button.

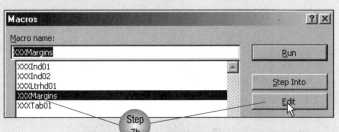

   c. At the Visual Basic Editor, make the following changes:
      1) Edit the step *.LeftMargin = InchesToPoints(1.5)* so it displays as *.LeftMargin = InchesToPoints(1)*.
      2) Edit the step *.RightMargin = InchesToPoints(1.5)* so it displays as *.RightMargin = InchesToPoints(1)*.
   d. Click the Save Normal button on the Visual Basic Editor Standard toolbar (third button from the left).
   e. Close the Visual Basic Editor by clicking File and then Close and Return to Microsoft Word.
8. Run the XXXMargins macro.
9. Save, print, and then close EWd C04 Ex08.

Formatting Text with Styles

A Word document, by default, is based on the Normal template document. Within a normal template document, a Normal style is applied to text by default. This Normal style sets text in the default font (this may vary depending on what you have selected or what printer you are using), uses left alignment and single spacing, and turns on the widow/orphan control. In addition to this Normal style, other predesigned styles are available in a document based on the Normal template document. These styles can be displayed by clicking the down-pointing triangle to the right of the Style button on the Formatting toolbar.

Normal

Style

Other template documents also contain predesigned styles. If you choose a different template document from the Templates dialog box, click the down-pointing triangle to the right of the Style button on the Formatting toolbar to display the names of styles available for that particular template document.

Styles can be changed and/or applied to text in three ways. The quickest way to apply styles to text in a document is with Word's AutoFormat feature. The advantage to using AutoFormat is that Word automatically applies the styles without you having to select them. The disadvantage is that you have less control over the styles that are applied.

Another method you can use to apply styles is to select a new template at the Style Gallery dialog box. The advantage to this is that you can preview your document as it will appear if formatted with various templates, and then apply the desired template. The disadvantage is that you have less control over the selection of styles.

A third method for applying styles to text is to make changes to those styles available in the template upon which your document is based. The advantage to this method is that you can format a document any way you want by creating and selecting styles. The disadvantage is that you have to create and/or select a style for each element in the document that you want formatted.

Formatting with AutoFormat

Word provides a variety of predesigned styles in the Normal template document that can be applied to text in a document. With this feature, called AutoFormat, Word goes through a document paragraph by paragraph and applies appropriate styles. For example, Word changes the font and size for heading text and adds bullets to listed items. The formatting is done automatically; all you do is sit back and watch Word do the work. Format a document with options at the AutoFormat dialog box shown in figure 4.9. Display this dialog box by clicking Format and then AutoFormat.

FIGURE

4.9 *AutoFormat Dialog Box*

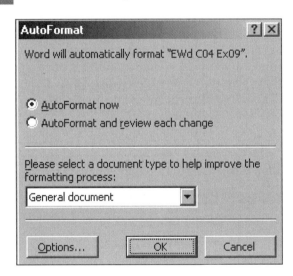

When AutoFormat applies styles to a document, it also makes corrections as follows:

- Uses formatting rules to find and format headings, body text, lists, superscript, subscript, addresses, and letter closings.
- Replaces straight quotes and apostrophes with typesetting quotation marks.
- Deletes extra paragraph marks.
- Replaces horizontal spaces inserted with the spacebar or the Tab key with indents.
- Replaces hyphens, asterisks, or other characters used to list items with a bullet (•).

If, after automatically formatting a document, you want to undo the changes, immediately click the Undo button on the Standard toolbar.

FORMATTING A DOCUMENT WITH AUTOFORMAT

1. Open Word Report 01.
2. Save the document with Save As and name it EWd C04 Ex09.
3. Automatically format the document by completing the following steps:
    a. Click Format and then AutoFormat.
    b. At the AutoFormat dialog box, make sure the AutoFormat now option is selected (if not, click this option), and then click OK.
4. Save, print, and then close EWd C04 Ex09.

Step 3b

Formatting Text with the Style Gallery

As you learned earlier in this chapter, each document is based on a template, with the Normal template document the default. The styles applied to text with AutoFormat are the styles available with the Normal template document. Word also provides predesigned styles with other template documents. You can use the Style Gallery dialog box to apply styles from other templates to the current document. This provides you with a large number of predesigned styles for formatting text. To display the Style Gallery dialog box shown in figure 4.10, click Format and then Theme. At the Theme dialog box, click the Style Gallery button (located towards the bottom of the dialog box).

FIGURE

4.10 *Style Gallery Dialog Box*

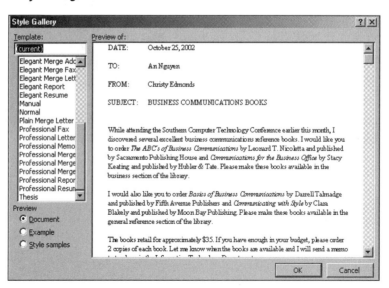

At the Style Gallery dialog box, the template documents are displayed in the Template list box. The open document is displayed in the Preview of section of the dialog box. With this section, you can choose templates from the Template list box and see how the formatting is applied to the open document.

At the bottom of the Style Gallery dialog box, the Document option is selected in the Preview section. If you click Example, Word will insert a sample document in the Preview of section that displays the formatting applied to the document. Click Style samples and styles will display in the Preview of section of the dialog box rather than the document or sample document.

exercise 10

FORMATTING A MEMO WITH STYLES FROM A MEMO TEMPLATE

1. Open Word Memo 01.
2. Save the document with Save As and name it EWd C04 Ex10.
3. Format the memo at the Style Gallery by completing the following steps:
   a. Click Format and then Theme.
   b. At the Theme dialog box, click the Style Gallery button (located at the bottom of the dialog box).
   c. At the Style Gallery dialog box, click *Elegant Memo* in the Template list box. (You may need to scroll up the list.)

   Step 3c

   d. Click OK.
   e. At the memo, properly align the text after the *FROM:* heading.
4. Save, print, and then close EWd C04 Ex10.

When you select a template at the Style Gallery, the template styles are available at the Style button on the Formatting toolbar and at the Styles and Formatting Task Pane. Paragraph styles are followed by the ¶ symbol and character styles are followed by the <u>a</u> symbol. Use the template styles to format specific text in a document.

exercise 11

APPLYING SPECIFIC STYLES TO A REPORT

1. Open Word Report 01.
2. Save the document with Save As and name it EWd C04 Ex11.
3. Select a template at the Style Gallery by completing the following steps:
   a. Click Format and then Theme.
   b. At the Theme dialog box, click the Style Gallery button.
   c. At the Style Gallery dialog box, click *Elegant Report* in the Template list box.
   d. Click OK.
4. Click the Styles and Formatting button on the Formatting toolbar to turn on the display of the Styles and Formatting Task Pane.
5. Apply the Body Text style by completing the following steps:

a. Select text from the beginning of the first heading *Defining Desktop Publishing* to the end of the document.

b. Click the *Body Text* paragraph style in the Pick formatting to apply list box.

6. Click anywhere in the title *DESKTOP PUBLISHING* and then click the <u>CHAPTER LABEL</u> paragraph style in the Pick formatting to apply list box.

7. Select the heading *Defining Desktop Publishing* and then click the EMPHASIS character style in the Pick formatting to apply list box.

8. Select each of the remaining headings individually (*Initiating the Desktop Publishing Process*, *Planning the Publication*, and *Creating the Content*) and apply the EMPHASIS character style.

9. Save, print, and then close EWd C04 Ex11.

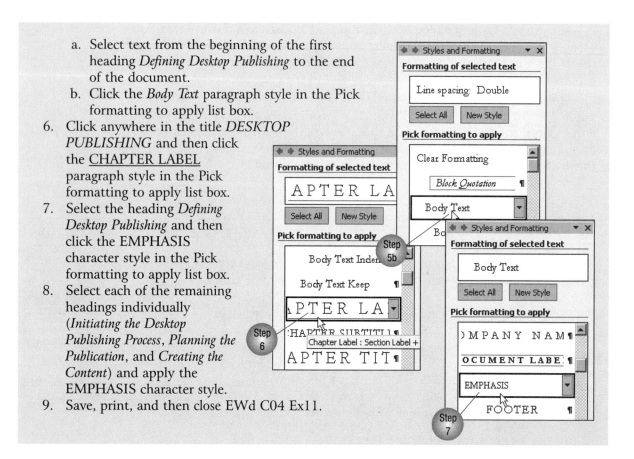

Creating Styles

If all of the styles predesigned by Word do not contain the formatting you desire, you can create your own style. A style can be created in two ways. You can either apply the desired formatting instructions to a paragraph and then save those instructions in a style, or you can specify the formatting instructions for a particular style without applying them to text. The first method is useful if you want to see how text appears when certain formatting instructions are applied to it. The second method is often used when you know the particular format that you want to use for certain paragraphs.

When you create your own style, you must give the style a name. When naming a style, avoid using the names already used by Word. The list of style names will display in the <u>S</u>tyles list box at the Style dialog box if *All styles* is selected in the <u>L</u>ist text box. When naming a style, try to name it something that gives you an idea what the style will accomplish. Consider the following when naming a style:

- A style name can contain a maximum of 213 characters.
- A style name can contain spaces and commas.
- A style name is case-sensitive. Uppercase and lowercase letters can be used.
- Do not use the backslash (\), brackets ({}), or a semicolon (;) when naming a style.

Creating a Style by Example

A style can be created by formatting text first and then using the Style button on the Formatting toolbar or the New Style dialog box to create the style. To do this, position the insertion point in a paragraph of text containing the formatting you wish to include in the style, and then click the down-pointing triangle to the right of the Style button on the Formatting toolbar. Key a unique name for the style and then press Enter. This creates the style and also displays the style in the Style button. The new style will be visible in the Style drop-down list from the Formatting toolbar as well as the Style dialog box.

Styles and
Formatting

You can create a style by example using the New Style dialog box. To do this, position the insertion point in a paragraph of text containing the desired formatting, and then click the Styles and Formatting button on the Formatting toolbar (or click Format and then Styles and Formatting). At the Styles and Formatting Task Pane, click the New Style button. At the New Style dialog box, key a name for the style in the Name text box, and then click OK.

exercise **12**

CREATING STYLES BY EXAMPLE

1. Open Word Style.
2. Save the document with Save As and name it Sty 01.
3. Create a style by example named Title 1 by completing the following steps:
   a. Position the insertion point anywhere in the text *TITLE OF DOCUMENT*.
   b. Click the down-pointing triangle to the right of the Style button on the Formatting toolbar.
   c. Key **Title 1** and then press Enter.
4. Create a style by example named Subtitle 1 using the *Subtitle of Document* text by completing steps similar to those in 3.
5. Select all of the text in the document and then delete it. (This removes the text but keeps the styles you created.)
6. Save and then close Sty 01.

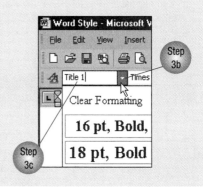

Creating a Style Using the New Style Dialog Box

You can create a style before you use it rather than creating it by example. To do this, use options from the New Style dialog box shown in figure 4.11. To display the New Style dialog box, click the New Style button in the Styles and Formatting Task Pane. At the New Style dialog box, key a name for the style in the Name text box, and specify whether you are creating a paragraph or character style at the Style type option. Click the Format button and then click the desired formatting options.

4.11 *New Style Dialog Box*

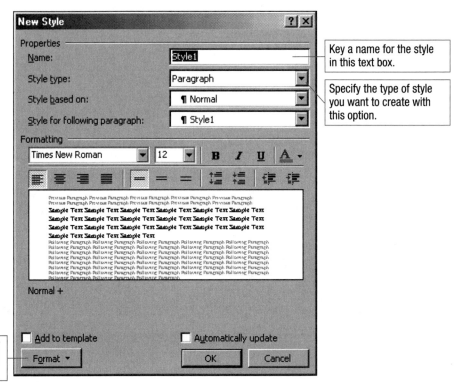

Key a name for the style in this text box.

Specify the type of style you want to create with this option.

Click this button to display a pop-up list of formatting choices.

exercise 13

CREATING STYLES AT THE NEW STYLE DIALOG BOX

1. Open Sty 01.
2. Using the New Style dialog box, create a style named Indent 1 that indents text 0.5 inch and adds 12 points of space after the paragraph by completing the following steps:
   a. Click the Styles and Formatting button on the Formatting toolbar (first button from the left).
   b. At the Styles and Formatting Task Pane, click the New Style button.
   c. At the New Style dialog box, key **Indent 1** in the Name text box.
   d. Click the Format button that displays toward the bottom of the dialog box and then click Paragraph at the pop-up list.
   e. At the Paragraph dialog box, click the up-pointing triangle to the right of the Left text box until *0.5″* displays in the text box.
   f. Click the up-pointing triangle to the right of the After text box until *12 pt* displays in the text box.

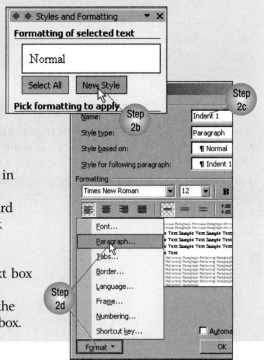

g. Click OK to close the Paragraph dialog box.
h. Click OK to close the New Style dialog box.

3. Create a style named Font 1, using the New Style dialog box, that changes the font to Century Schoolbook by completing the following steps:

a. Click the New Style button in the Styles and Formatting Task Pane.

b. At the New Style dialog box, key **Font 1** in the Name text box.

c. Click the down-pointing triangle at the right side of the Style type text box and then click *Character* at the drop-down list.

d. Click the Format button that displays toward the bottom of the dialog box and then click Font at the pop-up list.

e. At the Font dialog box, click *Bookman Old Style* (or a similar serif typeface) in the Font list box, *Regular* in the Font style list box, and *12* in the Size list box.

f. Click OK to close the Font dialog box.

g. Click OK to close the New Style dialog box.

h. Close the Styles and Formatting Task Pane.

4. Save and then close Sty 01.

Applying a Style

A style can be applied to the paragraph where the insertion point is positioned. You can also select several paragraphs and then apply a paragraph style. If you are applying a style that contains character formatting, you must select the text first, and then apply the style. A style can be applied using the Style button on the Formatting toolbar or the Styles and Formatting Task Pane.

To apply a style using the Style button, position the insertion point in the paragraph to which you want the style applied, or select the text, and then click the down-pointing triangle to the right of the Style button. At the drop-down list of styles, click the desired style. To apply a style using the Styles and Formatting Task Pane, display the task pane, and then click the desired style in the Pick formatting to apply list box.

APPLYING STYLES IN A DOCUMENT

1. Open Sty 01.
2. Save the document with Save As and name it EWd C04 Ex14.
3. Insert the document named Word Quiz into the EWd C04 Ex14 document. *(Hint: Use the File option from the Insert drop-down menu to do this.)*
4. Apply a style to the title by completing the following steps:

a. Position the insertion point on any character in the title *CHAPTER QUIZ*.

b. Click the down-pointing triangle at the right side of the Style button on the Formatting toolbar and then click *Title 1* at the drop-down list.

5. Apply styles to text in the document by completing the following steps:

a. Click F<u>o</u>rmat and then <u>S</u>tyles and Formatting. (This displays the Styles and Formatting Task Pane.)

b. Select the text in the document (except the title).

c. Click *Font 1* in the Pick formatting to apply list box in the Styles and Formatting Task Pane.

d. Click *Indent 1* in the Pick formatting to apply list box in the Styles and Formatting Task Pane.

e. Deselect the text.

6. Save, print, and then close EWd C04 Ex14.

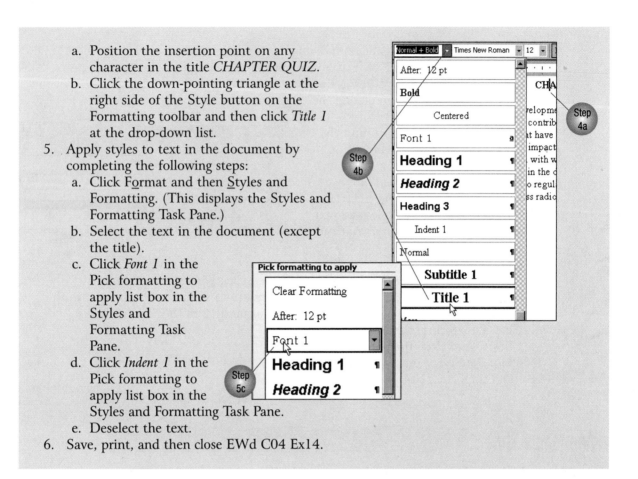

Modifying a Style

Once a style has been created, you can modify the style by changing the formatting instructions that it contains. When you modify a style by changing the formatting instructions, all text to which that style has been applied is changed accordingly. To modify a style, you would click the down-pointing triangle at the right side of the style name in the Styles and Formatting Task Pane, and then click <u>M</u>odify at the drop-down list. At the Modify Style dialog box shown in figure 4.12, you would add or delete formatting options.

4.12 *Modify Style Dialog Box*

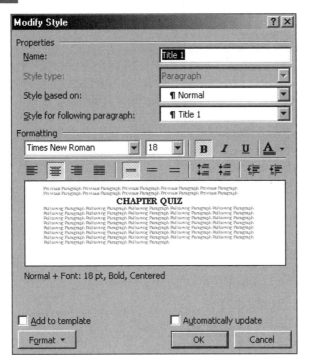

exercise 15

MODIFYING STYLES

1. Open EWd C04 Ex14.
2. Save the document with Save As and name it EWd C04 Ex15.
3. Modify the Title 1 style by completing the following steps:
   a. Click the Styles and Formatting button on the Formatting toolbar.
   b. At the Styles and Formatting Task Pane, position the mouse pointer on the *Title 1* style in the Pick formatting to apply list box, and then click the down-pointing triangle at the right side of the style name.
   c. At the drop-down menu that displays, click Modify.
   d. At the Modify Style dialog box, change the font to 20-point Arial bold by completing the following steps:
      1) Click the Format button located toward the bottom of the dialog box.

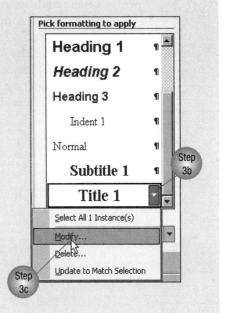

2) At the pop-up list that displays, click <u>F</u>ont.

3) At the Font dialog box, click *Arial* in the <u>F</u>ont list box, *Bold* in the Font st<u>y</u>le list box, and *20* in the <u>S</u>ize list box.

4) Click OK to close the Font dialog box.

5) Click OK to close the Modify Style dialog box.

4. Modify the Indent 1 style by completing the following steps:

a. Position the mouse pointer on the *Indent 1* style in the Pick formatting to apply list box and then click the down-pointing triangle.

b. At the drop-down menu, click <u>M</u>odify.

c. At the Modify Style dialog box, change the left indent and spacing after by completing the following steps:

1) Click the F<u>o</u>rmat button located toward the bottom of the dialog box.

2) Click <u>P</u>aragraph at the pop-up list.

3) At the Paragraph dialog box, click the down-pointing triangle at the right side of the <u>L</u>eft option until *0.3″* displays in the <u>L</u>eft text box.

4) Click the up-pointing triangle to the right of the Aft<u>e</u>r text box until *36 pts* displays in the text box.

5) Click OK to close the Paragraph dialog box.

6) Click OK to close the Modify Style dialog box.

5. Save, print, and then close EWd C04 Ex15.

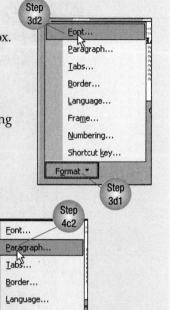

Assigning a Shortcut Key Combination to a Style

A style can be applied quickly in a document if a shortcut key has been assigned to the style. You can use the letters *A* through *Z*, numbers *0* through *9*, the Delete and Insert keys, combined with the Ctrl, Alt, and Shift keys to create a shortcut key combination. Word has already assigned shortcut key combinations to many features. If you assign a shortcut key combination to a style that is already used by Word, the message *Currently assigned to (name of feature)* displays. When this happens, choose another shortcut key combination. Create a shortcut key combination for a style with options at the Customize Keyboard dialog box shown in figure 4.13.

W O R D

4.13 *Customize Keyboard Dialog Box*

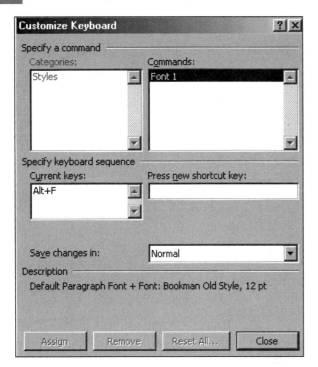

exercise 16

ASSIGNING SHORTCUT KEY COMBINATIONS TO STYLES

1. Open Sty 01.
2. Save the document with Save As and name it Sty 02.
3. Create the shortcut key combination, Alt + F, for the Font 1 style by completing the following steps:
   a. Click the Styles and Formatting button on the Formatting toolbar.
   b. At the Styles and Formatting Task Pane, position the mouse pointer on the *Font 1* style in the Pick formatting to apply list box, and then click the down-pointing triangle at the right side of the style name.
   c. At the drop-down menu that displays, click Modify.
   d. At the Modify Style dialog box, click the Format button that displays toward the bottom of the dialog box, and then click Shortcut key at the pop-up list.
   e. At the Customize Keyboard dialog box, press Alt + F. (This inserts *Alt + F* in the Press new shortcut key text box.)
   f. Click the Assign button.

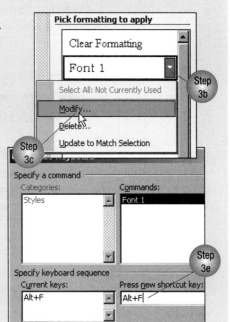

g. Click the Close button to close the Customize Keyboard dialog box.

h. Click OK to close the Modify Style dialog box.

4. Create the shortcut key combination, Alt + I, for the Indent 1 style by completing steps similar to those in 3.

5. Create the shortcut key combination, Alt + S, for the Subtitle 1 style by completing steps similar to those in 3.

6. Create the shortcut key combination, Alt + T, for the Title 1 style by completing steps similar to those in 3.

7. Save and then close Sty 02.

exercise 17

APPLYING STYLES IN A DOCUMENT WITH SHORTCUT KEY COMBINATIONS

1. Open Sty 02.

2. Save the document with Save As and name it EWd C04 Ex17.

3. Insert the document Word Report 01 into the EWd C04 Ex17 document.

4. Select the entire document and then change line spacing to single.

5. Position the insertion point on any character in the title *DESKTOP PUBLISHING* and then apply the Title 1 style by pressing Alt + T.

6. Position the insertion point on any character in the heading *Defining Desktop Publishing* and then apply the Subtitle 1 style by pressing Alt + S. (The Subtitle 1 style applies font formatting and also centers the heading.)

7. Apply the Subtitle 1 style to the following headings:

> *Initiating the Desktop Publishing Process*
> *Planning the Publication*
> *Creating the Content*

8. Save, print, and then close EWd C04 Ex17.

To remove a shortcut key combination from a style, display the Customize Keyboard dialog box for the specific style and then click the Remove button.

exercise 18

REMOVING A SHORTCUT KEY COMBINATION

1. Open Sty 02.

2. Save the document with Save As and name it Sty 03.

3. Remove the shortcut key combination, Alt + I, by completing the following steps:

a. Click the Styles and Formatting button on the Formatting toolbar.

b. At the Styles and Formatting Task Pane, position the mouse pointer on the *Indent 1* style in the Pick formatting to apply list box, and then click the down-pointing triangle at the right side of the style name.

c. At the drop-down menu that displays, click Modify.

d. At the Modify Style dialog box, click the Format button that displays toward the bottom of the dialog box, and then click Shortcut key at the pop-up list.

WORD

e. At the Customize Keyboard dialog box, click *Alt + I* in the Current keys list box.

f. Click the Remove button.

g. Click the Close button to close the Customize Keyboard dialog box.

h. At the Modify Style dialog box, click OK.

4. Save and then close Sty 03.

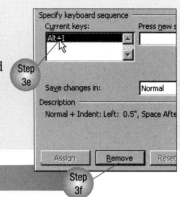

Step 3e

Step 3f

Removing a Style from Text

You may apply a style to text in a document and then change your mind and wish to remove the style. If you decide to remove the style immediately after applying it (before performing some other action), click the Undo button on the Standard toolbar. You can also click <u>E</u>dit and then <u>U</u>ndo Style. When a style is removed, the style that was previously applied to the text is applied once again (usually this is the Normal style).

You can also remove a style from text by applying a new style. Only one style can be applied at a time to the same text. For example, if you applied the Heading 1 style to text and then later decide you want to remove it, position the insertion point in the text containing the Heading 1 style, and then apply the Normal style.

Clearing Formatting

Word contains a Clear Formatting style you can use to remove all formatting from selected text. To use this style, position the insertion point in the paragraph of text or select specific text, click the down-pointing triangle at the right side of the Style button on the Formatting toolbar, and then click *Clear Formatting* at the drop-down list. The Styles and Formatting Task Pane also contains a Clear Formatting style in the Pick formatting to apply list box. You can also clear formatting by clicking <u>E</u>dit, pointing to Cle<u>a</u>r, and then clicking <u>F</u>ormats.

exercise 19

CLEARING FORMATTING

1. Open EWd C04 Ex17.

2. Save the document with Save As and name it EWd C04 Ex19.

3. Clear all character and paragraph formatting from the text by completing the following steps:

a. Press Ctrl + A to select the entire document.

b. Click the down-pointing triangle at the right side of the Style button on the Formatting toolbar and then click *Clear Formatting*. (You will need to scroll up the list to display this option.)

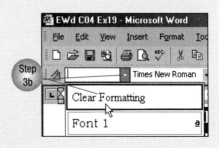

Step 3b

4. Make the following changes to the document:
   a. Select the entire document, change to a serif typeface other than Times New Roman (you choose the typeface), and then deselect the document.
   b. Bold and center the title.
   c. Bold the headings.
5. Save, print, and then close EWd C04 Ex19.

Deleting a Style

Delete a style in a document and any style to which that style is applied is returned to the Normal style. To delete a style, display the Styles and Formatting Task Pane, position the mouse pointer on the style name, and then click the down-pointing triangle at the right side of the style name. At the drop-down list that displays, click <u>D</u>elete. At the message asking if you want to delete the style, click <u>Y</u>es. You can delete styles that you create, but you cannot delete Word's standard styles.

 *exercise* **20**

1. Open Sty 03.
2. Insert the document named Word Report 02 into the Sty 03 document.
3. Save the document with Save As and name it EWd C04 Ex20.
4. Select the entire document and then change the line spacing to single.
5. Delete the Indent 1 style by completing the following steps:
   a. Click the Styles and Formatting button on the Formatting toolbar.
   b. At the Styles and Formatting Task Pane, position the mouse pointer on the *Indent 1* style in the Pick formatting to apply list box, and then click the down-pointing triangle at the right side of the style name.
   c. At the drop-down menu that displays, click <u>D</u>elete.
   d. At the message asking if you want to delete the style, click <u>Y</u>es.

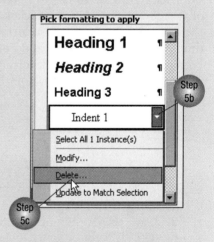

6. Select the entire document and then apply the Font 1 style.
7. Apply the Title 1 style to the title, *DESKTOP PUBLISHING DESIGN*.
8. Apply the Subtitle 1 style to the headings *Designing a Document* and *Creating Focus*.
9. Save, print, and then close EWd C04 Ex20.

Creating a Cross-Reference

A cross-reference in a Word document refers the reader to another location within the document. This feature is useful in a long document or a document containing related information. Insert a cross-reference to move to a specific location within the document. Key introductory text and then click Insert, point to Reference, and then click Cross-reference. At the Cross-reference dialog box shown in figure 4.14, identify the reference type, where to refer, and the specific text, and then click the Insert button and then the Close button.

FIGURE

4.14 *Cross-reference Dialog Box*

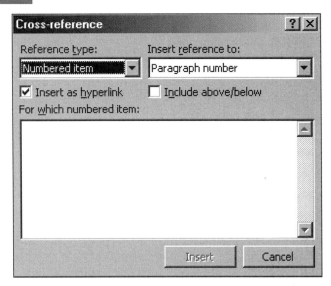

The reference identified in the Cross-reference dialog box displays immediately after the introductory text. To move to the specified reference, hold down the Ctrl key, position the mouse pointer over the introductory text (pointer turns into a hand), and then click the left mouse button.

exercise 21

INSERTING A CROSS-REFERENCE IN A DOCUMENT

1. Open Word Report 03.
2. Save the document with Save As and name it EWd C04 Ex21.
3. Apply the specified styles to the following headings:

THE TECHNOLOGY OF DESKTOP PUBLISHING	=	Heading 1
WHAT IS DESKTOP PUBLISHING?	=	Heading 2
BASIC HARDWARE	=	Heading 2

4. Insert a cross-reference by completing the following steps:
   a. Position the insertion point immediately following the period at the end of the last sentence in the document.
   b. Press the spacebar once and then key **(For more information, refer to**.
   c. Press the spacebar once.

d. Click Insert, point to Reference, and then click Cross-reference.
e. At the Cross-reference dialog box, click the down-pointing triangle at the right side of the Reference type list box, and then click *Heading* at the drop-down list.
f. Click *BASIC HARDWARE* in the For which heading list box.
g. Click the Insert button.
h. Click the Close button to close the dialog box.
i. At the document, key a period followed by the right parenthesis.

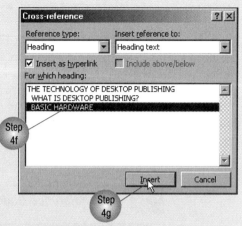

5. Move to the reference text by holding down the Ctrl key, positioning the mouse pointer over *BASIC HARDWARE* until the mouse pointer turns into a hand, and then clicking the left mouse button.
6. Save, print, and then close EWd C04 Ex21.

Navigating in a Document

Word offers several methods for navigating to specific locations in a document. Navigating is particularly useful in lengthy, multiple-paged documents. Three navigating techniques to consider are navigating in Outline view, using the Document Map feature, and inserting bookmarks in specific locations in a document.

HINT

Click the minus sign next to a heading in the Document Map pane to collapse the subordinate headings or click the plus symbol next to a heading to display subordinate headings.

Navigating in Outline View

In this chapter, you have learned how to apply styles to specific text in a document. If you apply the heading styles offered by the Normal template document to headings in a document, you can navigate to specific headings in Outline view. To do this, display the document in Outline view, collapse the document so only headings display, click the desired heading, and then expand the document.

exercise

NAVIGATING IN A DOCUMENT IN OUTLINE VIEW

1. Open Word Report 06.
2. Save the document with Save As and name it EWd C04 Ex22.
3. Apply the following styles to the following titles and headings:

SECTION 1: COMPUTERS IN COMMUNICATIONS	=	Heading 1
Telecommunications	=	Heading 2
Publishing	=	Heading 2
News Services	=	Heading 2
SECTION 2: COMPUTERS IN ENTERTAINMENT	=	Heading 1

WORD

Television and Film	=	Heading 2
Home Entertainment	=	Heading 2
SECTION 3: COMPUTERS IN PUBLIC LIFE	=	Heading 1
Government	=	Heading 2
Law	=	Heading 2
Education	=	Heading 2

4. Change to Outline view by clicking <u>V</u>iew and then <u>O</u>utline.
5. Collapse the outline so only the headings display by clicking the down-pointing triangle at the right side of the Show Level button, and then clicking *Show Level 2* at the drop-down list.
6. Move the insertion point to the third section by completing the following steps:
   a. Click anywhere in the title *SECTION 3: COMPUTERS IN PUBLIC LIFE*.
   b. Expand the outline so all text displays by clicking the down-pointing triangle at the right side of the Show Level button and then clicking *Show All Levels*.
7. Move the insertion point to the second section by collapsing the outline headings and then clicking anywhere in the title *SECTION 2: COMPUTERS IN ENTERTAINMENT*.

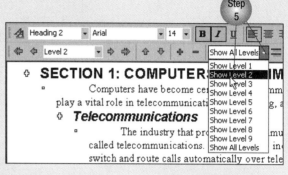

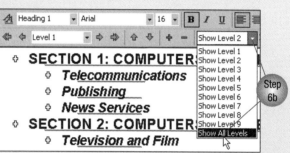

8. Print the document. (Only the titles and headings print.)
9. Expand the outline so all text displays.
10. Change to the Print Layout view.
11. Save and then close EWd C04 Ex22.

Navigating with Document Map

Use Word's Document Map feature to navigate easily in a document and keep track of your location within the document. The Document Map displays any headings that are formatted with heading styles or outline-level paragraph format. If no headings are formatted with headings styles or outline levels, Document Map searches for paragraphs that look like headings, such as short lines set in a larger type size. If no headings are found, the Document Map pane is blank.

The Document Map is a separate pane that displays the outline of a document. To display the Document Map pane, click the Document Map button on the Standard toolbar. This displays the Document Map pane at the left side of the document as shown in figure 4.15. Figure 4.15 displays the document you formatted with heading styles in exercise 22. In figure 4.15 not all of the heading text is visible in the Document Map pane. To display the entire heading, position the arrow pointer on the heading and the heading text displays in a yellow box.

Document Map

4.15 *Document Map Pane*

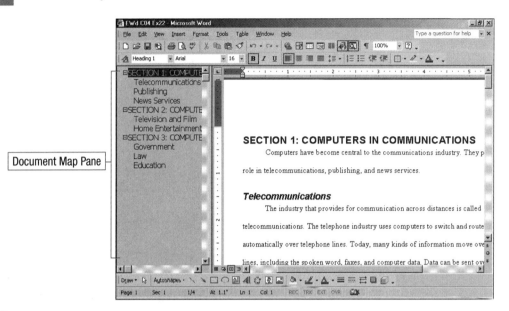

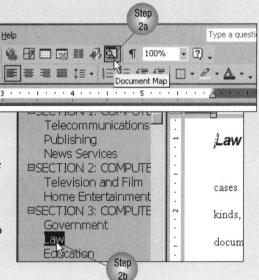

exercise 23

DISPLAYING THE DOCUMENT MAP PANE IN A DOCUMENT

1. Open EWd C04 Ex22.
2. Display the Document Map pane and move to different locations in the document by completing the following steps:
   a. Click the Document Map button on the Standard toolbar.
   b. Click the heading *Law* that displays in the Document Map pane.
   c. Click the heading *SECTION 2: COMPUTERS IN ENTERTAINMENT* that displays in the Document Map pane.
   d. Remove the Document Map pane by clicking the Document Map button on the Standard toolbar.
3. Close EWd C04 Ex23.
4. Open Word Report 04.
5. Display the Document Map pane and move to different locations in the document by completing the following steps:
   a. Click the Document Map button on the Standard toolbar.
   b. Click the heading *MODULE 2: PLANNING A NEWSLETTER.*
   c. Click the heading *MODULE 1: DEFINING NEWSLETTER ELEMENTS.*
   d. Remove the Document Map pane by clicking the Document Map button on the Standard toolbar.
6. Close Word Report 04.

W O R D

Navigating Using Bookmarks

In long documents, you may find marking a location in a document useful so you can quickly move the insertion point to the location. Create bookmarks for locations in a document at the Bookmark dialog box. When you create bookmarks, you can insert as many as needed in a document. To create a bookmark, position the insertion point at the location in the document where the bookmark is to appear, click Insert and then Bookmark. At the Bookmark dialog box shown in figure 4.16, key a name for the bookmark in the Bookmark name text box, and then click the Add button. Repeat these steps as many times as needed in a document to insert bookmarks.

FIGURE

4.16 **Bookmark Dialog Box**

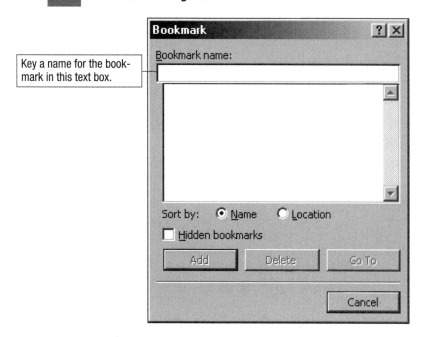

Key a name for the bookmark in this text box.

Make sure you give each bookmark a unique name. A bookmark name can contain a maximum of 40 characters and can include letters, numbers, and the underscore character (_). You cannot use spaces in a bookmark name. When you insert a bookmark in a document, the bookmark displays as an I-beam marker. If the bookmark is not visible, turn on the display by clicking Tools and then Options. At the Options dialog box, click the View tab. Insert a check mark in the Bookmarks check box in the Show section of the dialog box and then close the dialog box.

You can also create a bookmark for selected text. To do this, select the text first and then complete the steps to create a bookmark. When you create a bookmark for selected text, a left bracket ([) indicates the beginning of the selected text and a right bracket (]) indicates the end of the selected text.

After bookmarks have been inserted in a document, you can move the insertion point to a specific bookmark. To do this, click Insert and then Bookmark. At the Bookmark dialog box, double-click the bookmark name in the list box. When Word stops at the location of the bookmark, click the Close button to close the Bookmark dialog box. If you move the insertion point to a bookmark created with selected text, Word moves the insertion point to the bookmark and selects the text.

Bookmarks in a document are deleted at the Bookmark dialog box (not the document). To delete a bookmark, display the Bookmark dialog box, click the bookmark to be deleted in the list box, and then click the <u>D</u>elete button.

exercise

INSERTING BOOKMARKS IN A DOCUMENT

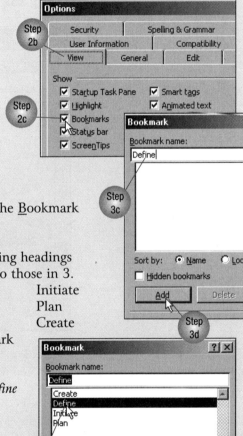

1. Open Word Report 01.
2. Make sure the display of bookmarks is turned on by completing the following steps:
   a. Click <u>T</u>ools and then <u>O</u>ptions.
   b. At the Options dialog box, click the View tab.
   c. Make sure a check mark appears in the Boo<u>k</u>marks check box in the Show section.
   d. Click OK or press Enter.
3. Insert a bookmark at the beginning of the heading *Defining Desktop Publishing* by completing the following steps:
   a. Position the insertion point at the beginning of the line containing the heading *Defining Desktop Publishing*.
   b. Click <u>I</u>nsert and then Boo<u>k</u>mark.
   c. At the Bookmark dialog box, key **Define** in the <u>B</u>ookmark name text box.
   d. Click the <u>A</u>dd button.
4. Insert a bookmark at the beginning of the following headings with the names listed by following steps similar to those in 3.

Initiating the Desktop Publishing Process	=	Initiate
Planning the Publication	=	Plan
Creating the Content	=	Create

5. Position the insertion point at the *Define* bookmark by completing the following steps:
   a. Click <u>I</u>nsert and then Boo<u>k</u>mark.
   b. At the Bookmark dialog box, double-click *Define* in the list box.
   c. When Word stops at the heading *Defining Desktop Publishing*, click the Close button to close the Bookmark dialog box.
6. Complete steps similar to those in 5 to move the insertion point to the *Initiate*, *Plan*, and *Create* bookmarks.
7. Close the report without saving the changes.

CHAPTER summary

- A macro contains recorded commands that can be applied to a document.
- Recording a macro involves turning on the macro recorder, performing the steps to be recorded, and then turning off the recorder.
- To record a macro, click Tools, point to Macro, and then click Record New Macro, or double-click the REC button on the Status bar.
- At the Record Macro dialog box, specify a name and description for the macro.
- Run a macro by displaying the Macros dialog box and double-clicking the desired macro name.
- You can temporarily suspend the recording of a macro by clicking the Pause Recording button on the Macro Record toolbar.
- Delete a macro by displaying the Macros dialog box, clicking the macro name to be deleted, and then clicking the Delete button.
- Assign a keyboard command to a macro at the Record Macro dialog box. To run a macro that has been assigned a keyboard command, press the keys assigned to the macro.
- You can add a macro as a button to a toolbar and then run the macro by clicking the button.
- Insert a Fill-in field in a macro that requires keyboard entry during the running of the macro.
- A macro is created with Visual Basic and can be edited using the Visual Basic Editor. To display a macro in the Visual Basic Editor, display the Macros dialog box, click the macro to be edited, and then click the Edit button.
- In addition to the Normal style that is applied to text by default, other predesigned styles are available in a document based on the Normal template document. Other template documents also contain predesigned styles.
- Styles can be changed and/or applied to text in three ways: 1) use Word's AutoFormat feature; 2) select a new template at the Style Gallery dialog box; or 3) make changes to styles available in the template upon which your document is based.
- The AutoFormat feature automatically applies styles to text in the document.
- Apply styles to a document from other templates with options at the Style Gallery dialog box.
- Create a new style by applying the desired formatting instructions to a paragraph and then saving the instructions in a style, or by specifying the formatting instructions for a style without applying the formatting.
- Apply a style to a paragraph of text where the insertion point is positioned or select text and then apply a style.
- Apply a style using the Style button on the Formatting toolbar or at the Styles and Formatting Task Pane.
- Modify a style by changing the formatting instructions that it contains with options at the Modify Style dialog box.
- A style can be applied quickly in a document if a shortcut key combination has been assigned to the style.
- Remove a style from text by clicking the Undo button, clicking Edit and then Undo style, applying the Normal style, or applying the Clear Formatting style. Only one style at a time can be applied to text.

- Delete a style by positioning the mouse pointer on the style name in the Styles and Formatting Task Pane, clicking the down-pointing triangle, and then clicking Delete at the drop-down list.
- Create a cross-reference in a document to refer the reader to another location within the document.
- Word offers features such as the Outline view, Document Map, and bookmarks you can use to navigate quickly to specific locations in lengthy documents.

COMMANDS review

Command	Mouse/Keyboard
Display Record Macro dialog box	Tools, Macro, Record New Macro; or double-click REC button on Status bar
Display Macros dialog box	Tools, Macro, Macros
Display Customize dialog box	Tools, Customize
Display Field dialog box	Insert, Field
Display Visual Basic Editor	At Macros dialog box, click desired macro, then click Edit button
Display AutoFormat dialog box	Format, AutoFormat
Display Style Gallery dialog box	Format, Theme, click Style Gallery button
Display Styles and Formatting Task Pane	Format, Styles and Formatting; or click Styles and Formatting button on Formatting toolbar
Display New Style dialog box	Click New Style button at Styles and Formatting Task Pane
Display Modify dialog box	At the Styles and Formatting Task Pane, click down-pointing triangle at right side of style to be modified, then click Modify
Display Cross-reference dialog box	Insert, Reference, Cross-reference
Display Outline view	View, Outline
Turn on/off Document Map	View, Document Map; or click Document Map button on Standard toolbar
Display Bookmark dialog box	Insert, Bookmark

CONCEPTS check

Completion: On a blank sheet of paper, indicate the correct term, command, or number for each item.

1. Double-click this button on the Status bar to display the Record Macro dialog box.
2. To run a macro, double-click the macro name at this dialog box.
3. Assign a keyboard command to a macro at this dialog box.
4. Assign a macro to a toolbar with options from this dialog box.
5. Insert this field in a macro that requires keyboard entry during the running of the macro.

6. Edit a macro using this editor.
7. By default, a Word document is based on this template document.
8. The predesigned styles based on the default template document are displayed by clicking this button on the Formatting toolbar.
9. The quickest way to apply styles to an entire document is with this feature.
10. Display this dialog box to apply styles from other templates to the current document.
11. Character styles display followed by this symbol in the Pick formatting to apply list box at the Styles and Formatting Task Pane.
12. Insert this in a document to refer the reader to another location within the document.
13. This is the name of a separate pane that displays the outline of a document at the left side of the screen.
14. Insert this in a document to mark a specific location.
15. List the steps you would complete to create a style named Document Format that changes the font to 12-point Bookman Old Style (or a similar serif typeface).

SKILLS check

Assessment 1

1. At a clear document screen, record a macro named XXXLtrhd02 (where your initials are used instead of the *XXX*) that contains the letterhead text shown in figure 4.17 and assign it the keyboard command Alt + Ctrl + G. (The text in figure 4.17 is set in 18-point Goudy Old Style bold.)
2. Close the document without saving it.
3. At a clear window, run the XXXLtrhd02 macro.
4. With the insertion point a double space below the letterhead, insert the document named Word Letter 02 into the current document. *(Hint: Do this by clicking Insert and then File.)*
5. Save the letter and name it EWd C04 SA01.
6. Print and then close EWd C04 SA01.

FIGURE

| 4.17 | *Assessment 1* |

GOOD SAMARITAN HOSPITAL
1201 James Street
St. Louis, MO 62033
(816) 555-1201

Assessment 2

1. At a clear document screen, run the XXXTab01 macro and then create the document shown in figure 4.18. (Key the text in the first column at the first tab stop, not the left margin.)
2. After creating the document, save it and name it EWd C04 SA02.
3. Print and then close EWd C04 SA02.

F I G U R E

4.18 *Assessment 2*

STRADFORD FUNDS CORPORATION

Public Relations Department, Extension Numbers

Roger Maldon 129

Kimberly Holland 143

Richard Perez 317

Sharon Rawlins 211

Earl Warnberg 339

Susan Fanning 122

Assessment 3

1. At a clear document screen, record a macro named XXXNotSig that includes the information shown in figure 4.19. Include Fill-in fields in the macro where you see the text in parentheses.
2. After recording the macro, close the document without saving it.
3. Open Word Contract.
4. Save the document with Save As and name it EWd C04 SA03.
5. Make the following changes to the document:
   a. Move the insertion point to the end of the document, press the Enter key twice and then insert the following information at the left margin:

LLOYD KOVICH, President
Reinberg Manufacturing

JOANNE MILNER, President
Labor Worker's Union

   b. Move the insertion point to the end of the document, press the Enter key three times, and then run the XXXNotSig macro and key the following information when prompted:

(name 1)	=	**LLOYD KOVICH**
(name 2)	=	**JOANNE MILNER**
(county)	=	**Ramsey County**

6. Save, print, and then close EWd C04 SA03.

F I G U R E

4.19 *Assessment 3*

STATE OF MINNESOTA   )
) ss.
COUNTY OF RAMSEY   )

   I certify that I know or have satisfactory evidence that (name 1) and (name 2) are the persons who appeared before me, and said persons acknowledge that they signed the foregoing Contract and acknowledged it to be their free and voluntary act for the uses and purposes therein mentioned.

                                             _____
                                             NOTARY PUBLIC in and for the State of
                                             Minnesota residing in (county)

Assessment 4

1. At a clear document screen, record a macro named XXXQuizFormat that does the following:
   a. Changes the font to 12-point Bookman Old Style (or a similar serif typeface).
   b. Changes the left paragraph indent to 0.3 inch.
   c. Adds 12 points of spacing before paragraphs.
2. Close the document without saving it.
3. Open Word Quiz.
4. Save the document with Save As and name it EWd C04 SA04.
5. Select the entire document and then run the XXXQuizFormat macro.
6. Save and then print EWd C04 SA04.
7. With EWd C04 SA04 still open, edit the XXXQuizFormat macro as follows:
   a. At the Visual Basic Editor, edit the step *.LeftIndent = InchesToPoints (0.3)* so it displays as *.LeftIndent = InchesToPoints (0.5)*. (You may need to scroll down the macro to display this macro line.)

     b. Edit the step *.RightIndent = InchesToPoints (0)* so it displays as *.RightIndent = InchesToPoints (0.5)*.

     c. Edit the step *.SpaceBefore = 12* so it displays as *.SpaceBefore = 24*.

8. After closing the Visual Basic Editor, select the entire document, and then run the XXXQuizFormat macro.
9. Center and bold the title *CHAPTER QUIZ*.
10. Save, print, and then close EWd C04 SA04.
11. At a clear document screen, display the Macros dialog box, delete all macros that begin with your initials, and then close the dialog box.

Assessment 5

1. Open Word Report 03.
2. Save the document with Save As and name it EWd C04 SA05.
3. Automatically format the document at the AutoFormat dialog box.
4. Save, print, and then close EWd C04 SA05.

Assessment 6

1. Open Word Letter 03.
2. Save the document with Save As and name it EWd C04 SA06.
3. Display the Style Gallery, choose the *Contemporary Letter* template, and then close the Style Gallery.
4. Turn on the display of the Styles and Formatting Task Pane.
5. Make sure the insertion point is positioned at the beginning of the document and then key **Plains Community College**.
6. Apply the Company Name paragraph style to the text *Plains Community College*.
7. Select the text *Re: Desktop Publishing Course* and then apply the EMPHASIS character style.
8. Save, print, and then close EWd C04 SA06.

Assessment 7

1. At a clear document screen, create the following styles:
     a. Create a style named Document Title that applies 16-point Tahoma bold.
     b. Create a style named Paragraph Spacing that applies 24 points of spacing after the paragraph.
2. Save the document and name it EWd C04 SA07.
3. With the document still open, insert the document named Word Document 07.
4. Apply the following styles:
     a. Apply the Document Title style to the text *ARE YOU PREPARING FOR RETIREMENT?*.
     b. Select the paragraphs of text (excluding the title and the blank line below the title) and then apply the Paragraph Spacing style.
5. Save, print, and then close EWd C04 SA07.

Assessment 8

1. Open EWd C04 SA07.
2. Save the document with Save As and name it EWd C04 SA08.
3. Make the following changes to the styles:
     a. Modify the Document Title style so it applies 16-point Times New Roman bold and also center aligns the text.

    b. Modify the Paragraph Spacing style so the space after is 18 points rather than 24 points.
 4. Save, print, and then close EWd C04 SA08.

Assessment 9

 1. Open Word Report 04.
 2. Save the document with Save As and name it EWd C04 SA09.
 3. Select the entire document and then change to single line spacing.
 4. Apply the specified styles to the following headings:

MODULE 1: DEFINING NEWSLETTER ELEMENTS	=	Heading 1
Designing a Newsletter	=	Heading 2
Defining Basic Newsletter Elements	=	Heading 2
MODULE 2: PLANNING A NEWSLETTER	=	Heading 1
Defining the Purpose of a Newsletter	=	Heading 2

 5. Insert a cross-reference following the period at the end of the first paragraph that contains the text *For more information, refer to* and refers readers to the *Defining the Purpose of a Newsletter* heading.
 6. Move to the reference text using the cross-reference.
 7. Save, print, and then close EWd C04 SA09.

WORK IN Progress

Managing Data and Documents

ASSESSING proficiencies

In this unit, you learned to format Word documents with features such as mail merge, sorting and selecting, AutoText, footnotes and endnotes, bookmarks, and cross-references. You also learned to add visual appeal to documents by inserting images, watermark text, shapes, and objects.

(Before completing unit assessments, delete the Word Chapter 04E *folder on your disk. Next, copy to your disk the* Word Unit 01E *subfolder from the CD that accompanies this textbook and then make* Word Unit 01E *the active folder.)*

Assessment 1

1. Look at the information shown in figures U1.1 and U1.2. Use the Mail Merge Wizard to prepare six letters using the information shown in the figures. When completing the steps, consider the following:
   a. At step 3, create a data source document using the information shown in figure U1.1. Save the data source document in the Word Unit 01E folder on your disk and name it Sound Med DS.
   b. At step 6, complete the following steps:
      1) Click the *Edit individual letters* hyperlink in the task pane.
      2) At the Merge to New Document dialog box, make sure All is selected, and then click the OK button.
      3) Save the merged letters in the normal manner in the *Word Unit 01E* folder on your disk and name the document Sound Med Letters.
      4) Print Sound Med Letters. (This document will print six letters.)
      5) Close Sound Med Letters.
      6) Save the main document in the normal manner on your disk in drive A and name it Sound Med MD.

Mrs. Antonio Mercado
3241 Court G
Tampa, FL 33623

Ms. Kristina Vukovich
1120 South Monroe
Tampa, FL 33655

Ms. Alexandria Remick
909 Wheeler South
Tampa, FL 33620

Mr. Minh Vu
9302 Lawndale Southwest
Tampa, FL 33623

Mr. Curtis Iverson
10139 93rd Court South
Tampa, FL 33654

Mrs. Holly Bernard
8904 Emerson Road
Tampa, FL 33620

Figure U1.1 • Assessment 1

December 9, 2002

««AddressBlock»»

««GreetingLine»»

Sound Medical is switching hospital care in Tampa to St. Jude's Hospital beginning January 1, 2003. As mentioned in last month's letter, St. Jude's Hospital was selected because it meets our requirements for high-quality, customer-pleasing care that is also affordable and accessible. Our physicians look forward to caring for you in this new environment.

Over the past month, staff members at Sound Medical have been working to make this transition as smooth as possible. Surgeries planned after January 1 are being scheduled at St. Jude's Hospital. Mothers delivering babies any time after January 1 are receiving information about delivery room tours and prenatal classes available at St. Jude's. Your Sound Medical doctor will have privileges at St. Jude's and will continue to care for you if you need to be hospitalized.

You are a very important part of our patient family, «Title» «Last_Name», and we hope this information is helpful. If you have any additional questions or concerns, please call our hospital transition manager, Jeff Greenswald, at (813) 555-9886, between 8:00 a.m. and 4:30 p.m.

Sincerely,

Jody Tiemann
District Administrator

XX:Sound Med MD

Figure U1.2 • Assessment 1

Assessment 2

1. Use the Mail Merge Wizard to prepare envelopes for the letters created in assessment 1.
2. Specify Sound Med DS as the data source document.
3. Save the merged envelope document on your disk and name the document Sound Med Envs.
4. Print the Sound Med Envs document.
5. Do not save the envelope main document.

Assessment 3

1. Open Word Tab 03.
2. Save the document with Save As and name it EWd U01 PA03.
3. Sort the columns of text alphabetically by last name in the first column. (Display the Sort Options dialog box and make sure Tabs is selected in the Separate fields at section.)
4. Print EWd U01 PA03.
5. Sort the second column of text alphabetically by the title in the second column and then alphabetically by last name in the first column. (This is one sort.)
6. Print and then close EWd U01 PA03.

Assessment 4

1. Open Word Table 03.
2. Save the document with Save As and name it EWd U01 PA04.
3. Sort the text alphabetically in the first column.
4. Use the AutoFit feature to make the columns in the table automatically fit the contents.
5. Apply the Table Contemporary table formatting to the table.
6. Save, print, and then close EWd U01 PA04.

Assessment 5

1. Create the following autotext entries:
   a. Create an autotext entry for *Government Obligations Fund* and use the initials *gof*.
   b. Create an autotext entry for *Prime Obligations Fund* and use the initials *pof*.
   c. Create an autotext entry for *Tax Free Obligations Fund* and use the initials *tfof*.
2. Key the document shown in figure U1.3 using the autotext entries you created.
3. Save the document and name it EWd U01 PA05.
4. Print and then close EWd U01 PA05.
5. At a clear document screen, delete the *gof*, *pof*, and the *tfof* autotext entries.

STRADFORD FUNDS CORPORATION

The Board of Directors and Shareholders

gof

pof

tfof

We have audited the statements of net assets of the *gof, pof,* and *tfof* as of September 30, 2002, and the related statements of operations, the statements of changes in net assets and the financial highlights for each of the periods presented.

In our opinion, the financial statements and the financial highlights present fairly, in all material respects, the financial position of the *gof, pof,* and *tfof* as of September 30, 2002, and the results of their operations, changes in their net assets, and the financial highlights for each of the periods are in conformity with generally accepted accounting principles.

Figure U1.3 • Assessment 5

Assessment 6

1. Open Word Report 05.
2. Save the document with Save As and name it EWd U01 PA06.
3. Make the following changes to the document:
   a. Bold the titles and headings in the document.
   b. Change the left and right margins to 1 inch.
   c. Insert a page break that begins a new page at the line containing the title *MODULE 4: CREATING NEWSLETTER LAYOUT*.
   d. Make sure the widow/orphan control is turned on.
   e. Create the first footnote shown in figure U1.4 at the end of the first paragraph in the Applying Desktop Publishing Guidelines section of the document.
   f. Create the second footnote shown in figure U1.4 at the end of the third paragraph in the Applying Desktop Publishing Guidelines section of the document.
   g. Create the third footnote shown in figure U1.4 at the end of the last paragraph in the Applying Desktop Publishing Guidelines section of the document.
   h. Create the fourth footnote shown in figure U1.4 at the end of the only paragraph in the Choosing Paper Weight section of the document.
4. Check page breaks in the document and, if necessary, adjust the page breaks.
5. Save, print, and then close EWd U01 PA06.

Fellers, Laurie, *Desktop Publishing Design,* Cornwall & Lewis Publishing, 2000, pages 67-72.

Moriarity, Joel, "Adding Emphasis to Documents," *Desktop Publishing,* August 2001, pages 3-6.

Wong, Chun Man, *Desktop Publishing with Style,* Monroe-Ackerman Publishing, 2000, pages 87-93.

Jaquez, Andre, *Desktop Publishing Tips and Tricks,* Aurora Publishing House, 2001, pages 103-106.

Figure U1.4 • Assessment 6

Assessment 7

1. Open EWd U01 PA06.
2. Save the document with Save As and name it EWd U01 PA07.
3. Make the following changes to the document:
   a. Edit the third footnote and change the publication year from *2000* to *2001* and change the pages from *87-93* to *61-68.*
   b. Move the first footnote to the end of the only paragraph in the Choosing Paper Size and Type section of the document.
   c. Delete the fourth footnote.
4. Save, print, and then close EWd U01 PA07.

Assessment 8

1. Open Word Report 06.
2. Save the document with Save As and name it EWd U01 PA08.
3. Make the following changes to the document:
   a. Delete text in the document from the beginning of the title *SECTION 2: COMPUTERS IN ENTERTAINMENT* (located on page 2) to the end of the document.
   b. Select the entire document, change the line spacing to 1.5, change the font size to 13 points, and then deselect the text.
   c. Move the insertion point immediately past the title *SECTION 1: COMPUTERS IN COMMUNICATIONS* and then press the Enter key once.
   d. Set the title in 14-point Arial bold.
   e. Center the title.
   f. Set the headings *Telecommunications, Publishing,* and *News Services* in 14-point Arial bold.
   g. Format the text in the document beginning with the first paragraph (begins with *Computer have become central...*) into two evenly spaced columns.
   h. Balance the columns on the last page of the document.
   i. Move the insertion point to the beginning of the document and then insert a clip art image of a computer (you choose the image) with the following specifications:
      1) Change the wrapping style to <u>T</u>ight.
      2) Change the width of the image to 1 inch.
      3) Change the horizontal alignment of the image to *Left* relative to the *Column.*

       4) Change the vertical absolute position to *1.6˝* below *Page.*

   j. Check column breaks in the document and, if necessary, insert your own column break.

4. Save, print, and then close EWd U01 PA08.

Assessment 9

1. At a clear document screen, create the document shown in figure U1.5 with the following specifications:

   a. Set the title *CORPORATE COMMITMENT* in 24-point Times New Roman bold.

   b. Create the top box with the following specifications:

       1) Use the Rectangle tool to draw the box.

       2) Add light green fill to the box.

       3) Click the 3-D Style button on the Drawing toolbar and then click the 3-D Style 11 option (third option from the left in the third row).

       4) Click the Text Box button and then draw a text box inside the first box.

       5) Set the text inside the text box in 20-point Times New Roman bold.

       6) Add light green fill to the text box.

       7) Remove the line around the text box. (Do this with the Line Color button on the Drawing toolbar.)

   c. After creating the top box, copy the box two times so a total of three boxes appear in the document as shown in figure U1.5.

   d. Make sure the text appears in the boxes as shown in figure U1.5.

   e. Make sure the boxes are center aligned. To do this, select all three boxes, click the D<u>r</u>aw button on the Drawing toolbar, point to <u>A</u>lign or Distribute, and then click Align <u>C</u>enter.

2. Save the completed document and name it EWd U01 PA09.

3. Print and then close EWd U01 PA09.

Figure U1.5 • Assessment 9

Assessment 10

1. Create a certificate with the following specifications:
   a. Change the page orientation to Landscape.
   b. Change the top, bottom, left, and right margins to 0.75 inch.
   c. Insert a page border of your choosing.
   d. Insert the following text (you determine the typeface, typestyle, and type size of the text):

   Volunteer of the Year Award
   Presented to Simone Moore
   Sun Valley School District
   June 2003

   e. Insert either an appropriate clip art image in the certificate or an appropriate autoshape.
   f. Include at least four small sun autoshapes that are aligned and distributed. (Find the sun shape by clicking the AutoShapes button on the Drawing toolbar and then pointing to Basic Shapes. The Sun shape is the third shape from the left in the sixth row.)
2. Save the completed certificate and name it EWd U01 PA10.
3. Print and then close EWd U01 PA10.

Assessment 11

1. At a clear document screen, use WordArt to create the flyer letterhead shown in figure U1.6 by completing the following steps:
   a. Press the Enter key seven times and then move the insertion back to the beginning of the document.
   b. Display the WordArt Gallery and then double-click the second option from the left in the third row.
   c. At the Edit WordArt Text dialog box, key **Newbury News**, and then click OK.
   d. Make the following changes to the WordArt text:
      1) Click the WordArt text to select it.
      2) Change the text wrapping to Through.
      3) Change the shape to Arch Up (Curve).
      4) Change the height and width to 2 inches.
      5) Change the horizontal alignment to left.
   e. Deselect the WordArt text.
   f. Move the insertion point to the end of the document and then insert the border line shown in figure U1.6. *(Hint: Do this at the Borders and Shading dialog box. Choose the fourth option from the end of the Style list box and change the color to Lavender.)*
2. Save the document and name it EWd U01 PA11.
3. Print and then close EWd U01 PA11.

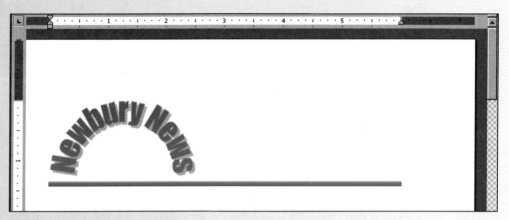

Figure U1.6 • Assessment 11

Assessment 12

1. At a clear document screen, record a macro named CWInfo that includes the copyright information shown in figure U1.7. Include Fill-in fields in the macro where you see the text in parentheses.
2. After recording the macro, close the document without saving it.
3. Open Word Contract.
4. Save the document with Save As and name it EWd U01 PA12.
5. Change the top, bottom, left, and right margins to 0.8 inch.
6. Move the insertion point to the end of the document, press the Enter key once, and then run the CWInfo macro and insert the following information when prompted:
   (name) = **Oliver Middleton**
   (date) = **March 20, 2003**
7. Save, print, and then close EWd U01 PA12.

This document is the sole property of Reinberg Manufacturing and may not be reproduced, copied, or sold without express written consent of a legal representative of Reinberg Manufacturing.

Prepared by: (name)
Date: (date)

Figure U1.7 • Assessment 12

Assessment 13

1. Open Word Report 05.
2. Save the document with Save As and name it EWd U01 PA13.
3. Select from the title *MODULE 4: CREATING NEWSLETTER LAYOUT* (located on page 2) to the end of the document and then delete the selected text.
4. Display the Style Gallery, choose the *Elegant Report* template, and then close the Style Gallery.
5. Turn on the display of the Styles and Formatting Task Pane.
6. Select the text from the beginning of the heading *Applying Desktop Publishing Guidelines* to the end of the document and then apply the Body Text style.
7. Apply the <u>CHAPTER LABEL</u> paragraph style to the title *MODULE 3: DESIGNING A NEWSLETTER*.
8. Apply the Heading 1 style to the heading *Applying Desktop Publishing Guidelines*.
9. Save, print, and then close EWd U01 PA13.

Assessment 14

1. At a clear document screen, create the following styles:
   a. Create a style named Title Formatting that applies the following formatting:
      1) 16-point Arial bold
      2) 6 points of spacing before and after paragraph
   b. Create a style named Heading Formatting that applies the following:
      1) 12-point Arial bold
      2) 6 points of spacing before and after paragraph
2. Save the document and name it EWd U01 PA14.
3. With EWd U01 PA14 open, insert the document named Word Report 04 into EWd U01 PA14.
4. Make the following changes to the document:
   a. Select the entire document and change the line spacing to single.
   b. Apply the Title Formatting style to the following titles:
      MODULE 1: DEFINING NEWSLETTER ELEMENTS
      MODULE 2: PLANNING A NEWSLETTER
   c. Apply the Heading Formatting style to the following headings:
      Designing a Newsletter
      Defining Basic Newsletter Elements
      Defining the Purpose of a Newsletter
5. Check the page break and, if necessary, adjust the page break.
6. Save and then print EWd U01 PA14.
7. With EWd U01 PA14 still open, save the document with Save As and name it EWd U01 PA14 Second.
8. Edit the Title Formatting style so it applies the following formatting:
   a. 14-point Times New Roman bold
   b. 12 points of spacing before and after paragraph
   c. center alignment
9. Edit the Heading Formatting style so it applies 12-point Times New Roman bold (leave the 6 point before and after spacing).
10. Save, print, and then close EWd U01 PA14 Second.

WRITING activities

Activity 1

Situation: You have just opened a new mailing and shipping business and need letterhead stationery. Create a letterhead for your company that includes *at least* one of the following: a drawn shape, an autoshape, a line, and/or a 3-D object. Include the following information in the letterhead:

> Global Mailing
> 4300 Jackson Avenue
> Toronto, Ontario M4C 3X4
> (416) 555-0095
> www.emcp.com/gmail.ca

Save the completed letterhead and name it EWd U01 Act01. Print and then close EWd U01 Act01.

Activity 2

Situation: You are interested in learning more about the Microsoft Design Gallery Live Web site and specifically how to limit searches. Make sure you are connected to the Internet, display the Insert Clip Art Task Pane, and then click the *Clips Online* hyperlink. At the Microsoft Design Gallery Live Web site, experiment with the options at the left side of the page including the Search in, Results should be, and Order by options. Then create a document that includes the following:

- An appropriate title.
- A brief description of the Search in, Results should be, and Order by options.
- Steps required to search for images of the sun and limiting the search to the *Nature* category.

Save the completed document and name it EWd U01 Act02. Print and then close EWd U01 Act02.

INTERNET project

Make sure you are connected to the Internet and then use a search engine (you choose the search engine) to search for companies on the Web that provide information, services, and/or products for designing documents. Key words you might consider using to search the Web include:

desktop publishing	typeface
document design	electronic design

Find at least three Web sites that interest you and then create a report in Word about the sites that includes the following:

- Type of site (company, personal, magazine, etc.)
- Site name, address, and URL
- A brief description of the site
- Products, services, and/or information available at the site

Include any other additional information pertinent to the sites. Apply formatting to enhance the document. Print a copy of the final document.

JOB study

Preparing Guidelines for E-mail Communications

With the daily use of e-mail in the corporate environment, it is essential for employees to know the rules of electronic communication. You have prepared the Pacific Northwest Technologies corporate guidelines for e-mail communications. You will distribute the guidelines to all departments in a report via e-mail. In addition, in keeping with Pacific's marketing strategy, you will use the same information to prepare a newsletter to be mailed to a select list of clients.

Using the concepts and techniques you learned in unit 1, complete the following tasks:

1. Key the text in figure U1.8 in appropriate report format, correcting all errors in style and word usage. Use the special features you learned in chapter 2 to enhance the format of the document. Then use the AutoSummarize feature to automatically summarize the completed document. Save and print the document.
2. Create a newsletter based on the report you prepared in step 1. Add visual appeal to the newsletter by incorporating the graphic and drawing techniques presented in chapter 3. Save and print the document.
3. Use the Mail Merge Wizard to prepare six letters enclosing the newsletter you created in step 2. Use the same data source to create mailing labels. Utilize the concepts and techniques you learned in unit 1 to design a custom letterhead for the main document. Save and print the main document and data source.
4. Create a macro that will open, print and close the merged letters and labels you created in step 3. Assign the macro to the toolbar.

When you communicate by letter, you follow a certain etiquette, including rules for formatting the letter and addressing the recipient. When you communicate by e-mail, you need to follow a similar set of rules, informally referred to as "netiquette."[1] Simply stated, netiquette is network etiquette?the etiquette of cyberspace. And "etiquette" means "the forms required by good breeding or prescribed by authority to be required in social or official life." In other words, netiquette is a set of rules for behaving properly online.[2]

Following netiquette can enhance the effectiveness of your e-mail. More important, not following it can jeopardize valuable relationships with Pacific Northwest Technologies' clients and colleagues. In general, rules of common courtesy for interaction with people should be in force for any situation. These rules are even more important on the Internet. Written communication does not convey the same expression as face-to-face communication, so we must have some standardized conventions for politeness. At Pacific Northwest Technologies, the rapport we have with clients and colleagues is important. The tone of a message will build it or destroy it. We must use netiquette to build/maintain rapport.[3]

To avoid breaches of netiquette in your e-mail, follow these guidelines for e-mail communication before you clicking the Send button:

1 http://www.text100.com/news/nettiquite.asp
2 www.albion.com
3 http://www.tamu-commerce.edu

Security. Pacific Northwest Technologies uses encryption software. However, you should assume that mail on the Internet is not secure. Never put in a mail message anything you would not put on a postcard. You don't have to be engaged in criminal activity to want to be careful. Any message you send could be saved or forwarded by its recipient. You have no control over where it goes.

Bandwidth. Bandwidth is the information-carrying capacity of the wires and channels that connect everyone in cyberspace. There is a limit to the amount of data that any piece of wiring can carry at any given moment?even a state-of-the-art fiber-optic cable systems such as that employed by Pacific Northwest Technologies.

Chain Letters. Never send chain letters via electronic mail. Chain letters are forbidden on the Internet. Your network privileges will be revoked. Notify the Pacific Northwest Technology System Administrator if your ever receive one.

Signature. Your e-mail signature is the equivalent of a business card that tells the reader who you are, what you do, and were to find you. In Internet parlance, this is known as a ".sig" or "signature" file. Your .sig file takes the place of your business card. (And you can have more than one to apply in different circumstances.) It is Pacific Northwest Technologies' policy to include a signature. Keep it short. The rule of thumb is no longer than four lines.[4] This can include your name, title, company name, company URL, mailing address, and telephone and fax numbers.

Subject Line. Mail should have a short (four to six words) subject heading which reflects the content of the message. This heading, or subject line, appears in your e-mail browser describing the contents of the e-mail. All Pacific Northwest Technology e-mail should include the word "Long" in the subject header so the recipient knows the message will take time to read and respond to. Over 100 lines is considered "long."

Message Body. Be sure that the message conveys information effectively and concisely. While we at Pacific Northwest Technology encourage the use of timely e-mail to respond to customers and colleagues, we also recognize that sometimes e-mail is not the best way to deliver a message. Does your message include information that would be better communicated using a different medium, such as a phone call or a link to a Web page? When replying to a message, address all points and answer all questions in the original message.

4 http://www.workz.com/content/233.asp

Figure U1.8 • Guidelines for E-mail Communications

Kathleen Richardson, President
Widden Communications
566 Longview Avenue
Bluestone, NY 12345

Raymond Lopez, CEO
United Freight, Inc.
887 Woodhaven Road
Garwood, NY 22355

Leonard Gothez, Chairman
Gothez Engineering
334 Bonhampton Avenue
Union Plains, NJ 12335

Cynthia Hu, Director
Hu Industrial Graphics, Inc.
908 Pinelawn Road
West Orange, NY 33425

Barbara Garwood, Dean
Information Technology
Fairfield Community College
Fairfield, IN 12445

Peter Young, President
On-line Now
664 West 57th Street
New York, NY 22335

Figure U1.9 • Mail Merge Recipients

WORD

Working with Shared Documents

Creating Specialized Tables and Indexes

Preparing and Protecting Forms

Sharing Data

MICROSOFT® WORD 2002

EXPERT BENCHMARK MOUS SKILLS-UNIT 2

WORKING WITH SHARED DOCUMENTS

PERFORMANCE OBJECTIVES

Upon successful completion of chapter 5, you will be able to:
- **Track changes to a document**
- **Accept/reject changes to a document**
- **Create, view, delete, and print comments**
- **Create multiple versions of a document**
- **Send and route documents**
- **Set the file location for Workgroup templates**
- **Create a master document and subdocuments**
- **Expand, collapse, open, close, rearrange, split, combine, remove, and rename subdocuments**

Word Chapter 05E

Some employees in a company may be part of a *workgroup*, which is a networked collection of computers sharing files, printers, and other resources. In a workgroup, you generally make your documents available to your colleagues. With the Windows operating system and Office applications, you can share and distribute your documents quickly and easily to members of your workgroup from your desktop computer.

If you are part of a workgroup, several options are available for distributing documents to colleagues. You can make the document available on the shared network drive for anyone in your workgroup to open and edit; members in your workgroup can open and edit copies of a document; or you can route a document to specific members in your workgroup.

In this chapter, you will learn how to track changes in a document from multiple users, create and insert comments in documents, create multiple versions of a document, send and route documents, and create a master document and subdocuments.

Tracking Changes to a Document

If more than one person in a workgroup needs to review and edit a document, consider using the tracking feature. With the tracking feature on, each deletion, insertion, or formatting change made to the document is tracked. For example, deleted text is not removed from the document but instead displays with a line through it and in a different color. Word uses a different color (up to eight) for each person in the workgroup making changes to the document. In this way, the person looking at the document can identify which author made what change.

Track Changes

Turn on tracking by clicking the Track Changes button on the Reviewing toolbar. To display this toolbar, shown in figure 5.1, click <u>V</u>iew, point to <u>T</u>oolbars, and then click *Reviewing* or right-click any currently displayed toolbar and then click *Reviewing* at the drop-down menu.

FIGURE

5.1 *Reviewing Toolbar*

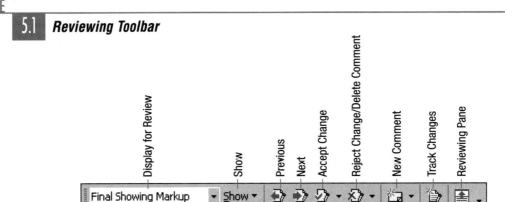

You can also turn on tracking by clicking <u>T</u>ools and then <u>T</u>rack Changes. When tracking is on, the letters *TRK* display in black on the Status bar (located toward the bottom of the screen). To turn off tracking, click the Track Changes button on the Reviewing toolbar or click <u>T</u>ools and then <u>T</u>rack Changes.

The display of tracked changes varies depending on the view. In Normal view, with tracking on, inserted text displays underlined while deleted text displays with a line through it. In Print Layout view, inserted text displays underlined while deleted text displays in a balloon in the right margin. In either view, Word inserts a vertical line outside the left margin beside the line containing a change.

Display for Review

Control how changes display in the document with the Display for Review button on the Reviewing toolbar. Click the down-pointing triangle at the right side of the Display for Review button and a drop-down list displays with the options *Final Showing Markup*, *Final*, *Original Showing Markup*, and *Original*. Choose a final option if you want the document to display in its final form with or without changes or choose an original option if you want the document to display in its original form with or without changes.

Show

Click the down-pointing triangle at the right side of the <u>S</u>how button on the Reviewing toolbar and a drop-down list displays with options for controlling what changes display in the document. By default, comments, insertions, deletions, and formatting changes display in the document. Remove the check mark from those options you want inactive.

1. Open Word Contract.
2. Save the document with Save As and name it EWd C05 Ex01.
3. Change to the Print Layout view.
4. Turn on the display of the Reviewing toolbar by *right-clicking* the Standard toolbar and then clicking *Reviewing* at the drop-down list. (Skip this step if the Reviewing toolbar is already displayed.)
5. Click the down-pointing triangle at the right side of the Display for Review button on the Reviewing toolbar and then click *Original Showing Markup* at the drop-down list.
6. Make changes to the contract and track the changes by completing the following steps:
   a. Click the Track Changes button on the Reviewing toolbar.
   b. Delete *4,000* in paragraph number 3 in the TRANSFERS AND MOVING EXPENSES section (the text will not be removed from the screen—instead, a line will display through the text).
   c. Position the insertion point immediately to the right of *4,000* and then key **6,000** in the Inserted balloon. (The balloon displays as soon as you begin keying *6,000*.)
   d. Click in the document (outside the balloon).
   e. Delete *two (2)* in paragraph number 3 in the SICK LEAVE section.
   f. Position the insertion point immediately to the right of *two (2)* and then key **three (3)** in the Inserted balloon.
   g. Click in the document (outside the balloon).
   h. Turn off tracking by clicking the Track Changes button on the Reviewing toolbar.
7. Save, print, and then close EWd C05 Ex01.

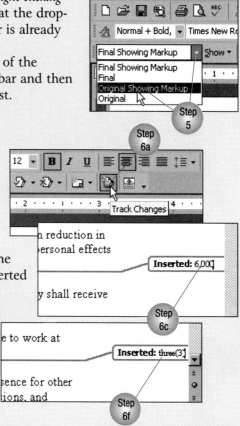

You can display information on tracking changes by positioning the mouse pointer on a change. After approximately one second, a box displays above the change containing the author's name, date, time, and the type of change (for example, whether it was a deletion or insertion). You can also display information on tracking changes by displaying the Reviewing pane. To do this, click the Reviewing Pane button on the Reviewing toolbar or click the <u>S</u>how button and then click Reviewing <u>P</u>ane at the drop-down list. Each change is listed separately in the Reviewing pane as shown in figure 5.2. Use the arrow keys at the right side of the Reviewing pane to scroll through the pane and view each change. To remove the Reviewing pane, click the Reviewing Pane button.

Reviewing
Pane

5.2 **Reviewing Pane**

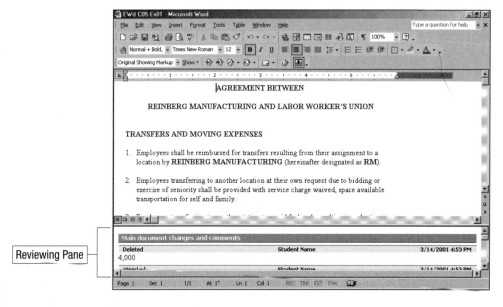

Reviewing Pane

If changes are made to the document by another person with different User Information, the changes display in a different color. In the next exercise, you will pretend to be another author, change User Information, and then make changes to the contract. Change user information at the Options dialog box with the User Information tab selected.

exercise 2

TRACKING CHANGES TO A DOCUMENT MADE BY ANOTHER AUTHOR

(Note: Check with your instructor before completing this exercise to determine if you can change User Information.)

1. Open EWd C05 Ex01.
2. Save the document with Save As and name it EWd C05 Ex02.
3. Change User Information by completing the following steps:
   a. Click Tools and then Options.
   b. At the Options dialog box, click the User Information tab.
   c. At the Options dialog box with the User Information tab selected, make a note of the current name, initials, and mailing address. (You will reenter this information later in this exercise.)
   d. Key **David Wells** in the Name text box.
   e. Press the Tab key. (This moves the insertion point to the Initials text box.)
   f. Key **DW**.
   g. Click OK to close the Options dialog box.

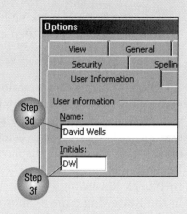

4. Make additional changes to the contract and track the changes by completing the following steps:
   a. Make sure the Reviewing toolbar is displayed.
   b. Make sure the Display for Review button contains the *Final Showing Markup* option.
   c. Turn on tracking by clicking the Track Changes button on the Reviewing toolbar.
   d. Add the text **up to $5,000** to the end of the sentence in paragraph number 4 in the TRANSFERS AND MOVING EXPENSES section. (Notice that the change displays in a different color than the changes you made in exercise 1.)
   e. Delete paragraph number 5 in the SICK LEAVE section. (The paragraph is removed and inserted in a balloon in the right margin.)
5. Turn off tracking by clicking the Track Changes button on the Reviewing toolbar.
6. View the changes in the Reviewing pane by completing the following steps:
   a. Click the Reviewing Pane button on the Reviewing toolbar.
   b. Use the arrows at the right side of the Reviewing pane to scroll through the pane and review the changes. (Notice that the changes made in the first exercise are in a different color than the changes made in this exercise.)
   c. Click the Reviewing Pane button to turn off the display of the Reviewing pane.
7. Change the User Information back to the information that displayed before you keyed *David Wells* and the initials *DW* by completing the following steps:
   a. Click <u>T</u>ools and then <u>O</u>ptions.
   b. At the Options dialog box, make sure the User Information tab is selected.
   c. At the Options dialog box with the User Information tab selected, key the original name in the <u>N</u>ame text box.
   d. Press the Tab key and then key the original initials in the <u>I</u>nitials text box.
   e. Click OK to close the dialog box.
8. Save, print, and then close EWd C05 Ex02.

Moving to the Next/Previous Change

In a longer document containing several changes, use buttons on the Reviewing toolbar to move the insertion point to a change in the document. Click the Previous button on the Reviewing toolbar to move to the previous change in the document or click the Next button to move to the next change in the document.

Previous

Next

Accepting/Rejecting Changes

Changes made to a document can be accepted or rejected. Click the Accept Change button on the Reviewing toolbar to accept the change or click the Reject Change/Delete Comment button to specify changes you want to reject. You can also position the mouse pointer over the change and then click the *right* mouse button. This causes a pop-up menu to display with options for accepting or rejecting the change.

Accept Change

Reject Change/Delete Comment

1. Open EWd C05 Ex02.
2. Save the document with Save As and name it EWd C05 Ex03.
3. Accept some changes and reject others by completing the following steps:
   a. Accept the change from *4,000* to *6,000* by completing the following steps:
      1) Make sure the Reviewing toolbar is displayed. (If not, *right-click* on the Standard toolbar and then click *Reviewing*.)
      2) Click the Next button on the Reviewing toolbar.
      3) With *4,000* selected in the Deleted balloon, click the Accept Change button on the Reviewing toolbar.

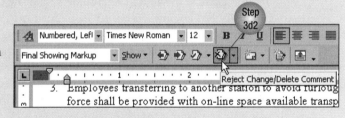

   b. Acccpt the <u>6,000</u> by completing steps similar to those in 3a.
   c. Click the Next button on the Reviewing toolbar and then accept the change adding **up to $5,000** to the end of the sentence in paragraph number 4 in the TRANSFERS AND MOVING EXPENSES section.
   d. Reject the change from *two (2)* to *three (3)* by completing the following steps:
      1) Click the Next button on the Reviewing toolbar.
      2) With *two (2)* selected in the Deleted balloon, click the Reject Change/Delete Comment button.
      3) Click the Next button on the Reviewing toolbar.
      4) Reject the change inserting *three (3)* by clicking the Reject Change/Delete Comment button on the Reviewing toolbar.
   e. Reject the change deleting paragraph number 5 in the SICK LEAVE section.
   f. Deselect the text.
4. Save, print, and then close EWd C05 Ex03.

Inserting Comments

In some situations, people in a workgroup may want to make comments on a document rather than make editing changes. You can insert a comment in a document in a Comment balloon or in the Reviewing pane. More than one person in a workgroup can insert comments in a document. Word distinguishes comments from users by color. Comments from the first user are inserted in a pink balloon or with a pink shading in the Reviewing pane. Blue is used for comments from the second user.

Creating a Comment

To create a comment, select the text or item on which you want to comment or position the insertion point at the end of the text, click Insert, and then click Comment, or click the New Comment button on the Reviewing toolbar. If you are in Print Layout view, a Comment balloon displays in the right margin and the Reviewing toolbar. Key the desired comment in the Comment balloon. If you are in Normal view, the Reviewing pane automatically opens and the Reviewing toolbar displays. Key the desired comment in the Reviewing pane. The Reviewing pane displays the complete text of all tracked changes and comments. Close the Reviewing pane by clicking the Reviewing Pane button on the Reviewing toolbar.

New Comment

Editing a Comment

To edit a comment in Print Layout view, click in the Comment balloon, make the desired changes, and then click outside the balloon. To edit a comment in the Normal view, first turn on the display of the Reviewing Pane. To do this, display the Reviewing toolbar and then click the Reviewing Pane button on the Reviewing toolbar. Click in the comment text in the Reviewing pane, make the desired changes, and then click in the document.

HINT
Use the ScreenTips to quickly view comments in a document.

Deleting a Comment

Delete a comment by clicking the Next button on the Reviewing toolbar (this moves the insertion point to the next comment in the document) and then clicking the down-pointing triangle at the right side of the Reject Change/Delete Comment button. At the drop-down list that displays, click the Reject Change/Delete Comment to delete the current comment, or click Reject All Comments to delete all comments in the document.

In Print Layout view, you can also delete a comment by right-clicking the Comment balloon and then clicking Delete Comment at the pop-up list. This deletes the Comment balloon as well as the comment text in the Reviewing pane.

Printing a Comment

Print a document containing comments with the comments or print just the comments and not the document. To print a document and comments, display the Print dialog box, click the down-pointing triangle at the right side of the Print what option, and then click *Document showing markup* at the drop-down list. To print only comments, display the Print dialog box, click the down-pointing triangle at the right side of the Print what option, and then click *List of markup* at the drop-down list. This prints the contents of the Reviewing pane including comments as well as any tracked changes or changes to headers, footers, text boxes, footnotes, or endnotes.

1. Open Word Report 02.
2. Save the document with Save As and name it EWd C05 Ex04.
3. Make sure the Reviewing toolbar displays.
4. Make sure that the document displays in Normal view.
5. Create a comment by completing the following steps:
   a. Position the insertion point at the end of the first paragraph below the bulleted items on the first page in the report.
   b. Press the spacebar once and then key **Source?**.
   c. Select *Source?*.
   d. Click the New Comment button on the Reviewing toolbar. (This opens the Reviewing pane.)
   e. Key **Please add the source for the information in this paragraph.** in the Reviewing pane.

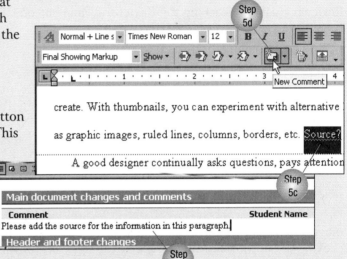

6. Turn off the display of the Reviewing pane by clicking the Reviewing Pane button on the Reviewing toolbar.
7. Create another comment by completing the following steps:
   a. Move the insertion point to the end of the last paragraph in the Designing a Document section of the report.
   b. Press the spacebar once, key **Examples?** and then select *Examples?*.
   c. Click the New Comment button on the Reviewing toolbar.
   d. Key **Include several examples of flyers containing graphic elements and color.** in the Reviewing pane.
   e. Click the Reviewing Pane button to turn off the display of the Reviewing pane.
8. Change to the Print Layout view.
9. Create another comment by completing the following steps:
   a. Move the insertion point to the end of the last paragraph in the report.
   b. Press the spacebar once, key **Illustrations,** and then select *Illustrations*.
   c. Click the New Comment button on the Reviewing toolbar.
   d. Key **Add several illustrations of focal points in a document.** in the Comment balloon.
   e. Click in the document.
10. Edit the first comment by completing the following steps:
    a. Scroll up the document until the first Comment balloon is visible and then click in the text located inside the balloon.

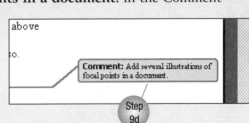

WORD

b. Move the insertion point immediately left of the period at the end of the sentence and then key **and include any pertinent Web sites**.

c. Click in the document, outside any Comment balloons.

11. Save the document again with the same name (EWd C05 Ex04).

12. Print the document and the comments by completing the following steps:

   a. Display the Print dialog box.

   b. At the Print dialog box, make sure the Print <u>w</u>hat option displays as *Document showing markup*. (If not, click the down-pointing triangle at the right side of the Print <u>w</u>hat option, and then click *Document showing markup*.)

   c. Click OK.

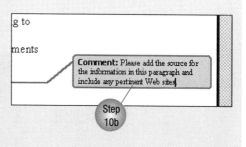

13. Print just the information in the Reviewing pane by completing the following steps:

   a. Display the Print dialog box.

   b. At the Print dialog box, click the down-pointing triangle at the right side of the Print <u>w</u>hat option, and then click *List of markup* at the drop-down list.

   c. Click OK.

14. Delete a comment by completing the following steps:

   a. Move the insertion point to the beginning of the document and then click the Next button on the Reviewing toolbar.

   b. Click the Next button again. (This moves the insertion point to the second comment balloon.)

   c. Click the down-pointing triangle at the right side of the Reject Change/Delete Comment button.

   d. At the drop-down list, click <u>R</u>eject Change/Delete Comment.

   e. Select and then delete *Examples?*.

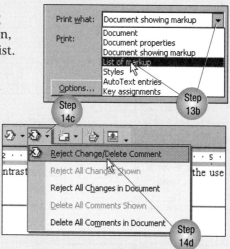

15. Turn off the display of the Reviewing toolbar.

16. Print only the comments.

17. Save and then close EWd C05 Ex04.

Creating Multiple Versions of a Document

Use Word's versioning feature to save multiple versions of a document in the same document. This saves disk space because only the differences between the versions are saved, not the entire document. You can create, review, open, and delete versions of a document. Creating versions is useful in a situation where you want to maintain the original document and use it as a "baseline" to compare with future versions of the document.

Saving a Version of a Document

To save a version of a document, click <u>F</u>ile and then Ver<u>s</u>ions. This displays the Versions in (Document Name) dialog box shown in figure 5.3.

5.3 *Versions in (Document Name) Dialog Box*

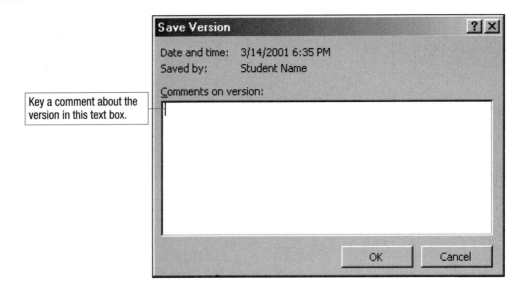

At the Versions in (Document Name) dialog box, click the <u>S</u>ave Now button. This displays the Save Version dialog box shown in figure 5.4. At this dialog box, key a comment about the version in the <u>C</u>omments on version text box, and then click OK. This removes the dialog box and returns you to the document. When a version is saved, a *File Versions* icon displays at the right side of the Status bar. To review the version information, display the Versions in (Document Name) dialog box.

5.4 *Save Version Dialog Box*

1. Open Word Contract.
2. Save the document with Save As and name it EWd C05 Ex05.
3. Create a version of the original document by completing the following steps:
   a. Click File and then Versions.
   b. At the Versions in EWd C05 Ex05 dialog box, click the Save Now button.
   c. At the Save Version dialog box, key **First draft of contract** in the Comments on version text box.
   d. Click OK.
4. Make the following editing changes to the contract:
   a. Delete paragraph number 5 in the TRANSFERS AND MOVING EXPENSES section.
   b. Add the text **and ten (10) hours of sick leave after 10 years of employment with RM** at the end of the sentence in paragraph number 1 in the SICK LEAVE section.
5. Create another version of the document that contains the edits by completing the following steps:
   a. Click File and then Versions.
   b. At the Versions in EWd C05 Ex05 dialog box, click the Save Now button.
   c. At the Save Version dialog box, key **Second draft of contract** in the Comments on version text box.
   d. Click OK.
6. Make the following editing changes to the contract:
   a. Change *4,000* to *8,000* in paragraph number 3 in the TRANSFERS AND MOVING EXPENSES section.
   b. Delete paragraph number 2 in the SICK LEAVE section. (When you delete paragraph number 2, the remaining paragraphs are automatically renumbered.)
7. Create another version of the document with the comment **Third draft of contract**.
8. Close EWd C05 Ex05.

Versions in EWd C05 Ex05

New versions

Save Now...

Step 3b

Existing versions

Save Version

Date and time: 3/14/2001 6:31 PM
Saved by: Student Name

Comments on version:

First draft of contract

Step 3c

Opening an Earlier Version

You can open an earlier version of a document and view it next to the current version. To do this, open the document containing the versions, and then display the Versions in (Document Name) dialog box. Click the desired earlier version in the Existing versions list box and then click the Open button. This opens the earlier version in a new window and tiles the two documents.

Saving a Version as a Separate Document

If you try to save an earlier version, the Save As dialog box will display. This dialog box displays so you will key a new name for the version document rather than overwriting the original. Key a new name for the version at the Save As dialog box and then press Enter or click the Save button.

HINT

When saving multiple versions of a document, you are archiving the document. You cannot modify a saved version of the document. To make changes to an earlier version, open the version, then save it with File and then Save As.

Deleting a Version

Delete a version of a document at the Versions in (Document Name) dialog box. To delete a version, display the dialog box, click the version name in the Existing versions list box, and then click the Delete button. At the Confirm Version Delete message, click Yes.

exercise 6

1. Open EWd C05 Ex05.
2. Open an earlier version by completing the following steps:
   a. Click File and then Versions.
   b. At the Versions in EWd C05 Ex05 dialog box, click the First draft of contract version in the Existing versions list box.
   c. Click the Open button. (This opens the earlier version in a new window and tiles the two documents.)
3. After viewing the documents, save the earlier version as a separate document by completing the following steps:
   a. Make sure the earlier version document window is active (and no text is selected). (The earlier version will probably display in the bottom window and will contain the word *version* somewhere in the Title bar.)
   b. Click File and then Save As.
   c. At the Save As dialog box, key **Contract First Draft**.
   d. Press Enter or click the Save button.
4. Close the Contract First Draft document.
5. Maximize the EWd C05 Ex05 window.
6. Delete the second draft version of the document by completing the following steps:
   a. Click File and then Versions.
   b. At the Versions in EWd C05 Ex05 dialog box, click the Second draft of contract version in the Existing versions list box.
   c. Click the Delete button.
   d. At the Confirm Version Delete message, click Yes.
   e. At the Versions in EWd C05 Ex05 dialog box, click the Close button.
7. Save and then close EWd C05 Ex05.
8. Compare the first draft document with the latest version by completing the following steps:
   a. Open the document named Contract First Draft.
   b. Click Tools and then Compare and Merge Documents.

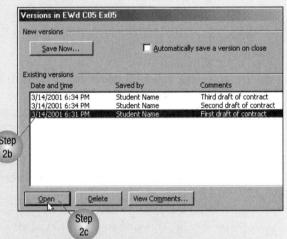

Step 2b

Step 2c

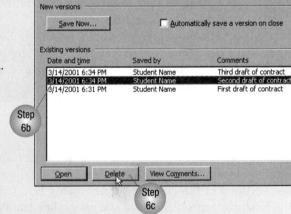

Step 6b

Step 6c

c. At the Compare and Merge Documents dialog box, click once on EWd C05 Ex05.

d. Click the down-pointing triangle at the right side of the Merge button and then click *Merge into new document* at the drop-down list.

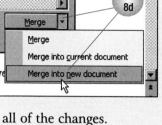

9. Change to the Print Layout view. (Notice the results of the compare and merge.)

10. Print the document with the marked changes.

11. Make sure the Reviewing toolbar is displayed and then accept all of the changes.

12. Save the document and name it EWd C05 Ex06.

13. Print and then close EWd C05 Ex06.

14. Close Contract First Draft.

Sending and Routing Documents

In a corporate or business setting, you may work on a project with others in a group. In a situation where a number of people are working on individual documents that will be combined into a larger document, sending and routing documents can be very helpful. In Word, you can send a document to a project member in an Outlook e-mail message or route a document to several project members, one after the other.

To complete exercises in this section, you will need to have Outlook available on your system. System configurations can be quite varied. You may find that your screen does not exactly match what you see in figures in this section. Steps in exercises may need to be modified to accommodate your system. Before completing exercises in this section, please check with your instructor for any modifications or changes to information and exercises.

Sending a Document in an E-mail

You can send a document in an e-mail, as an attachment to the e-mail, or as the body of the e-mail message. To send a document as an e-mail attachment, click File, point to Send To, and then click Mail Recipient (as Attachment). (To send a document as an e-mail attachment, you must be using Microsoft Outlook, Microsoft Outlook Express, Microsoft Exchange, or an e-mail program compatible with the Messaging Application Programming Interface (MAPI).) To send a document as the body of an e-mail message, click the E-mail button on the Standard toolbar or click File, point to Send to, and then click Mail Recipient. (You must be using Outlook 2002 to use this procedure.)

E-mail

To send a document as the body of an e-mail message, click the E-mail button on the Standard toolbar and the e-mail header displays below the Formatting toolbar as shown in figure 5.5. When the e-mail header displays, Outlook is automatically opened. The E-mail header contains buttons you can use to perform functions such as sending a copy of the document to the recipient, specifying a document attachment, setting the message priority, and flagging the e-mail.

FIGURE

5.5 **E-mail Header**

E-mail Header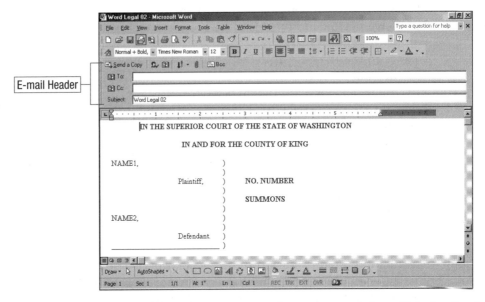

At the e-mail header, fill in the recipient information and then click the Send a Copy button. Word sends a copy of the document to the recipient and closes the e-mail header. The original document remains open for editing. When the document is saved, the e-mail information is saved with the document.

In the To text box in the e-mail header, key the e-mail address of the person to receive the document. If the e-mail name and address have been established in an address folder, click the book icon that displays immediately before To and the Select Recipients dialog box displays. At this dialog box, shown in figure 5.6, select the name to receive the document in the list box that displays at the left side of the dialog box, and then click the To:-> button. This inserts the name in the Message recipients list box. Click OK to close the dialog box.

FIGURE

5.6 **Select Recipients Dialog Box**

Click the name in this list box and then click the To: -> button.

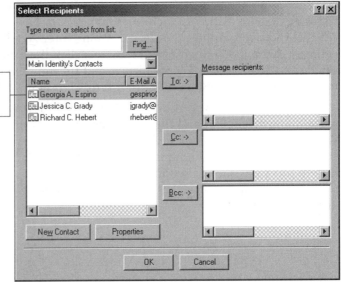

In the exercises in this chapter, you will send the e-mail to your instructor. If your system is networked and your computer is not part of an intranet system, skip the step instructing you to click the Send a Copy button.

exercise 7

(Note: Before completing this exercise, check to see if you can send e-mail messages. If you cannot, consider completing all of the steps in the exercise except step 3d.)

1. Open Word Legal 02.
2. Save the document with Save As and name it EWd C05 Ex07.
3. Create the EWd C05 Ex07 document as an Outlook e-mail by completing the following steps:
   a. Click the E-mail button on the Standard toolbar.
   b. At the e-mail header, key your instructor's name in the To text box. (Depending on how the system is configured, you may need to key your instructor's e-mail address.)
   c. Click the down-pointing triangle at the right side of the Set Priority button in the E-mail header and then click *High Priority* at the drop-down list. (This button may vary.)
   d. Click the Send a Copy button.
   e. If necessary, click the E-mail button on the Standard toolbar to turn off the display of the e-mail header.
4. Save, print, and then close EWd C05 Ex07.

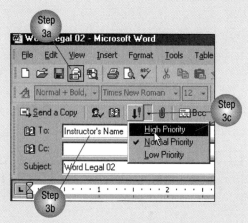

Routing a Document

Routing a document differs from sending a document in that the first recipient receives the document, makes comments or changes, and then it is sent to the next person on the list. In this way, one document is edited by several people rather than several people editing versions of the same document.

To route a document, open the document, click File, point to Send To, and then click Routing Recipient. This displays the Routing Slip dialog box shown in figure 5.7. At the Routing Slip dialog box, click the Address button and the Address Book dialog box shown in figure 5.8 displays.

HINT

Routing is the process of sending a document to a person or several people and then getting the document back when they are done reading and commenting on it.

5.7 *Routing Slip Dialog Box*

Click the Address button to
display the Address Book
dialog box.

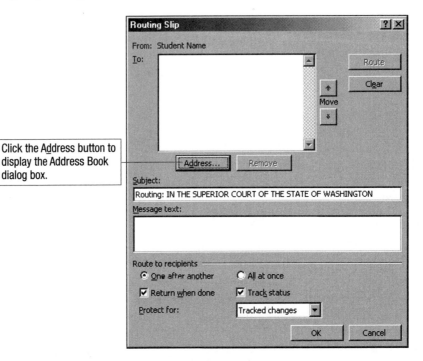

5.8 *Address Book Dialog Box*

Click the name of the
person to receive the
document and then click
the To: -> button or double-
click the name.

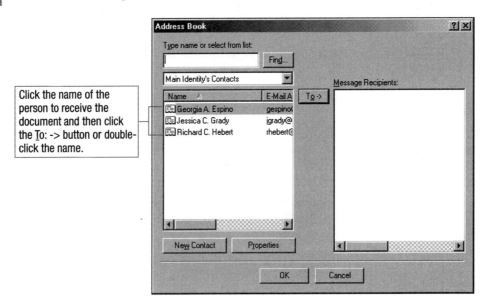

At the Address Book dialog box, double-click the name of each recipient in
the order they are to receive the document. Double-clicking a name inserts the
name in the list box that displays at the right side of the dialog box. When all
names are displayed in the list box, click OK. At the Routing Slip dialog box,
make sure the names are displayed in the proper order. (If not, click one of the
Move buttons to move the names into the proper order.) Key a message in the

Message text box. Make sure <u>O</u>ne after another is selected in the Route to recipients section, and then click the <u>R</u>oute button that displays at the right side of the dialog box.

1. Open EWd C05 Ex07.
2. Route the document by completing the following steps:
   a. Click <u>F</u>ile, point to Sen<u>d</u> To, and then click <u>R</u>outing Recipient.
   b. At the Routing Slip dialog box, click the A<u>d</u>dress button.
   c. At the Address Book dialog box, double-click any names that display in the list box at the left side of the dialog box. (If there are no names, skip this step.)
   d. Click OK to close the Address Book dialog box.
   e. At the Routing Slip dialog box, click the <u>R</u>oute button to route the document to the first recipient. (Depending on your system configuration, you may not be able to send this e-mail. If that is the case, click the Cancel button instead of the <u>R</u>oute button.)
3. Close EWd C05 Ex07.

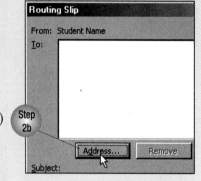

Creating a Template

A document that will be used in the future as a framework for other documents can be saved as a template. To save a document as a template, display the Save As dialog box, change the Save as <u>t</u>ype option to *Document Template*, key a name for the template, and then press Enter.

Changing the Default File Location for Workgroup Templates

By default, a template is saved in the *Templates* folder and will display at the Templates dialog box with the General tab selected. You can save a template in a folder other than the default by specifying the folder. If you are working in a company setting with an intranet, consider saving templates that will be shared on the network in the *Workgroup templates* file location. You can specify the file location for Workgroup templates at the Options dialog box. To do this, you would complete the following steps:

1. At a clear document screen, click <u>T</u>ools and then <u>O</u>ptions.
2. At the Options dialog box, click the File Locations tab.
3. At the Options dialog box with the File Locations tab selected as shown in figure 5.9, click *Workgroup templates* in the <u>F</u>ile types list box.
4. Click the <u>M</u>odify button.
5. At the Modify Location dialog box, specify the desired drive and/or folder in the Look <u>i</u>n option box, and then click OK.
6. Click OK to close the Options dialog box.

5.9 *Options Dialog Box with File Locations Tab Selected*

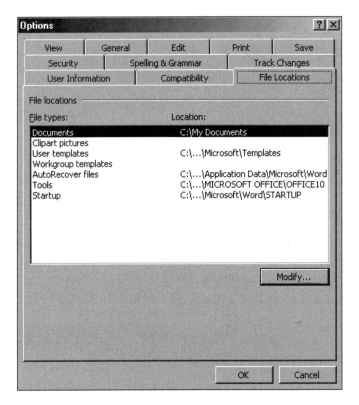

In exercise 9 you will change the location of Workgroup templates to a *Templates* folder you will create on your disk. In a company setting, the Workgroup templates location would probably be a folder on the network. Before completing exercise 9, check with your instructor to determine if you can change file locations.

CHANGING FILE LOCATION AND CREATING A TEMPLATE DOCUMENT

1. Create a *Templates* folder on your disk by completing the following steps:
   a. Display the Open dialog box.
   b. Make active the drive where your disk is located (do not make *Word Chapter 05E* the active folder).
   c. Click the Create New Folder button on the Open dialog box toolbar.
   d. At the New Folder dialog box, key **Templates** in the Name text box.
   e. Click OK or press Enter to close the dialog box.
   f. Click the Cancel button to close the Open dialog box.
2. At a clear document screen, specify the *Templates* folder on your disk as the location for Workgroup templates by completing the following steps:
   a. Make sure your disk (containing the *Templates* folder) is inserted in the appropriate drive.
   b. Click Tools and then Options.
   c. At the Options dialog box, click the File Locations tab.

d. At the Options dialog box with the File Locations tab selected, make a note of the current location for *Workgroup templates* that displays in the File types list box (the location may be blank). (You will be returning the location back to this default at the end of the exercise.)

e. Click *Workgroup templates* in the File types list box.

f. Click the Modify button.

g. At the Modify Location dialog box, click the down-pointing triangle at the right side of the Look in option box and then click *3½ Floppy (A:)* (or the drive letter where your disk is located).

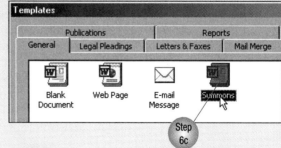

h. Double-click the *Templates* folder.

i. Click OK to close the Modify Location dialog box.

j. Click OK to close the Options dialog box.

3. Open Word Legal 02.

4. Save the document as a template named Summons in the *Templates* folder on your disk by completing the following steps:

a. Click File and then Save As.

b. At the Save As dialog box, click the down-pointing triangle at the right side of the Save as type option box, and then click *Document Template*. (This automatically changes the folder to the *Microsoft Templates* folder.)

c. Change to the *Templates* folder on your disk by completing the following steps:

1) Click the down-pointing triangle at the right side of the Save in option box.

2) At the drop-down list that displays, click the drive where your disk is located.

3) Double-click the *Templates* folder.

d. Select the name in the File name text box and then key **Summons**.

e. Press Enter or click the Save button.

5. Close the Summons template.

6. Open the Summons template by completing the following steps:

a. Click File and then New.

b. Click the *General Templates* hyperlink in the New Document Task Pane.

c. At the Templates dialog box with the General tab selected, double-click on the *Summons* icon.

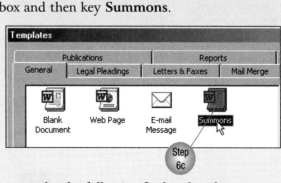

7. With the Summons template document open, make the following find and replaces:

a. Find *NAME1* and replace with *AMY GARCIA*.

b. Find *NAME2* and replace with *NEIL CARLIN*.

c. Fine *NUMBER* and replace with *C-98002*.

8. Save the document in the *Word Chapter 05E* folder on your disk and name it EWd C05 Ex09.

9. Print and then close EWd C05 Ex09.
10. Remove the Summons template from the Templates dialog box by completing the following steps:
    a. Click File and then New.
    b. Click the *General Templates* hyperlink in the New Document Task Pane.
    c. At the Templates dialog box with the General tab selected, *right-click* on the *Summons* icon.
    d. At the shortcut menu that displays, click the Delete option.
    e. At the Confirm File Delete message, click Yes.
    f. Click Cancel to close the New dialog box.
11. Return the Workgroup templates back to the default location by completing the following steps:
    a. At a document screen, click Tools and then Options.
    b. At the Options dialog box, click the File Locations tab.
    c. At the Options dialog box with the File Locations tab selected, click *Workgroup templates* in the File types list box.
    d. Click the Modify button.
    e. At the Modify Location dialog box, change to the default Workgroup templates folder. (If the default location was blank, select any text currently displayed in the Folder name text box and then press the Delete key.)
    f. Click OK to close the Modify Location dialog box.
    g. Click OK to close the Options dialog box.

Creating a Master Document and Subdocuments

HINT
By setting up a master document and saving it to a network, several people can work simultaneously on subdocuments within the master document.

For projects containing a variety of parts or sections such as a reference guide or book, consider using a *master document*. A master document contains a number of separate documents referred to as *subdocuments*. A master document might be useful in a situation where several people are working on one project. Each person prepares a document for their part of the project and then the documents are included in a master document. A master document allows for easier editing of subdocuments. Rather than opening a large document for editing, you can open a subdocument, make changes, and those changes are reflected in the master document.

Create a new master document or format an existing document as a master document at the Outline view and the Master Document view. When you change to the Outline view, the Outlining toolbar displays with buttons for working with master documents and subdocuments. These buttons are shown in figure 5.10. The names and functions of some of the Outlining toolbar buttons for working with master documents and subdocuments may vary depending on what is selected in the document. Some buttons may display activated and others deactivated. An activated button displays on the toolbar with a blue border.

5.10 *Outlining Toolbar Master Document Buttons*

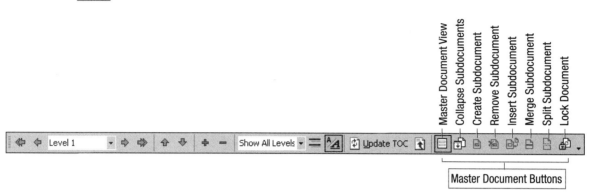

When Outline View is selected, the Master Document View button on the Outlining toolbar is automatically activated. With this button activated, collapsed subdocuments display surrounded by a light gray border line, and subdocument icons display.

Master Document View

Creating a Master Document

To create a master document, start at a clear document screen, and then key the text for the document; or, open an existing document. Identify the subdocuments by completing the following steps:

1. Change to the Outline view.
2. Make sure the Master Document View button is activated.
3. Make sure heading level styles are applied to headings in the document.
4. Select the heading and text to be divided into a subdocument.
5. Click the Create Subdocument button on the Outlining toolbar. (Text specified as a subdocument displays surrounded by a thin gray line border and a subdocument icon displays in the upper left corner of the border.)

Create Subdocument

Word creates a subdocument for each heading at the top level within the selected text. For example, if selected text begins with Heading 1 text, Word creates a new subdocument at each Heading 1 in the selected text.

Save the master document in the same manner as a normal document. Word automatically assigns a document name to each subdocument using the first characters in the subdocument heading.

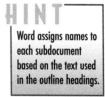

HINT

Word assigns names to each subdocument based on the text used in the outline headings.

Opening and Closing a Master Document and Subdocument

Open a master document at the Open dialog box in the same manner as a normal document. Subdocuments in a master document display collapsed in the master document as shown in figure 5.11. This figure displays the master document named Master Doc C05 Ex10 you will create in exercise 10. Notice that Word automatically converts subdocument names into hyperlinks. To open a subdocument, hold down the Ctrl key and then click the subdocument hyperlink. This displays the subdocument and also displays the Web toolbar.

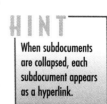

HINT

When subdocuments are collapsed, each subdocument appears as a hyperlink.

5.11 *Master Doc C05 Ex10*

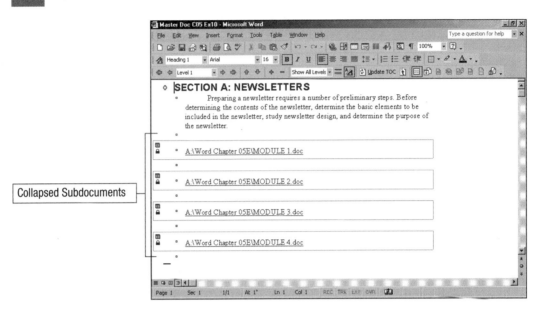

Collapsed Subdocuments

To close a subdocument, click File and then Close or click the Close button that displays at the right side of the Menu bar. If you made any changes to the document, you will be asked if you want to save the changes. Closing a subdocument redisplays the master document and the subdocument hyperlink displays in a different color (identifying that the hyperlink has been used). Close a master document in the normal manner. You may also want to turn off the display of the Web toolbar.

Expand
Subdocuments

Expanding/Collapsing Subdocuments

Open a master document and subdocuments are automatically collapsed. To expand subdocuments, click the Expand Subdocuments button on the Outlining toolbar. To collapse expanded subdocuments, click the Collapse Subdocuments button on the Outlining toolbar.

Collapse
Subdocuments

Locking/Unlocking a Subdocument

By default, a subdocument is unlocked so that the subdocument can be viewed or edited. If you want a subdocument available for viewing but not editing, lock the subdocument by clicking the Lock Document button on the Outlining toolbar. Word will automatically lock a subdocument if the subdocument name is set as a read-only document or if another user is currently working on the subdocument.

Lock
Document

When subdocuments are collapsed, all subdocuments appear to be locked. A lock icon displays below the subdocument icon at the left side of the subdocument name. A document is locked only if the lock icon displays below the subdocument icon when subdocuments are expanded.

WORD

CREATING A MASTER DOCUMENT AND EXPANDING/COLLAPSING SUBDOCUMENTS

1. At a clear document screen, change the line spacing to double, and then key the text shown in figure 5.12. (Press the Enter key after keying the text.)
2. With the insertion point positioned below the text, insert the document named Word Report 04. (To do this, click Insert and then File. At the Insert File dialog box, make sure the *Word Chapter 05E* folder is active and then double-click *Word Report 04*.)
3. Move the insertion point to the end of the document, press the Backspace key once, and then insert the document named Word Report 05. (Use Insert and then File. After inserting the document, press the Backspace key once.)
4. Make the following changes to the document:
   a. Move the insertion point to the beginning of the document.
   b. Change to Outline view.
   c. Make sure the Master Document View button on the Outlining toolbar is active (displays with a blue border). If it is not active, click the Master Document View button.
   d. Format the title with a style by completing the following steps:
      1) Position the insertion point on any character in the title *SECTION A: NEWSLETTERS*.
      2) Click the down-pointing triangle at the right side of the Style button (located at the left side of the Formatting toolbar).
      3) At the drop-down menu that displays, click *Heading 1*.
   e. Complete steps similar to those in 4d to apply the specified styles to the following headings:

MODULE 1: DEFINING NEWSLETTER ELEMENTS	=	Heading 2
Designing a Newsletter	=	Heading 3
Defining Basic Newsletter Elements	=	Heading 3
MODULE 2: PLANNING A NEWSLETTER	=	Heading 2
Defining the Purpose of a Newsletter	=	Heading 3
MODULE 3: DESIGNING A NEWSLETTER	=	Heading 2
Applying Desktop Publishing Guidelines	=	Heading 3
MODULE 4: CREATING NEWSLETTER LAYOUT	=	Heading 2
Choosing Paper Size and Type	=	Heading 3
Choosing Paper Weight	=	Heading 3
Creating Margins for Newsletters	=	Heading 3

5. Save the document and name it Master Doc C05 Ex10.
6. Create subdocuments with the module text by completing the following steps:
   a. Position the mouse pointer on the selection symbol (white plus sign) that displays immediately left of the heading *MODULE 1: DEFINING NEWSLETTER ELEMENTS* until the pointer turns into a four-headed arrow, and then click the left mouse button.
   b. Scroll through the document until the *MODULE 4: CREATING NEWSLETTER LAYOUT* heading displays.
   c. Hold down the Shift key, position the mouse pointer on the selection symbol (white plus sign) immediately left of the title until the pointer turns into a four-headed arrow, and then click the left mouse button. (This selects all of the text in modules 1, 2, 3, and 4.)

Step 4d2

Step 4d3

d. With the text selected, click the Create Subdocument button on the Outlining toolbar.

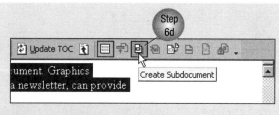
Step 6d

7. Save and then close Master Doc C05 Ex10.
8. Open Master Doc C05 Ex10 and then complete the following steps:
   a. Print Master Doc C05 Ex10 by completing the following steps:
      1) Click the Print button on the Standard toolbar.
      2) At the question asking if you want to open the subdocuments, click No. (The document will print collapsed as shown on the document screen.)
   b. Edit the MODULE 1 subdocument by completing the following steps:
      1) Hold down the Ctrl key and then click the *A:\Word Chapter 05E\MODULE 1.doc* hyperlink.
      2) With the *MODULE 1.doc* document displayed, edit the title so it reads *MODULE 1: DEFINING ELEMENTS*.
      3) Change the heading *Designing a Newsletter* so it displays as *Designing*.
      4) Change the heading *Defining Basic Newsletter Elements* so it displays as *Defining Basic Elements*.

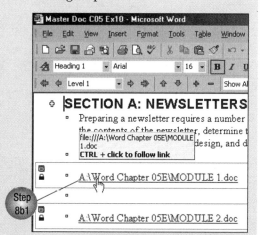
Step 8b1

   c. Save the subdocument by clicking the Save button on the Standard toolbar.
   d. Close the subdocument.
   e. Clicking the module hyperlink automatically turned on the display of the Web toolbar. Turn off this toolbar by clicking View, pointing to Toolbars, and then clicking *Web*.
   f. Expand the subdocuments by clicking the Expand Subdocuments button on the Outlining toolbar.
   g. Print page 1 of the master document.
   h. Collapse the subdocuments by clicking the Collapse Subdocuments button on the Outlining toolbar.
9. Save and then close Master Doc C05 Ex10.

FIGURE

5.12 *Exercise 10*

SECTION A: NEWSLETTERS

Preparing a newsletter requires a number of preliminary steps. Before determining the contents of the newsletter, determine the basic elements to be included in the newsletter, study newsletter design, and determine the purpose of the newsletter.

WORD

Rearranging Subdocuments

Many of the features of a master document are similar to an outline. For example, expanding and collapsing an outline is very similar to expanding and collapsing subdocuments. Also, like headings in an outline, expanded subdocuments in a master document can be moved or rearranged.

To rearrange the order of a subdocument, collapse the subdocuments. Position the mouse pointer on the subdocument icon, hold down the left mouse button (mouse pointer turns into a four-headed arrow), drag to the location where you want the subdocument moved, and then release the mouse button. As you drag with the mouse, a dark gray horizontal line displays identifying where the subdocument will be inserted. Use this dark gray line to insert the subdocument in the desired location.

Removing a Subdocument

Remove a subdocument from a master document by clicking the subdocument icon and then pressing the Delete key. This removes the subdocument from the master document but not from the original location. For example, in exercise 11, you will remove the MODULE 3 subdocument from the Master Doc C05 Ex10 master document, but the document named MODULE 3 remains on your disk.

Splitting/Combining Subdocuments

A subdocument can be split into smaller subdocuments or subdocuments can be combined into one. To split a subdocument, expand subdocuments, select the specific text within the subdocument, and then click the Split Subdocument button on the Outlining toolbar. Word assigns a document name based on the first characters in the subdocument heading.

Split
Subdocument

To combine subdocuments, expand subdocuments, and then click the subdocument icon of the first subdocument to be combined. Hold down the Shift key and then click the subdocument icon of the last subdocument (subdocuments must be adjacent). With the subdocuments selected, click the Merge Subdocument button on the Outlining toolbar. Word saves the combined subdocuments with the name of the first subdocument.

Merge
Subdocument

Renaming a Subdocument

If you need to rename a subdocument, do it through the master document. To rename a subdocument, display the master document containing the subdocument, and then click the subdocument hyperlink. With the subdocument displayed, click File and then Save As. At the Save As dialog box, key a new name for the subdocument, and then press Enter or click the Save button. This renames the document in its original location as well as within the master document.

1. Open Master Doc C05 Ex10.
2. Save the document with Save As and name it Master Doc C05 Ex11.
3. Make the following changes to the master document:
   a. Move the Module 4 subdocument above the Module 3 subdocument by completing the following steps:
      1) Make sure the Lock Document button (last button on the Outlining toolbar) is not active.
      2) Position the mouse pointer on the Module 4 subdocument icon.
      3) Hold down the left mouse button (mouse pointer turns into a four-headed arrow), drag up so the dark gray horizontal line displays between the MODULE 2 and MODULE 3 subdocuments (above the white square between the modules), and then release the mouse button.
   b. Print Master Doc C05 Ex11. (At the prompt asking if you want to open the subdocuments, click No.)
   c. Remove the A:\Word Chapter 05E\MODULE 3.doc subdocument by completing the following steps:
      1) Click the subdocument icon that displays to the left of the A:\Word Chapter 05E\MODULE 3.doc subdocument.
      2) Press the Delete key.
   d. Split the MODULE 1 subdocument by completing the following steps:
      1) Click the Expand Subdocuments button on the Outlining toolbar.
      2) Move the insertion point to the MODULE 1 subdocument.
      3) In the MODULE 1 subdocument, edit the heading *Defining Basic Elements* so it displays as *MODULE 2: DEFINING BASIC ELEMENTS*.
      4) Change the heading style of the heading *MODULE 2: DEFINING BASIC ELEMENTS* from *Heading 3* to *Heading 2*. (Hint: Use the Style button on the Formatting toolbar.)
      5) Position the mouse pointer on the selection symbol (white plus sign) that displays immediately left of the heading *MODULE 2: DEFINING BASIC ELEMENTS* until the pointer turns into a four-headed arrow, and then click the left mouse button.

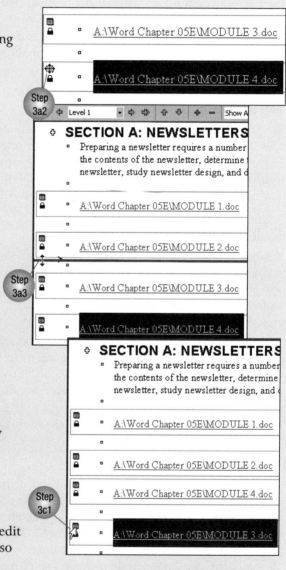

6) With the text selected, click the Split Subdocument button on the Outlining toolbar.

7) Click the Collapse Subdocuments button on the Outlining toolbar. At the question asking if you want to save the changes to the master document, click OK.

e. Rename the MODULE 1 subdocument by completing the following steps:

1) Hold down the Ctrl key and then click the *A:\Word Chapter 05E\MODULE 1.doc* hyperlink.

2) With the subdocument open, click File and then Save As.

3) At the Save As dialog box, key **NEW MOD 1** and then press Enter.

4) Close the subdocument.

f. Rename the MODULE 5 subdocument by completing the following steps:

1) Hold down the Ctrl key and then click the *A:\Word Chapter 05E\MODULE 5.doc* hyperlink.

2) With the subdocument open, click File and then Save As.

3) At the Save As dialog box, key **NEW MOD 2** and then press Enter.

4) Close the subdocument.

g. Rename and edit the MODULE 2 subdocument by completing the following steps:

1) Hold down the Ctrl key and then click the *A:\Word Chapter 05E\MODULE 2.doc* hyperlink.

2) With the subdocument open, edit the *MODULE 2: PLANNING A NEWSLETTER* heading so it reads *MODULE 3: PLANNING A NEWSLETTER*.

3) Click File and then Save As.

4) At the Save As dialog box, key **NEW MOD 3** and then press Enter.

5) Close the subdocument.

h. Rename the MODULE 4 subdocument by completing the following steps:

1) Hold down the Ctrl key and then click the *A:\Word Chapter 05E\MODULE 4.doc* hyperlink.

2) With the subdocument open, click File and then Save As.

3) At the Save As dialog box, key **NEW MOD 4** and then press Enter.

4) Close the subdocument.

4. Save the master document and then print the master document with the subdocuments collapsed.

5. Close Master Doc C05 Ex11.

CHAPTER summary

- Use the tracking feature when more than one person is reviewing a document and making editing changes. Turn on tracking by clicking the Track Changes button on the Reviewing toolbar.

- The display of tracked changes varies depending on the view. In Normal view, with tracking on, text inserted displays underlined while deleted text displays with a line through it. In Print Layout view, inserted text displays underlined while deleted text displays in a balloon in the right margin.

- Display information on tracking changes such as author's name, date, time, and type of change by positioning the mouse pointer on a change. After approximately one second, a box displays with the information. You can also display information on tracking changes by displaying the Reviewing pane. Display this pane by clicking the Reviewing Pane button on the Reviewing toolbar.

- If changes are made to a document by another person with different user information, the changes display in a different color. Change user information at the Options dialog box with the User Information tab selected.

- Move to the next change in a document by clicking the Next button on the Reviewing toolbar or click the Previous button to move to the previous change.

- Changes made to a document can be accepted or rejected.

- If you want to make comments in a document you are creating, or if a reviewer wants to make comments in a document written by someone else, insert a comment. Insert a comment by clicking the New Comment button on the Reviewing toolbar.

- Click the New Comment button in Print Layout view and a Comment balloon displays in the right margin where you key the comment. Click the New Comment button in Normal view and the Reviewing pane opens where you key the comment.

- Edit a comment in Print Layout view by clicking in the Comment balloon and edit a comment in Normal view by clicking in the comment text in the Reviewing pane.

- Delete a comment by right-clicking the Comment balloon and then clicking Delete Comment at the pop-up list.

- A document containing comments can be printed with the comments, or you can choose to print just the comments and not the document.

- Use the versioning feature to save multiple versions of a document in the same document.

- Save a version of a document and delete a version of a document at the Versions in (Document Name) dialog box.

- An earlier version of a document can be opened and then viewed next to the current version.

- Send a document in an Outlook e-mail for others to review, as an attachment to an e-mail, or as the body of the e-mail message.

- Click the E-mail button on the Standard toolbar to display the E-mail header. The E-mail header contains buttons you can use to customize the e-mail message.

- When a document is routed, one document is edited by several people rather than several people editing versions of the same document.

- Specify file locations with options at the Options dialog box with the File Locations tab selected.
- A master document contains a number of separate documents called subdocuments.
- Create a master document or format an existing document as a master document at the Outline view and the Master Document view.
- The Outlining toolbar contains buttons for working with master documents and subdocuments.
- Clicking the Create Subdocument button on the Outlining toolbar causes Word to create a subdocument for each heading at the top level within the selected text.
- Save a master document in the normal manner. Word automatically assigns a document name to each subdocument using the first characters in the subdocument heading.
- Using buttons on the Outlining toolbar, you can expand and collapse subdocuments, lock/unlock subdocuments, and rearrange, remove, split, combine, and rename subdocuments.

COMMANDS review

Command	Mouse/Keyboard
Turn on tracking	Click Track Changes button on Reviewing toolbar or click Tools, Track Changes
Display Options dialog box	Click Tools, Options
Display Comment balloon	In Print Layout view, click New Comment button on Reviewing toolbar
Display Reviewing pane	In Normal view, click Reviewing Pane button on Reviewing toolbar
Display Versions in (Document Name) dialog box	Click File, Versions
Display Save Version dialog box	Click Save Now button at Versions in (Document Name) dialog box
Display E-mail header	Click the E-mail button on Standard toolbar; or click File, point to Send To, then click Mail Recipient
Display Routing Slip dialog box	Click File, point to Send To, then click Routing Recipient
Display Address Book dialog box	Click Address button at Routing Slip dialog box
Change to Master Document view	Click the Master Document View button on the Outlining toolbar

CONCEPTS check

Completion: On a blank sheet of paper, indicate the correct term, command, or number for each item.

1. Turn on tracking by clicking this button on the Reviewing toolbar.
2. With tracking turned on in a document in Normal view, deleted text is not removed but instead displays in this manner.
3. When tracking is turned on in a document, these letters display in black on the Status bar.
4. To create a comment, click the New Comment button on this toolbar.
5. In Print Layout view, clicking the New Comment button causes this to display in the right margin.
6. In Normal view, clicking the New Comment button causes this to open.
7. Use this feature to save multiple versions of a document in the same document.
8. Display the Save Version dialog box by clicking this button at the Versions in (Document Name) dialog box.
9. Click this button on the Standard toolbar to display the E-mail header.
10. Click File, point to Send To, and then click Routing Recipient and this dialog box displays.
11. Specify a location for Workgroup templates with options at this dialog box with the File Locations tab selected.
12. Change to the Outline view and then to this view to create a master document.
13. Expand subdocuments with the Expand Subdocuments button on this toolbar.
14. List the steps you would complete to insert the comment *Please include additional resources.* into a document.

SKILLS check

Assessment 1

1. Open Word Mortgage.
2. Save the document with Save As and name it EWd C05 SA01.
3. Make changes to the document and track the changes by completing the following steps:
   a. Turn on tracking.
   b. Change *ten (10)* in the *Delinquency* paragraph to *fifteen (15)*.
   c. Delete the words *charge computed as if Buyers had prepaid in full* that display at the end of the *Demand for Full Payment* paragraph.
   d. Insert the words *and safe* between *good* and *condition* in the second sentence in the *Use of the Collateral* paragraph.
   e. Turn off tracking.
4. Save, print, and then close EWd C05 SA01.

Assessment 2

1. Open EWd C05 SA01.
2. Save the document with Save As and name it EWd C05 SA02.
3. Make additional changes to the document and track the changes by completing the following steps:
   a. Display the Options dialog box with the User Information tab selected and then complete the following steps:
      1) Make a note of the current name, initials, and mailing address. (You will reenter this information later in this assessment.)
      2) Key **Mildred Brown** in the Name text box.
      3) Key **MB** in the Initials text box.
   b. Close the Options dialog box.
   c. Turn on tracking.
   d. Make the following changes to the document:
      1) Insert the word *all* between *pay* and *reasonable* in the last sentence in the *Delinquency* paragraph.
      2) Delete the words *at the time of the default or any time after default,* in the first sentence in the *Demand for Full Payment* paragraph.
      3) Insert the words *unless agreed upon by Sellers* between *Contract* and the period that ends the last sentence in the *Use of the Collateral* paragraph.
   e. Turn off tracking.
   f. Display the Options dialog box with the User Information tab selected, change back to the information that displays before you keyed *Mildred Brown* and the initials *MB*, and then close the dialog box.
4. Save, print, and then close EWd C05 SA02.

Assessment 3

1. Open EWd C05 SA02.
2. Save the document with Save As and name it EWd C05 SA03.
3. Accept the following changes in the document:
   a. Accept the change from *ten (10)* to *fifteen (15)* in the *Delinquency* paragraph.
   b. Accept the change deleting the words *charge computed as if Buyers had prepaid in full* that display at the end of the *Demand for Full Payment* paragraph.
   c. Accept the change inserting the word *all* between *pay* and *reasonable* in the last sentence in the *Delinquency* paragraph.
   d. Accept the change inserting the words *unless agreed upon by Sellers* between *Contract* and the period that ends the last sentence in the *Use of the Collateral* paragraph.
4. Reject the following changes in the document:
   a. Reject the change inserting the words *and safe* between *good* and *condition* in the second sentence in the *Use of the Collateral* paragraph.
   b. Reject the change deleting the words *at the time of the default or any time after default,* in the first sentence in the *Demand for Full Payment* paragraph.
5. Save, print, and then close EWd C05 SA03.

Assessment 4

1. Open Word Report 01.
2. Save the document with Save As and name it EWd C05 SA04.
3. Make the following changes to the report:

    a. Select the entire document and then change the font to 13-point Garamond (or a similar serif typeface).

    b. Set the title and the headings in 14-point Arial bold.

    c. Select the text in the body of the report (everything except the title) and then make the following change:

       1) Change the line spacing to single.

       2) Change the spacing before and after paragraphs to 6 points.

       3) Change the paragraph alignment to justified.

    d. Create a comment at the end of the second paragraph in the Defining Desktop Publishing section of the report. Key the words **Color printers?**, select the words, and then create the comment with the following text: *Include information on color printers.*

    e. Create a comment at the end of the last paragraph in the Planning the Publication section of the report. Key the word **Examples**, select the word, and then create the comment with the following text: *Include examples of effective designs.*

4. Save and then print the document and the comments.

5. Close EWd C05 SA04.

Assessment 5

1. Open Word Legal 02.

2. Save the document with Save As and name it EWd C05 SA05.

3. Create a version of the original document by completing the following steps:

    a. Displays the Versions in EWd C05 SA05 dialog box.

    b. Click the <u>S</u>ave Now button to display the Save Version dialog box.

    c. At the Save Version dialog box, key **First draft of Summons** in the <u>C</u>omments on version text box.

    d. Click OK to close the dialog box.

4. Make the following editing changes to the document:

    a. Delete the words *a copy of which is* at the end of the first paragraph and replace them with *two copies of which are.*

    b. Insert the word *written* between the words *without* and *notice* located at the end of the first sentence in the second paragraph.

5. Create another version of the document with the comment *Second draft of Summons.*

6. Make the following editing changes to the document:

    a. Delete the sentence *A default judgment is one where the plaintiff, NAME1, is entitled to what plaintiff asks for because you have not responded.* that displays at the end of the second paragraph.

    b. Insert the words *null and* between the words *be* and *void* located at the end of the third paragraph.

7. Create another version of the document with the comment *Third draft of Summons.*

8. Open the First draft of Summons version of the document. *(Hint: Be sure to do this at the Versions in EWd C05 SA05 dialog box.)*

9. After viewing the first draft version, save the version as a separate document named Summons First Draft.

10. Close the Summons First Draft document.

11. Maximize the EWd C05 SA05 window.

12. Delete the second draft version of the document. *(Hint: Be sure to do this at the Versions in EWd C05 SA05 dialog box.)*

13. Save and then close EWd C05 SA05.

14. Open Summons First Draft and then compare the document with EWd C05 SA05. (Save the results in a new document.)
15. Save the new document and name it EWd C05 SA05 Com Doc.
16. Print and then close EWd C05 SA05 Com Doc.
17. Close Summons First Draft.

Assessment 6

1. Open Word Report 01.
2. Save the document with Save As and name it Master Doc C05 SA06.
3. Make the following changes to the document:
   a. Delete the title *DESKTOP PUBLISHING* and the blank line below the title.
   b. Change to the Outline view.
   c. Apply the Heading 1 style to the following headings:
      Defining Desktop Publishing
      Initiating the Desktop Publishing Process
      Planning the Publication
      Creating the Content
   d. Make sure the Master Document View button on the Outlining toolbar is active.
   e. Create subdocuments by selecting the entire document and then clicking the Create Subdocument button on the Outlining toolbar.
4. Save and then close Master Doc C05 SA06.
5. Open Master Doc C05 SA06 and then print the document. (At the prompt asking if you want to open the subdocuments, click <u>N</u>o.)
6. Close Master Doc C05 SA06.

Assessment 7

1. Open Master Doc C05 SA06.
2. Save the document with Save As and name it Master Doc C05 SA07.
3. Make the following changes to the document:
   a. Move the Planning the Publication subdocument above the Initiating the Desktop Publishing Process subdocument. (Make sure the dark gray horizontal line is positioned above the white square above the Initiating the Desktop Publishing Process subdocument before you release the mouse button.)
   b. Remove the Defining Desktop Publishing subdocument.
4. Save and then print Master Doc C05 SA07. (At the prompt asking if you want to open the subdocuments, click <u>N</u>o.)
5. Close Master Doc C05 SA07.

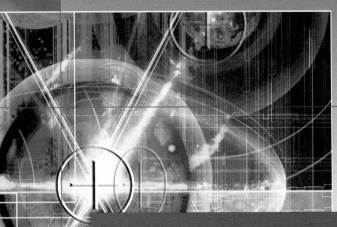

CREATING SPECIALIZED TABLES AND INDEXES

PERFORMANCE OBJECTIVES

Upon successful completion of chapter 6, you will be able to:
- **Create, compile, and update a table of contents**
- **Create, compile, and update an index**
- **Create, compile, and update a table of figures**
- **Create, compile, and update a table of authorities**

Word Chapter 06E

A book, textbook, report, or manuscript often includes sections such as a table of contents, index, and table of figures in the document. Creating these sections can be tedious when done manually. With Word, these functions can be automated to create the sections quickly and easily. In this chapter, you will learn the steps to mark text for a table of contents, index, table of figures, and table of authorities, and then compile the table or list.

Creating a Table of Contents

A table of contents appears at the beginning of a book, manuscript, or report and contains headings and subheadings with page numbers. Figure 6.1 shows an example of a table of contents. Text to be included in a table of contents can be identified by applying a heading style, assigning an outline level, or text can be marked as a field entry.

> **HINT**
> You can use a table of contents to quickly navigate in a document and to get an overview of the topics covered in the document.

FIGURE

6.1 *Table of Contents*

TABLE OF CONTENTS

Marking Table of Contents Entries as Styles

A table of contents can be created by applying heading styles to text to be included in the table of contents. Two steps are involved in creating the table of contents:

1. Apply the appropriate styles to the text that will be included in the table of contents.
2. Compile the table of contents in the document.

Word automatically includes text that is formatted with a heading style in a table of contents. In chapter 4, you learned that Word contains heading styles you can apply to text. If you have already applied styles to headings in a document, the same headings are included in the table of contents. If the styles have not previously been applied, you can apply them with the Style button on the Formatting toolbar, or with buttons on the Outlining toolbar in the Outline view. To apply styles for a table of contents, position the insertion point on any character in the text you want included in the table of contents, click the down-pointing triangle to the right of the Style button on the Formatting toolbar, and then click the desired style. Continue in this manner until all styles have been applied to titles, headings, and subheadings in the document.

Compiling a Table of Contents

After the necessary heading styles have been applied to text that you want included in the table of contents, the next step is to compile the table of contents. To do this, position the insertion point where you want the table to appear, click Insert, point to Reference, and then click Index and Tables. At the Index and Tables dialog box, click the Table of Contents tab. This displays the Index and Tables dialog box as shown in figure 6.2. At this dialog box, make any desired changes, and then click OK.

FIGURE

6.2 *Index and Tables Dialog Box with Table of Contents Tab Selected*

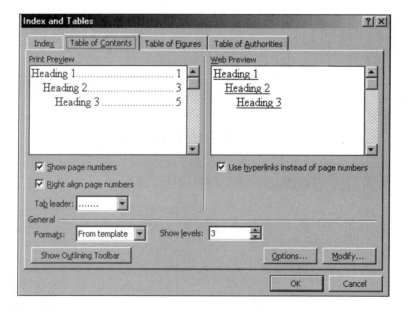

At the Index and Tables dialog box with the Table of Contents tab selected, a sample table of contents displays in the Print Preview section. You can change the table of contents format by clicking the down-pointing triangle at the right side of the Formats option box (located in the General section). At the drop-down list that displays, click the desired format. When a different format is selected, that format displays in the Print Preview section. Page numbers in a table of contents will display after the text or aligned at the right margin depending on what options are selected. The number of levels displayed depends on the number of heading levels specified in the document.

Tab leaders help guide the reader's eyes from the table of contents heading to the page number. The default tab leader is a period. To choose a different leader, click the down-pointing triangle at the right side of the Tab leader text box, and then click the desired leader character from the drop-down list.

If you want the table of contents to print on a page separate from the document text, insert a section break that begins a new page between the table of contents and the title of the document. If the beginning of the text in the document, rather than the table of contents, should be numbered as page 1, change the starting page number for the section. A table of contents is generally numbered with lowercase Roman numerals.

Word automatically identifies headings in a table of contents as hyperlinks. You can use these hyperlinks to move the insertion point to a specific location in the document. To move the insertion point, position the mouse pointer on the desired heading in a table of contents, hold down the Ctrl key (the mouse pointer turns into a hand), and then click the left mouse button.

(Before completing computer exercises, delete the Word Chapter 05E *folder on your disk. Next, copy to your disk the* Word Chapter 06E *subfolder from the Word 2002 Expert folder on the CD that accompanies this textbook and then make* Word Chapter 06E *the active folder.)*

exercise

APPLYING STYLES AND COMPILING A TABLE OF CONTENTS

1. Open Word Report 01.
2. Save the document with Save As and name it EWd C06 Ex01.
3. Apply heading styles to the title, headings, and subheadings by completing the following steps:
    a. With the insertion point positioned at the beginning of the document, press the Enter key once. (This adds room for the table of contents you will be inserting later.)
    b. Select the entire document and then change the line spacing to single.
    c. Position the insertion point on any character in the title *DESKTOP PUBLISHING*, click the down-pointing triangle to the right of the Style button on the Formatting toolbar, and then click *Heading 1*.
    d. Position the insertion point on any character in the heading *Defining Desktop Publishing*, click the down-pointing triangle to the right of the Style button on the Formatting toolbar, and then click *Heading 2*.

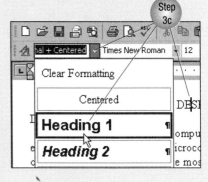

e. Apply the *Heading 2* style to the following headings:
   Initiating the Desktop Publishing Process
   Planning the Publication
   Creating the Content

4. Position the insertion point immediately left of the *D* in *DESKTOP PUBLISHING* and then insert a section break by completing the following steps:
   a. Click Insert and then Break.
   b. At the Break dialog box, click Next page.
   c. Click OK or press Enter.

5. With the insertion point positioned below the section break, insert page numbering and change the beginning number to 1 by completing the following steps:
   a. Click Insert and then Page Numbers.
   b. At the Page Numbers dialog box, click the down-pointing triangle at the right side of the Alignment option, and then click *Center* at the drop-down list.
   c. Click the Format button (in the dialog box, not on the Menu bar).
   d. At the Page Number Format dialog box, click Start at. (This inserts **1** in the Start at text box.)
   e. Click OK or press Enter to close the Page Number Format dialog box.
   f. At the Page Numbers dialog box, click OK or press Enter. (The view automatically changes to Print Layout.)

6. Compile and insert a table of contents at the beginning of the document by completing the following steps:
   a. Position the insertion point at the beginning of the document (on the new page).
   b. Turn on bold, key **TABLE OF CONTENTS** centered, and then turn off bold.
   c. Press the Enter key once and then change the paragraph alignment back to left.
   d. Click Insert, point to Reference, and then click Index and Tables.
   e. At the Index and Tables dialog box, click the Table of Contents tab.
   f. At the Index and Tables dialog box with the Table of Contents tab selected, click the down-pointing triangle at the right side of the Formats option box, and then click *Formal* at the drop-down list.
   g. Click OK or press Enter.

7. Position the insertion point on any character in the title, *TABLE OF CONTENTS*, and then apply the Heading 1 style. (This will change the font to 16-point Arial bold and also change the alignment to left.)

8. Insert page numbering in the Table of Contents page by completing the following steps:

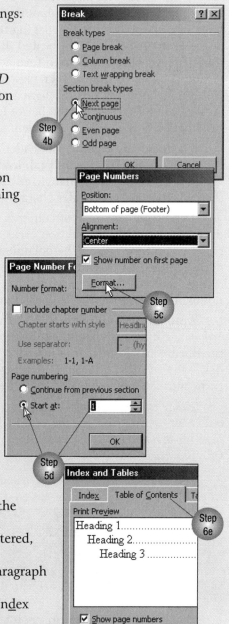

a. Click Insert and then Page Numbers.

b. At the Page Numbers dialog box, click the Format button.

c. At the Page Number Format dialog box, click the down-pointing triangle at the right side of the Number format text box, and then click *i, ii, iii, ...* at the drop-down list.

d. Click Start at. (This inserts *i* in the Start at text box.)

e. Click OK or press Enter to close the Page Number Format dialog box.

f. At the Page Numbers dialog box, click OK or press Enter.

9. Save the document again and then print the table of contents page. (Check with your instructor to see if you should print the other pages of the document.)

10. Close EWd C06 Ex01. (If a message displays asking if you want to save the changes to the document, click Yes.)

Assigning Levels to Table of Contents Entries

Applying styles to text applies specific formatting. If you want to identify titles and/or headings for a table of contents but you do not want heading style formatting applied, assign an outline level. To do this, open the document in Normal or Print Layout view, and then display the Outlining toolbar. Move the insertion point to a title or heading you want included in the table of contents. Click the down-pointing triangle at the right side of the Outline Level button on the Outlining toolbar and then click the desired level at the drop-down list. After assigning levels to titles and/or headings, compile the table of contents.

Outline
Level

exercise 2

ASSIGNING LEVELS AND COMPILING A TABLE OF CONTENTS

1. Open Word Report 04.

2. Save the document with Save As and name it EWd C06 Ex02.

3. Make sure the Normal view is selected.

4. With the insertion point positioned at the beginning of the document, press the Enter key once. (This adds room for the table of contents you will insert later.)

5. Turn on the display of the Outlining toolbar by clicking View, pointing to Toolbars, and then clicking *Outlining*.

6. Assign levels to titles and headings by completing the following steps:

a. Position the insertion point on any character in the title *MODULE 1: DEFINING NEWSLETTER ELEMENTS*, click the down-pointing triangle to the right of the Outline Level button on the Outlining toolbar, and then click *Level 1* at the drop-down list.

b. Assign level 1 to the title *MODULE 2: PLANNING A NEWSLETTER*. (This title is located approximately on the third page.)

c. Position the insertion point on any character in the heading *Designing a Newsletter* (located toward the beginning of the document), click the down-pointing triangle to the right of the Outline Level button on the Outlining toolbar, and then click *Level 2*.

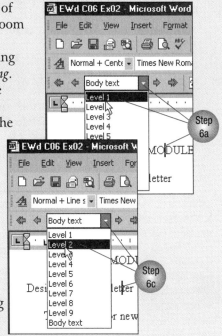

d. Assign level 2 to the following headings:
Defining Basic Newsletter Elements
Defining the Purpose of a Newsletter

7. Position the insertion point immediately left of the *M* in *MODULE 1: DEFINING NEWSLETTER ELEMENTS* and then insert a section break that begins a new page. *(Hint: Refer to exercise 1, step 4.)*

8. With the insertion point positioned below the section break, insert page numbering at the bottom center of each page of the section and change the starting number to 1. *(Hint: Refer to exercise 1, step 5.)*

9. Compile and insert a table of contents at the beginning of the document by completing the following steps:
   a. Position the insertion point at the beginning of the document (on the new page).
   b. Turn on bold, key **TABLE OF CONTENTS** centered, and then turn off bold.
   c. Press the Enter key once and then change the paragraph alignment back to left.
   d. Click Insert, point to Reference, and then click Index and Tables.
   e. At the Index and Tables dialog box, click the Table of Contents tab.
   f. At the Index and Tables dialog box with the Table of Contents tab selected, click the down-pointing triangle at the right side of the Formats option box, and then click *Distinctive* at the drop-down list.
   g. Click OK or press Enter.

10. Insert page numbering on the Table of Contents page at the bottom center. *(Hint: Refer to exercise 1, step 8.)*

11. Save the document again and then print the table of contents page. (Check with your instructor to see if you should print the other pages of the document.)

12. Close EWd C06 Ex02. (If a message displays asking if you want to save the changes to the document, click Yes.)

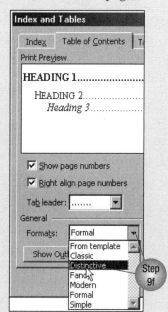

Step 9f

Marking Table of Contents Entries as Fields

Another method for marking text for a table of contents is to mark the text as a field entry. To do this, select the text you want included in the table of contents and then press Alt + Shift + O. This displays the Mark Table of Contents Entry dialog box shown in figure 6.3. The text you selected in the document displays in the Entry text box. At this dialog box, specify the text level using the Level option, and then click the Mark button. This turns on the display of nonprinting symbols in the document and also inserts a field code immediately after the selected text. For example, when you select the first title in exercise 3, the following code is inserted immediately after the title: { TC "MODULE 3: DESIGNING A NEWSLETTER" \f C \l " 1 " }. The Mark Table of Contents Entry dialog box also remains open. To mark the next entry for the table of contents, select the text, and then click the title bar of the Mark Table of Contents Entry dialog box. Specify the level and then click the Mark button. Continue in this manner until all table of contents entries have been marked.

6.3 *Mark Table of Contents Entry Dialog Box*

Mark Table of Contents Entry

Entry: MODULE 3: DESIGNING A NEWSLETTER

Table identifier: C

Level: 1

Click the Mark button to identify the text in the Entry text box as a table of contents field.

Mark   Cancel

If you mark table of contents entries as fields, you will need to activate the Table entry fields option when compiling the table of contents. To do this, display the Index and Tables dialog box with the Table of Contents tab selected, and then click the Options button. At the Table of Contents Options dialog box, click in the Table entry fields text box to insert a check mark, and then click OK.

exercise 3

MARKING HEADINGS AS FIELDS AND THEN COMPILING A TABLE OF CONTENTS

1. Open Word Report 05.
2. Save the document with Save As and name it EWd C06 Ex03.
3. Mark the titles and headings as fields for a table of contents by completing the following steps:
    a. With the insertion point positioned at the beginning of the document, press the Enter key once. (This adds room for the table of contents you will be inserting later.)
    b. Select the title *MODULE 3: DESIGNING A NEWSLETTER*.
    c. Press Alt + Shift + O.
    d. At the Mark Table of Contents Entry dialog box, make sure the Level is set at *1*, and then click the Mark button. (This turns on the display of nonprinting symbols.)
    e. Click in the document and then select the heading *Applying Desktop Publishing Guidelines*.
    f. Click the up-pointing triangle at the right side of the Level text box in the Mark Table of Contents Entry dialog box until *2* displays.
    g. Click the Mark button.
    h. Click in the document and then scroll down the document until the Module 4 title displays.
    i. Select the title *MODULE 4: CREATING NEWSLETTER LAYOUT*.

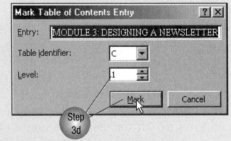

Step 3d

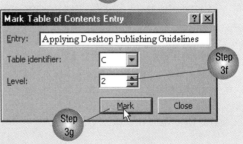

Step 3f

Step 3g

j. Click the down-pointing triangle at the right side of the Level text box in the Mark Table of Contents Entry dialog box until *1* displays.

k. Click the Mark button.

l. Mark the following headings as level 2:
Choosing Paper Size and Type
Choosing Paper Weight
Creating Margins for Newsletters

m. Click the Close button to close the Mark Table of Contents Entry dialog box.

4. Position the insertion point immediately left of the *M* in the title *MODULE 3: DESIGNING A NEWSLETTER* and then insert a section break that begins a new page. *(Hint: Refer to exercise 1, step 4.)*

5. With the insertion point positioned below the section break, insert page numbering at the bottom center of each page of the section and change the starting number to 1. *(Hint: Refer to exercise 1, step 5.)*

6. Compile and insert a table of contents at the beginning of the document by completing the following steps:

a. Position the insertion point at the beginning of the document (on the new page).

b. Key **TABLE OF CONTENTS** centered and bolded.

c. Press the Enter key once, turn off bold, and then change the paragraph alignment back to left.

d. Click Insert, point to Reference, and then click Index and Tables.

e. At the Index and Tables dialog box, click the Table of Contents tab.

f. At the Index and Tables dialog box with the Table of Contents tab selected, click the down-pointing triangle at the right side of the Formats option box, and then click *Fancy* at the drop-down list.

g. Click the Options button.

h. At the Table of Contents Options dialog box, click Table entry fields to insert a check mark in the check box. (This option is located in the bottom left corner of the dialog box.)

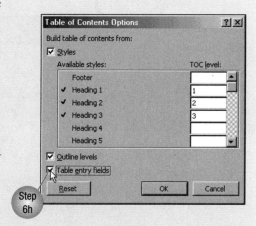

Step 6h

i. Click OK or press Enter to close the Table of Contents Options dialog box.

j. Click OK or press Enter to close the Index and Tables dialog box.

7. Insert page numbering on the Table of Contents page at the bottom center. *(Hint: Refer to exercise 1, step 8.)*

8. Turn off the display of nonprinting symbols.

9. Check the page breaks in the document and, if necessary, adjust the page breaks.

10. Save the document again and then print the table of contents page. (Before printing, make sure that hidden text will not print. To do this, click the Options button at the Print dialog box. At the Print dialog box with the Print tab selected, make sure there is no check mark in the Hidden text option.) (Check with your instructor to see if you should print the entire document.)

11. Close EWd C06 Ex03. (If a message displays asking if you want to save the changes to the document, click Yes.)

Updating a Table of Contents

If you make changes to a document after compiling a table of contents, update the table of contents. To do this, click anywhere within the current table of contents and then press F9 (the Update Field key) or click the Update TOC button on the Outlining toolbar. At the Update Table of Contents dialog box shown in figure 6.4, click Update page numbers only if changes occur only to the page numbers, or click Update entire table if changes were made to headings or subheadings within the table. Click OK or press Enter to close the dialog box.

Update TOC

Update TOC

F I G U R E

6.4 **Update Table of Contents Dialog Box**

H I N T

If you add, delete, move, or edit headings or other text in a document, update the table of contents.

exercise 4

UPDATING A TABLE OF CONTENTS

1. Open EWd C06 Ex01.
2. Save the document with Save As and name it EWd C06 Ex04.
3. Select the entire document and then change the line spacing to double.
4. Update the table of contents by completing the following steps:
    a. Click once in the table of contents.
    b. Press F9. (This is the Update Field key.)
    c. At the Update Table of Contents dialog box, make sure Update page numbers only is selected, and then click OK or press Enter.
5. Save the document again and then print the table of contents page. (Check with your instructor to see if you should print the entire document.)
6. Close EWd C06 Ex04. (If a message displays asking if you want to save the changes to the document, click Yes.)

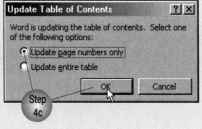

Step 4c

Deleting a Table of Contents

A table of contents that has been compiled in a document can be deleted. To do this, select the entire table of contents in the normal manner, and then press the Delete key. You can also select the table of contents by clicking the Go to TOC button on the Outlining toolbar.

Go to TOC

Creating an Index

An index is a list of topics contained in a publication, and the pages where those topics are discussed. Word lets you automate the process of creating an index in a manner similar to that used for creating a table of contents. When creating an index, you mark a word or words that you want included in the index. Creating an index takes some thought and consideration. The author of the book, manuscript, or report must determine the main entries desired and what subentries will be listed under main entries. An index may include such items as the main idea of a document, the main subject of a chapter or section, variations of a heading or subheading, and abbreviations. Figure 6.5 shows an example of an index.

FIGURE

6.5 *Index*

INDEX

A
Alignment, 12, 16
ASCII, 22, 24, 35
    data processing, 41
    word processing, 39

B
Backmatter, 120
    page numbering, 123
Balance, 67-69
Banners, 145

C
Callouts, 78
Captions, 156
Color, 192-195
    ink for offset printing, 193
    process color, 195

D
Databases, 124-129
    fields, 124
    records, 124
Directional flow, 70-71

Marking Text for an Index

A selected word or words can be marked for inclusion in an index. Before marking words for an index, determine what main entries and subentries are to be included in the index. Selected text is marked as an index entry at the Mark Index Entry text box.

To mark text for an index, select the word or words, and then press Alt + Shift + X. At the Mark Index Entry dialog box, shown in figure 6.6, the selected word(s) appears in the Main entry text box. Make any necessary changes to the dialog box, and then click the Mark button. (When you click the Mark button, Word automatically turns on the display of nonprinting symbols and displays the index field code.) Click the Close button to close the Mark Index Entry dialog box.

6.6 *Mark Index Entry Dialog Box*

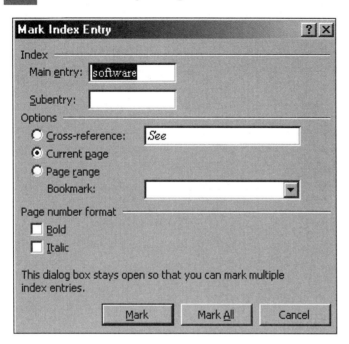

At the Mark Index Entry dialog box, the selected word or words displays in the Main entry text box. If the text is a main entry, leave it as displayed. If, however, the selected text is a subentry, key the main entry in the Main entry text box, click in the Subentry text box, and then key the selected text. For example, suppose a publication includes the terms *Page layout* and *Portrait*. The words *Page layout* are to be marked as a main entry for the index and *Portrait* is to be marked as a subentry below *Page layout*. To mark these words for an index, you would complete the following steps:

1. Select *Page layout*.
2. Press Alt + Shift + X.
3. At the Mark Index Entry dialog box, click the Mark button. (This turns on the display of nonprinting symbols.)
4. With the Mark Index Entry dialog box still displayed on the screen, click in the document to make the document active, and then select *Portrait*.
5. Click the Mark Index Entry dialog box Title bar to make it active.
6. Select *Portrait* in the Main entry text box and then key **Page layout**.
7. Click in the Subentry text box and then key **Portrait**.
8. Click the Mark button.
9. Click the Close button.

The main entry and subentry do not have to be the same as the selected text. You can select text for an index, type the text you want to display in the Main entry or Subentry text box, and then click Mark. At the Mark Index Entry dialog box, you can apply bold and/or italic formatting to the page numbers that will appear in the index. To apply formatting, click Bold and/or Italic to insert a check mark in the check box.

The Options section of the Mark Index Entry dialog box contains several options, with Current page the default. At this setting, the current page number will be listed in the index for the main and/or subentry. If you click Cross-reference, you would key the text you want to use as a cross-reference for the index entry in the Cross-reference text box. For example, you could mark the word *Serif* and cross reference it to *Typefaces*.

Click the Mark All button at the Mark Index Entry dialog box to mark all occurrences of the text in the document as index entries. Word marks only those entries whose uppercase and lowercase letters exactly match the index entry.

exercise 5

MARKING WORDS FOR AN INDEX

1. Open Word Report 01.
2. Save the document with Save As and name it EWd C06 Ex05.
3. Make the following changes to the document:
   a. Number pages at the bottom center of each page.
   b. Set the title *DESKTOP PUBLISHING* and the headings *Defining Desktop Publishing, Initiating the Desktop Publishing Process, Planning the Publication*, and *Creating the Content* in 14-point Times New Roman bold.
4. Mark the word *software* in the first paragraph for the index as a main entry and mark *word processing* in the first paragraph as a subentry below *software* by completing the following steps:
   a. Select *software* (located in the last sentence of the first paragraph).
   b. Press Alt + Shift + X.
   c. At the Mark Index Entry dialog box, click the Mark All button. (This turns on the display of nonprinting symbols.)
   d. With the Mark Index Entry dialog box still displayed, click in the document to make the document active, and then select *word processing* (located in the last sentence of the first paragraph). (You may want to drag the dialog box down the screen so more of the document text is visible.)
   e. Click the Mark Index Entry dialog box Title bar to make it active.
   f. Select *word processing* in the Main entry text box and then key **software**.
   g. Click in the Subentry text box and then key **word processing**.
   h. Click the Mark All button.
   i. With the Mark Index Entry dialog box still displayed, complete steps similar to those in 4d through 4h to mark the *first* occurrence of the following words as main entries or subentries for the index:

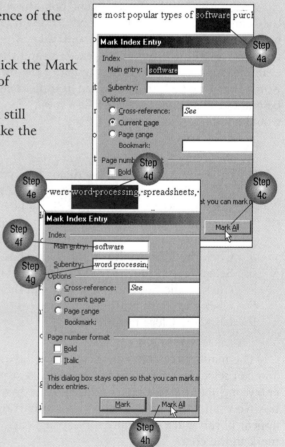

WORD

In the first paragraph in the Defining Desktop Publishing section:

| *spreadsheets* | = | subentry (main entry = *software*) |
| *database* | = | subentry (main entry = *software*) |

In the second paragraph in the Defining Desktop Publishing section:

publishing	=	main entry
desktop	=	subentry (main entry = *publishing*)
printer	=	main entry
laser	=	subentry (main entry = *printer*)

In the third paragraph in the Defining Desktop Publishing section:

| *design* | = | main entry |

In the fourth paragraph in the Defining Desktop Publishing section:

| *traditional* | = | subentry (main entry = *publishing*) |

In the first paragraph in the Initiating the Desktop Publishing Process section:

publication	=	main entry
planning	=	subentry (main entry = *publication*)
creating	=	subentry (main entry = *publication*)
intended audience	=	subentry (main entry = *publication*)
content	=	subentry (main entry = *publication*)

In the third paragraph in the Planning the Publication section:

| *message* | = | main entry |

    j. Click Close to close the Mark Index Entry dialog box.

    k. Click the Show/Hide ¶ button on the Standard toolbar to turn off the display of nonprinting symbols.

  5. Save and then close EWd C06 Ex05.

Compiling an Index

After all necessary text has been marked as a main entry or subentry for the index, the next step is to compile the index. An index should appear at the end of a document, generally beginning on a separate page. To compile the index, position the insertion point at the end of the document, and then insert a page break. With the insertion point positioned below the page break, key **INDEX** centered and bolded, and then press the Enter key. With the insertion point positioned at the left margin, click Insert, point to Reference, and then click Index and Tables. At the Index and Tables dialog box, click the Index tab. At the Index and Tables dialog box with the Index tab selected, as shown in figure 6.7, select the desired formatting, and then click OK or press Enter.

6.7 Index and Tables Dialog Box with Index Tab Selected

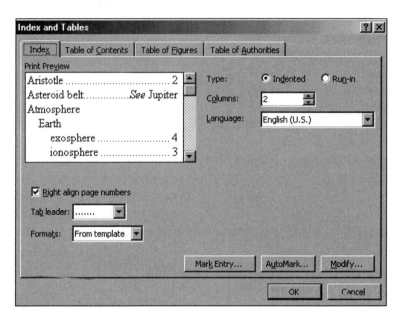

Word compiles the index and then inserts it at the location of the insertion point with the formatting selected at the Index and Tables dialog box. Word also inserts a section break above and below the index text.

At the Index and Tables dialog box with the Index tab selected, you can specify how the index entries will appear. The Print Preview section shows how the index will display in the document. The Columns option has a default setting of 2. At this setting, the index will display in two newspaper columns. This number can be increased or decreased.

By default, numbers are right aligned in the index. If you do not want numbers right aligned, click the Right align page numbers check box to remove the check mark. The Tab leader option is dimmed for all formats except *Formal*. If you click *Formal* in the Formats option box, the Tab leader option displays in black. The default tab leader character is a period. To change to a different character, click the down-pointing triangle at the right of the text box, and then click the desired character.

In the Type section, the Indented option is selected by default. At this setting, subentries will appear indented below main entries. If you click Run-in, subentries will display on the same line as main entries.

Click the down-pointing triangle at the right side of the Formats option box and a list of formatting choices displays. At this list, click the desired formatting and the Print Preview box will display how the index will appear in the document.

WORD

1. Open EWd C06 Ex05.
2. Save the document with Save As and name it EWd C06 Ex06.
3. Compile the index and insert it in the document by completing the following steps:
   a. Position the insertion point at the end of the document.
   b. Insert a page break.
   c. With the insertion point positioned below the page break, key **INDEX** centered and bolded.
   d. Press the Enter key twice, turn off bold, and then change the paragraph alignment back to left.
   e. Click Insert, point to Reference, and then click Index and Tables.
   f. At the Index and Tables dialog box, click the Index tab.
   g. At the Index and Tables dialog box with the Index tab selected, click the down-pointing triangle at the right side of the Formats option box, and then click *Modern* at the drop-down list.
   h. Click OK to close the dialog box.
   i. Select the title *INDEX* and then set it in 14-point Times New Roman bold.
4. Save the document again and then print the index (last page). (Check with your instructor to see if you should print the entire document.)
5. Close EWd C06 Ex06.

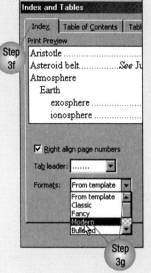

Creating a Concordance File

Words that appear frequently in a document can be saved as a concordance file. This saves you from having to mark each reference in a document. A concordance file is a regular Word document containing a single, two-column table with no text outside the table. In the first column of the table, you enter words you want to index. In the second column, you enter the main entry and subentry that should appear in the index. To create a subentry, separate each main entry from a subentry by a colon. Figure 6.8 shows an example of a completed concordance file.

6.8 *Concordance File*

World War I	World War I
Technology	Technology
technology	Technology
Teletypewriters	Technology: teletypewriters
motion pictures	Technology: motion pictures
Television	Technology: television
Radio Corporation of America	Radio Corporation of America
coaxial cable	Coaxial cable
Telephone	Technology: telephone
Communications Act of 1934	Communications Act of 1934
World War II	World War II
radar system	Technology: radar system
Computer	Computer
Atanasoff Berry Computer	Computer: Atanasoff Berry Computer
Korean War	Korean War
Columbia Broadcasting System	Columbia Broadcasting System
Cold War	Cold War
Vietnam	Vietnam
artificial satellite	Technology: artificial satellite
Communications Satellite Act of 1962	Communications Satellite Act of 1962

In the concordance file shown in figure 6.8, the text as it appears in the document is inserted in the first column (such as *World War I*, *Technology*, and *technology*). The second column contains the text as it should appear in the index specifying whether it is a main entry or subentry. For example, the text *motion pictures* in the concordance file will appear in the index as a subentry under the main entry *Technology*.

After a concordance file has been created, it can be used to quickly mark text for an index in a document. To do this, open the document containing text you want marked for the index, display the Index and Tables dialog box with the Index tab selected, and then click the AutoMark button. At the Open Index AutoMark File dialog box, double-click the concordance file name in the list box. Word turns on the display of nonprinting symbols, searches through the document for text that matches the text in the concordance file, and then marks it accordingly. After marking text for the index, insert the index in the document as described earlier.

When creating the concordance file in exercise 7, Word's AutoCorrect feature will automatically capitalize the first letter of the first word entered in each cell. In figure 6.9, you can see that several of the first words in the first column do not begin with a capital letter. Before completing the exercise, consider turning off this AutoCorrect capitalization feature. To do this, click Tools and then AutoCorrect Options. At the AutoCorrect dialog box click the *Capitalize first letter of table cells* check box to remove the check mark. Click OK to close the dialog box.

1. At a clear document screen, create the text shown in figure 6.9 as a concordance file by completing the following steps:
    a. Click the Insert Table button on the Standard toolbar.
    b. Drag down and to the right until *1 x 2 Table* displays at the bottom of the grid and then click the left mouse button.
    c. Key the text in the cells as shown in figure 6.9. Press the Tab key to move to the next cell. (If you did not remove the check mark before the *Capitalize first letter of table cells* option at the AutoCorrect dialog box, the *n* in the first word in the first cell *newsletters* is automatically capitalized. Delete the capital *N*, key an **n**, press the down arrow key [this will capitalize it again], and then click the Undo button. Repeat this for each cell entry in the first column that should begin with a lowercase letter.)
2. Save the document and name it EWd C06 Concord File.
3. Print and then close EWd C06 Concord File.

F I G U R E

6.9 *Exercise 7*

newsletters	Newsletters
Newsletters	Newsletters
Software	Software
desktop publishing	Software: desktop publishing
word processing	Software: word processing
Printers	Printers
Laser	Printers: laser
Design	Design
Communication	Communication
Consistency	Design: consistency
Elements	Elements
Nameplate	Elements: nameplate
Logo	Elements: logo
Subtitle	Elements: subtitle
Folio	Elements: folio
Headlines	Elements: headlines
Subheads	Elements: subheads
Byline	Elements: byline
Body Copy	Elements: body copy
Graphics Images	Elements: graphics images
Audience	Newsletters: audience
Purpose	Newsletters: purpose
focal point	Newsletters: focal point

If you removed the check mark before the *Capitalize first letter of table cells* option at the AutoCorrect dialog box, you may need to turn this feature back on. To do this, click Tools and then AutoCorrect Options. At the AutoCorrect dialog box, click the *Capitalize first letter of table cells* check box to insert the check mark, and then click OK to close the dialog box.

exercise 8

1. Open Word Report 04.
2. Save the document with Save As and name it EWd C06 Ex08.
3. Make the following changes to the document:
   a. Select the entire document and then change the font to 12-point Bookman Old Style (or a similar serif typeface).
   b. Set the titles and headings in the document in 14-point Bookman Old Style bold.
4. Mark text for the index using the concordance file by completing the following steps:
   a. Click Insert, point to Reference, and then click Index and Tables.
   b. At the Index and Tables dialog box with the Index tab selected, click the AutoMark button.
   c. At the Open Index AutoMark File dialog box, double-click *EWd C06 Concord File* in the list box. (This turns on the display of the nonprinting symbols.)
5. Compile and insert the index in the document by completing the following steps:
   a. Position the insertion point at the end of the document.
   b. Insert a page break.
   c. Key **INDEX** bolded and centered.
   d. Press the Enter key twice, turn off bold, and then return the paragraph alignment to left.
   e. Click Insert, point to Reference, and then click Index and Tables.
   f. At the Index and Tables dialog box, click the Index tab.
   g. At the Index and Tables dialog box with the Index tab selected, click the down-pointing triangle at the right side of the Formats option box, and then click *Formal* at the drop-down list.
   h. Click OK to close the dialog box.
   i. Click the Show/Hide ¶ button on the Standard toolbar to turn off the display of nonprinting symbols.
   j. Set the title *INDEX* in 14-point Bookman Old Style bold.
6. Check the page breaks in the document and, if necessary, adjust the page breaks.
7. Save the document again and then print the index (last page). (Check with your instructor to see if you should print the entire document.)
8. Close EWd C06 Ex08.

HINT

If you edit an index entry and move it to a different page, update the index.

Updating or Deleting an Index

If you make changes to a document after inserting an index, update the index. To do this, click anywhere within the index and then press F9. To delete an index, select the entire index using either the mouse or the keyboard, and then press the Delete key.

1. Open EWd C06 Ex08.
2. Save the document with Save As and name it EWd C06 Ex09.
3. Insert a page break at the beginning of the title *MODULE 2: PLANNING A NEWSLETTER*.
4. Update the index by clicking anywhere in the index and then pressing F9.
5. Save the document again and then print only the index. (Check with your instructor to see if you should print the entire document.)
6. Close EWd C06 Ex09.

Creating a Table of Figures

A document that contains figures should include a list (table) of figures so the reader can quickly locate a specific figure. Figure 6.10 shows an example of a table of figures. A table of figures can be created using a variety of methods. The easiest method is to mark figure names as captions and then use the caption names to create the table of figures.

FIGURE

6.10 *Table of Figures*

TABLE OF FIGURES

Creating Captions

A variety of methods are available for creating a caption for text. One method is to select the text, click Insert, point to Reference, and then click Caption. At the Caption dialog box shown in figure 6.11, make sure *Figure 1* displays in the Caption text box and the insertion point is positioned after *Figure 1*. Key the name for the caption, and then click OK or press Enter. Word inserts *Figure 1 (caption name)* below the selected text.

6.11 *Caption Dialog Box*

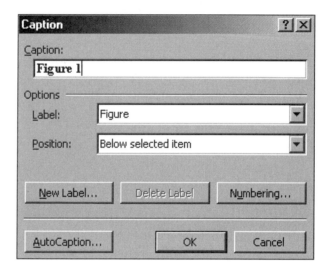

Compiling a Table of Figures

Once figures have been marked as captions in a document, compile the table of figures. A table of figures generally displays at the beginning of the document, after the table of contents. To compile the table of figures, display the Index and Tables dialog box with the Table of Figures tab selected as shown in figure 6.12, make any necessary changes, and then click OK to close the dialog box.

6.12 *Index and Tables Dialog Box with the Table of Figures Tab Selected*

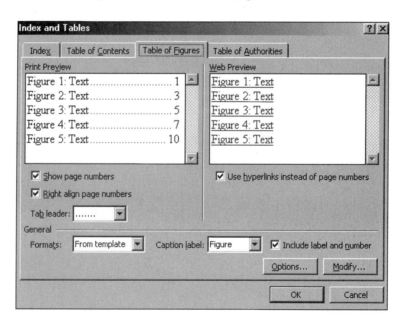

The options at the Index and Tables dialog box with the Table of Figures tab selected are similar to those options available at the dialog box with the Table of Contents tab selected. For example, you can choose a format for the table of figures from the Formats option box, change the alignment of the page number, or add leaders before page numbers.

CREATING A LIST OF FIGURES

1. Open Word Report 03.
2. Save the document with Save As and name it EWd C06 Ex10.
3. Add the caption *Figure 1 Basic Hardware* to the bulleted text, and the lines above and below the bulleted text, that displays in the middle of page 2 by completing the following steps:
   a. Move the insertion point to the middle of page 2 and then select the horizontal lines and the bulleted text between the two lines.
   b. Click Insert, point to Reference, and then click Caption.
   c. At the Caption dialog box, press the spacebar once, and then key **Basic Hardware**. (The insertion point is automatically positioned in the Caption text box, immediately after *Figure 1*.)
   d. Click OK or press Enter.

4. Complete steps similar to those in 3 to create the caption *Figure 2 Input Devices* for the bulleted text toward the bottom of the second page. (Be sure to include the lines above and below the bulleted text.)
5. Complete steps similar to those in 3 to create the caption *Figure 3 Output Devices* for the bulleted text that displays at the bottom of the second page and the top of the third page (the location may vary slightly). (Be sure to include the lines above and below the bulleted text.)
6. Compile and insert a table of figures at the beginning of the document by completing the following steps:
   a. Position the insertion point at the beginning of the document, press the Enter key, and then insert a page break.
   b. Move the insertion point above the page break and then key **TABLE OF FIGURES** bolded and centered.
   c. Press the Enter key, turn off bold, and then change the paragraph alignment back to left.
   d. Click Insert, point to Reference, and then click Index and Tables.
   e. At the Index and Tables dialog box, click the Table of Figures tab.
   f. At the Index and Tables dialog box with the Table of Figures tab selected, click the down-pointing triangle at the right side of the Formats option box, and then click *Formal* at the drop-down list.
   g. Click OK or press Enter.

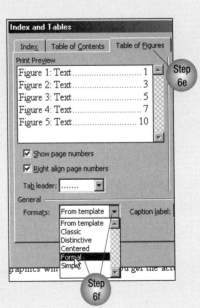

7. Check the page breaks in the document and, if necessary, adjust the page breaks.
8. Save the document again and then print the Table of Figures page. (Check with your instructor to see if you should print the entire document.)
9. Close EWd C06 Ex10.

Updating or Deleting a Table of Figures

If you make changes to a document after inserting a table of figures, update the table. To do this, click anywhere within the table of figures, and then press F9. At the Update Table of Figures dialog box, click Update page numbers only if the changes occur only to the page numbers, or click Update entire table if changes were made to headings or subheadings within the table. Click OK or press Enter to close the dialog box. To delete a table of figures, select the entire table using either the mouse or the keyboard, and then press the Delete key.

Creating a Table of Authorities

A table of authorities is a list of citations identifying the pages where the citations appear in a legal brief or other legal document. Word provides many common categories under which citations can be organized. Word includes Cases, Statutes, Other Authorities, Rules, Treatises, Regulations, and Constitutional Provisions. Within each category, Word alphabetizes the citations. Figure 6.13 shows an example of a table of authorities.

FIGURE

6.13 *Table of Authorities*

TABLE OF AUTHORITIES

CASES

Mansfield v. Rydell, 72 Wn.2d 200, 433 P.2d 723 (1983)...3

State v. Fletcher, 73 Wn.2d 332, 124 P.2d 503 (1981)..5

Yang v. Buchwald, 21 Wn.2d 385, 233 P.2d 609 (1991)..7

STATUTES

RCW 8.12.230(2)...4

RCW 6.23.590..7

RCW 5.23.103(3)...10

Some thought goes into planning a table of authorities. Before marking any text in a legal document, you need to determine what section headings you want and what should be contained in the sections. When marking text for a table of authorities, you need to find the first occurrence of the citation, mark it as a full citation with the complete name, and then specify a short citation. To mark a citation for a table of authorities, you would complete the following steps:

1. Select the first occurrence of the citation.
2. Press Alt + Shift + I.
3. At the Mark Citation dialog box shown in figure 6.14, edit and format the text in the Selected text box as you want it to appear in the table of authorities. Edit and format the text in the Short citation text box so it matches the short citation you want Word to search for in the document.
4. Click the down-pointing triangle at the right of the Category text box and then click the category from the drop-down list that applies to the citation.
5. Click the Mark button to mark the selected citation or click the Mark All button if you want Word to mark all long and short citations in the document that match those displayed in the Mark Citation dialog box.
6. The Mark Citation dialog box remains on the document screen so you can mark other citations. To find the next citation in a document, click the Next Citation button. (This causes Word to search through the document for the next occurrence of text commonly found in a citation such as *in re* or *v*.)
7. Select the text for the next citation and then complete steps 3 through 5.
8. After marking all citations, click the Close button to close the Mark Citations dialog box.

FIGURE

6.14 *Mark Citation Dialog Box*

Compiling a Table of Authorities

Once citations have been marked in a document, the table of authorities can be compiled and inserted in the document. A table of authorities is compiled in a document in a manner similar to a table of contents or figures. A table of authorities generally displays at the beginning of the document. To compile a table of authorities in a document containing text marked as citations, display the Index and Tables dialog box with the Table of Authorities selected, as shown in figure 6.15, make any necessary changes, and then click OK to close the dialog box.

FIGURE

6.15 *Index and Tables Dialog Box with the Table of Authorities Tab Selected*

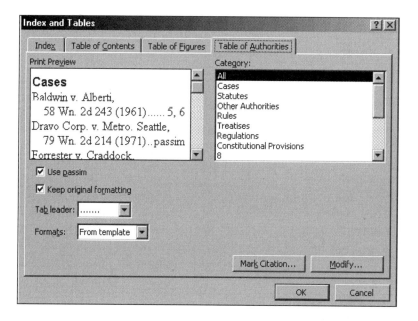

If you want the table of authorities to print on a page separate from the document text, insert a section break that begins a new page between the table of authorities and the title of the document. If the beginning of the text in the document, rather than the table of authorities, should be numbered as page 1, change the starting page number for the section.

The Index and Tables dialog box with the Table of Authorities tab selected contains options for formatting a table of authorities. The Use passim option is active by default (the check box contains a check mark). When it is active, Word replaces five or more page references to the same authority with *passim*. With the Keep original formatting check box active, Word will retain the formatting of the citation as it appears in the document. Click the Tab leader option if you want to change the leader character. By default, Word compiles all categories for the table of authorities. If you want to compile citations for a specific category, select that category from the Category drop-down list.

1. Open Word Legal Brief.
2. Save the document with Save As and name it EWd C06 Ex11.
3. Mark *RCW 7.89.321* as a statute citation by completing the following steps:
   a. Select *RCW 7.89.321*. (This citation is located toward the middle of the second page. *Hint: Use the Find feature to help you locate this citation.*)
   b. Press Alt + Shift + I.
   c. At the Mark Citation dialog box, click the down-pointing triangle at the right side of the Category text box, and then click *Statutes* at the drop-down list.
   d. Click the Mark All button. (This turns on the display of nonprinting symbols.)
   e. Click the Close button to close the Mark Citation dialog box.

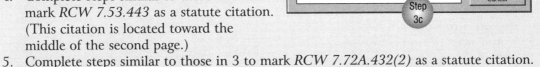

4. Complete steps similar to those in 3 to mark *RCW 7.53.443* as a statute citation. (This citation is located toward the middle of the second page.)
5. Complete steps similar to those in 3 to mark *RCW 7.72A.432(2)* as a statute citation. (This citation is located toward the top of the third page.)
6. Complete steps similar to those in 3 to mark *RCW 7.42A.429(1)* as a statute citation. (This citation is located toward the top of the third page.)
7. Mark *State v. Connors, 73 W.2d 743, 430 P.2d 199 (1974)* as a case citation by completing the following steps:
   a. Select *State v. Connors, 73 W.2d 743, 430 P.2d 199 (1974)*. (This citation is located toward the bottom of the second page. *Hint: Use the Find feature to help you locate this citation.*)
   b. Press Alt + Shift + I.
   c. At the Mark Citation dialog box, key **State v. Connors** in the Short citation text box.
   d. Click the down-pointing triangle at the right side of the Category text box, and then click *Cases* at the drop-down list.
   e. Click the Mark All button.
   f. Click the Close button to close the Mark Citation dialog box.

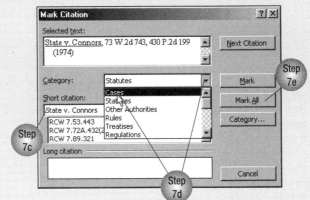

8. Complete steps similar to those in 7 to mark *State v. Bertelli, 63 W.2d 77, 542 P.2d 751 (1971)*. Enter **State v. Bertelli** as the short citation. (This citation is located toward the bottom of the second page.)
9. Complete steps similar to those in 7 to mark *State v. Landers, 103 W.2d 432, 893 P.2d 2 (1984)*. Enter **State v. Landers** as the short citation. (This citation is located toward the top of the third page.)

10. Turn on page numbering and compile the table of authorities by completing the following steps:

   a. Position the insertion point at the beginning of the document and then press the Enter key once.

   b. Position the insertion point immediately left of the *S* in *STATEMENT OF CASE* and then insert a section break that begins a new page.

   c. With the insertion point positioned below the section break, turn on page numbering at the bottom center of each page and change the starting number to 1.

   d. Position the insertion point above the section break and then key **TABLE OF AUTHORITIES** centered and bolded.

   e. Press the Enter key, turn off bold, and then change the paragraph alignment back to left.

   f. Click Insert, point to Reference, and then click Index and Tables.

   g. At the Index and Tables dialog box, click the Table of Authorities tab.

   h. At the Index and Tables dialog box with the Table of Authorities tab selected, click the down-pointing triangle at the right side of the Formats option box, and then click *Formal* at the drop-down list.

   i. Click OK or press Enter.

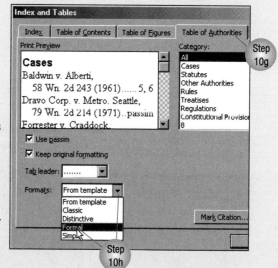

11. With the insertion point positioned anywhere in the table of authorities, turn on page numbering at the bottom center of each page and change the numbering format to lowercase Roman numerals.

12. Turn off the display of nonprinting symbols.

13. Save the document again and then print the table of authorities. (Check with your instructor to see if you should print the entire document.)

14. Close EWd C06 Ex11.

Updating or Deleting a Table of Authorities

If you make changes to a document after inserting a table of authorities, update the table. To do this, click anywhere within the table of authorities, and then press F9. To delete a table of authorities, select the entire table of authorities using either the mouse or the keyboard, and then press the Delete key.

HINT

If you need to make changes to a citation in a document containing a table of authorities, modify the citation in the body of the document and not the citation in the table of authorities; otherwise, the next time you update the table, your change will be lost.

WORD

CHAPTER summary

➤ Word contains options for automating the creation of a table of contents, index, list, or table of authorities.

➤ Text to be included in a table of contents can be identified by applying a heading style, assigning an outline level, or text can be marked as a field entry.

➤ One method for marking text for a table of contents is to mark the text as a field entry at the Mark Table of Contents dialog box. Display this dialog box by pressing Alt + Shift + O.

➤ Two steps are involved in creating a table of contents: apply the appropriate styles to the text that will be included, and compile the table of contents in the document.

➤ To compile the table of contents, position the insertion point where you want it to appear, display the Index and Tables dialog box with the Table of Contents tab selected, make any desired changes, and then click OK.

➤ If you want the table of contents to print on a page separate from the document text, insert a section break that begins a new page between the table of contents and the title of the document. You may need to adjust the page numbering also.

➤ If you make changes to a document after compiling a table of contents, update the table of contents by clicking anywhere in the table and then pressing F9. Update an index, table of figures, or table of authorities in a similar manner.

➤ To delete a table of contents, select the entire table of contents, and then press the Delete key. Delete an index, a table of figures, or a table of authorities in the same manner.

➤ An index is a list of topics contained in a publication and the pages where those topics are discussed. Word lets you automate the process of creating an index in a manner similar to that for creating a table of contents.

➤ Mark text for an index at the Mark Index Entry dialog box. Display this dialog box by pressing Alt + Shift + X.

➤ After all necessary text has been marked as a main entry or subentry for the index, the next step is to compile the index so that it appears at the end of the document beginning on a separate page.

➤ Word provides seven formatting choices for an index at the Formats option box at the Index and Tables dialog box.

➤ Words that appear frequently in a document can be saved as a concordance file so that you need not mark each reference in a document. A concordance file is a regular document containing a single, two-column table created at the Insert Table dialog box.

➤ Create a table of figures by marking specific text as captions and then using the caption names to create the table of figures. Mark captions at the Caption dialog box. Display this dialog box by clicking Insert, pointing to Reference, and then clicking Caption.

➤ A table of figures is compiled in a document in a manner similar to a table of contents and generally displays at the beginning of the document, after the table of contents.

➤ A table of authorities is a list of citations identifying the pages where the citations appear in a legal brief or other legal document.

➤ When marking text for a table of authorities, find the first occurrence of the citation, mark it as a full citation with the complete name, and then specify a short citation at the Mark Citation dialog box. Display this dialog box by pressing Alt + Shift + I.

➤ A table of authorities is compiled in a document in a manner similar to a table of contents or figures. A table of authorities generally displays at the beginning of the document.

COMMANDS review

Command	Mouse	Keyboard
Display Index and Tables dialog box	Insert, Reference Index and Tables	Insert, Reference Index and Tables
Display Mark Table of Contents Entry dialog box		Alt + Shift + O
Update table of contents	Click Update TOC button on Outlining toolbar	F9
Display Mark Index Entry dialog box		Alt + Shift + X
Update index, table of figures, or table of authorities		F9
Display Captions dialog box	Insert, Reference, Caption	Insert, Reference, Caption
Display Mark Citation dialog box		Alt + Shift + I

CONCEPTS check

Matching: On a blank sheet of paper, indicate the letter of the term that matches each description. (Terms may be used more than once.)

Ⓐ Alt + Shift + A
Ⓑ Alt + Shift + I
Ⓒ Alt + Shift + O
Ⓓ Alt + Shift + X
Ⓔ Alt + Shift + T
Ⓕ Captions

Ⓖ Compiling
Ⓗ Concordance
Ⓘ F9
Ⓙ F10
Ⓚ Index
Ⓛ Index and Tables dialog box

Ⓜ Subentries
Ⓝ Table of authorities
Ⓞ Table of contents
Ⓟ Table of figures

1. File that helps save time when marking text for an index.
2. Identifies citations in a legal brief.
3. Generally placed at the end of a document.
4. Generally placed at the beginning of a document.
5. This is a list of topics contained in a publication.
6. Pressing these keys displays the Mark Table of Contents Entry dialog box.
7. If included in a document, it usually follows the Table of Contents.
8. Pressing these keys displays the Mark Index Entry dialog box.
9. The easiest way to create a table of figures is to use these.
10. Choose a preformatted table of contents at this dialog box.
11. Pressing this key updates a table of authorities.

WORD

SKILLS check

Assessment 1

1. At a clear document screen, create the text shown in figure 6.16 as a concordance file.
2. Save the document and name it EWd C06 SAConcord File.
3. Print and then close EWd C06 SAConcord File.
4. Open Word Report 05.
5. Save the document with Save As and name it EWd C06 SA01.
6. Make the following changes to the document:
   a. Mark text for an index using the concordance file EWd C06 SAConcord File.
   b. Compile the index at the end of the document.
7. Save the document again and then print the index. (Check with your instructor to see if you should print the entire document.)
8. Close EWd C06 SA01.

Assessment 2

1. Open EWd C06 SA01.
2. Save the document with Save As and name it EWd C06 SA02.
3. Make the following changes to the document:
   a. Apply the following styles:

MODULE 3: DESIGNING A NEWSLETTER	=	Heading 1
Applying Desktop Publishing Guidelines	=	Heading 2
MODULE 4: CREATING NEWSLETTER LAYOUT	=	Heading 1
Choosing Paper Size and Type	=	Heading 2
Choosing Paper Weight	=	Heading 2
Creating Margins for Newsletters	=	Heading 2
INDEX	=	Heading 1

   b. Number the pages at the bottom center of each page.
   c. Compile the table of contents. (Include a title for the table of contents.)
   d. Number the table of contents page at the bottom center of the page. (Change the number to a lowercase Roman numeral.)
4. Save the document again and then print the table of contents page. (Check with your instructor to see if you should print the entire document.)
5. Close EWd C06 SA02.

FIGURE

6.16 *Assessment 1*

NEWSLETTER	Newsletter
Newsletter	Newsletter
Consistency	Newsletter: consistency
Element	Elements
Margins	Elements: margins
column layout	Elements: column layout
Nameplate	Elements: nameplate
Location	Elements: location
Logos	Elements: logo
Color	Elements: color
ruled lines	Elements: ruled lines
Focus	Elements: focus
Balance	Elements: balance
graphics images	Graphics images
Photos	Photos
Headlines	Newsletter: headlines
Subheads	Newsletter: subheads
White space	White space
directional flow	Newsletter: directional flow
Paper	Paper
Size	Paper: size
Type	Paper: type
Weight	Paper: weight
Stock	Paper: stock
margin size	Newsletter: margin size

Assessment 3

1. Open EWd C06 SA02.
2. Save the document with Save As and name it EWd C06 SA03.
3. Insert a page break at the beginning of the title *MODULE 4: CREATING NEWSLETTER LAYOUT.*
4. Update the table of contents and the index.
5. Save the document again, print the table of contents, and then print the index. (Check with your instructor to see if you should print the entire document.)
6. Close EWd C06 SA03.

7

PREPARING AND PROTECTING FORMS

PERFORMANCE OBJECTIVES

Upon successful completion of chapter 7, you will be able to:
- **Fill in a form document**
- **Print, edit, and customize a form**
- **Draw a table in a form template**
- **Protect and secure documents**

Word Chapter 07E

Many businesses use preprinted forms that are generally filled in by hand, with a typewriter, or using a computer. These forms require additional storage space and also cost the company money. With Word's form feature you can create your own forms, eliminating the need for preprinted forms.

In this chapter, you will learn how to create a template document for a form that includes text boxes, check boxes, and pull-down lists. You will learn how to save the form as a protected document and then open the form and key information in the fill-in boxes. You will create basic form documents in this chapter. For ideas on creating advanced forms, please refer to Word's Help guide.

In chapter 2, you learned how to create fill-in fields in a main document. The main document containing fill-in fields also required a data source for other variable information. Creating a form does not require a main document or a data source. The form is created as a template document that contains fill-in fields. Information is keyed in the fields when a document based on the form template is opened.

Creating a Form

In Word, a *form* is a protected document that includes fields where information is entered. A form document contains *form fields* that are locations in the document where one of three things is performed: text is entered, a check box is turned on or off, or information is selected from a drop-down list. Three basic steps are completed when creating a form:

1. Create a form document based on a template and build the structure of the form.

HINT

Before creating a form, sketch a layout of the form.

2. Insert form fields where information is to be entered at the keyboard.
3. Save the form as a protected document.

Creating the Form Template

A form is created as a template so that anyone who fills in the form is working on a copy of the form, not the original. The original is the template document that is saved as a protected document. In this way, a form can be used over and over again without changing the original form. When a form is created from the template form document that has been protected, information can be keyed only in the fields designated when the form was created.

HINT

Consider using an existing form as a guide for designing a new form.

Word provides a Forms toolbar with buttons you can use to easily insert a text box, check box, or other form fields into a form template document. To display the Forms toolbar shown in figure 7.1, position the arrow pointer on any currently displayed toolbar, click the *right* mouse button, and then click *Forms* at the drop-down list. You can also display the Forms toolbar by clicking <u>V</u>iew, pointing to <u>T</u>oolbars, and then clicking Forms.

FIGURE

7.1 *Forms Toolbar*

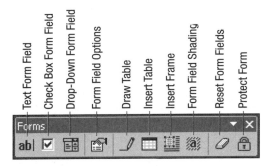

Figure 7.2 shows an example of a form document created with the form feature. (You will create this form in exercise 1.) You can create forms that contain fields for text, such as the fields *Name:*, *Address:*, *Date of Birth:*, and so on, shown in figure 7.2. Forms can also contain check boxes, such as the boxes after *Yes* and *No*, shown in figure 7.2. Forms can also contain drop-down lists (not used in the form shown in figure 7.2). You will learn about drop-down lists later in this chapter.

Generally, a form is created based on the default template document (called the Normal template). The form is created and then saved as a protected template document. To learn how to create a form document, complete exercise 1.

Changing File Locations

By default, Word saves template documents in a *Templates* subfolder within the Microsoft Office program. In this chapter, you will create form template documents and save them to this subfolder. In some situations, you may want to change the location of template documents. Do this at the Options dialog box with the File Locations tab selected. At the Options dialog box, click the *User templates* in the <u>F</u>ile types list box, and then click the <u>M</u>odify button. At the Modify Location dialog box, specify the desired folder, and then click OK. Click OK to close the Options dialog box.

1. Create the form shown in figure 7.2 as a template document by completing the following steps:
    a. Click File and then New.
    b. Click the *General Templates* hyperlink in the New Document Task Pane.
    c. At the Templates dialog box with the General tab selected, make sure *Blank Document* is selected in the list box.
    d. Click Template in the Create New section at the bottom right corner of the dialog box.
    e. Click OK or press Enter.
    f. Key the beginning portion of the form shown in figure 7.2 up to the colon after *Name:*. After keying the colon, press the spacebar once, and then insert a form field where the name will be keyed by completing the following steps:

        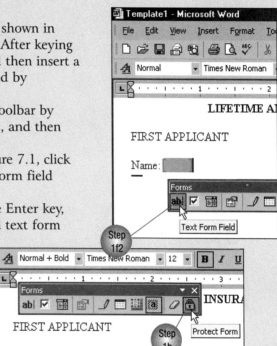

        1) Turn on the display of the Forms toolbar by clicking View, pointing to Toolbars, and then clicking Forms.
        2) At the Forms toolbar shown in figure 7.1, click the Text Form Field button. (The form field displays as a shaded area.)
    g. After inserting the form field, press the Enter key, and then create the remaining text and text form fields as shown in figure 7.2. To create the check boxes after *Yes* and *No*, position the insertion point where you want the check box to display, and then click the Check Box Form Field button on the Forms toolbar.
    h. After the form is completed, protect the document by clicking the Protect Form button on the Forms toolbar.
    i. Turn off the display of the Forms toolbar by clicking the Close button located at the right side of the Forms toolbar Title bar.
2. Save the document with Save As and name it XXX Template Document. (Use your initials in place of the *XXX*.)
3. Print and then close XXX Template Document. (The field gray shading does not print.)

LIFETIME ANNUITY INSURANCE APPLICATION

FIRST APPLICANT

Name:

Address:

Date of Birth:

Occupation:

SECOND APPLICANT

Name:

Address:

Date of Birth:

Occupation:

1. During the past 3 years, have you for any reason consulted a doctor or been hospitalized?

   First Applicant: Second Applicant:

   Yes ☐   No ☐   Yes ☐   No ☐

2. Have you ever been treated for or advised that you had any of the following: heart, lung, nervous, kidney, or liver disorder; high blood pressure; drug abuse, including alcohol; cancer or tumor; AIDS, or any disorder of your immune system; diabetes?

   First Applicant: Second Applicant:

   Yes ☐   No ☐   Yes ☐   No ☐

These answers are true and complete to the best of my knowledge and belief. To determine my insurability, I authorize any health care provider or insurance company to give any information about me or my physical or mental health.

FIRST APPLICANT'S SIGNATURE   SECOND APPLICANT'S SIGNATURE

Filling In a Form Document

After a template form document is created, protected, and saved, the template can be used to create a personalized form document. When you open a form template document that has been protected, the insertion point is automatically inserted in the first form field. Key the information for the data field and then press the Tab key to move the insertion point to the next form field. You can move the insertion point to a preceding form field by pressing Shift + Tab. To fill in a check box form field, move the insertion point to the check box, and then press the spacebar. Complete the same steps to remove an *X* from a check box form field. As an example of how to fill in a form template, complete exercise 2.

exercise 2

FILLING IN A TEMPLATE FORM DOCUMENT

1. Create a form with the XXX Template Document form template by completing the following steps:
   a. Click File and then New.
   b. Click the *General Templates* hyperlink in the New Document Task Pane.
   c. At the Templates dialog box with the General tab selected, double-click the *XXX Template Document* icon (where your initials display instead of the *XXX*).
   d. Word displays the form document with the insertion point positioned in the first form field after *Name*. Key the name **Dennis Utley** (as shown in figure 7.3), and then press the Tab key to move to the next form field.
   e. Fill in the remaining text and check box form fields as shown in figure 7.3. Press the Tab key to move the insertion point to the next form field. Press Shift + Tab to move the insertion point to the preceding form field. (To insert the *X* in a check box, move the insertion point to the check box, and then press the spacebar.)
2. When the form is completed, save the document and name it EWd C07 Ex02.
3. Print and then close EWd C07 Ex02.

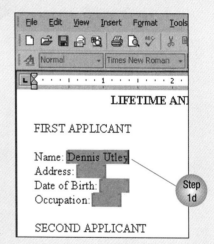

LIFETIME ANNUITY INSURANCE APPLICATION

FIRST APPLICANT

Name: **Dennis Utley**
Address: **11315 Lomas Drive, Seattle, WA 98123**
Date of Birth: **02/23/59**
Occupation: **Accountant**

SECOND APPLICANT

Name: **Geneva Utley**
Address: **11315 Lomas Drive, Seattle, WA 98123**
Date of Birth: **09/04/62**
Occupation: **Social Worker**

1. During the past 3 years, have you for any reason consulted a doctor or been hospitalized?

   First Applicant: Second Applicant:
   Yes ☐   No ☒   Yes ☐   No ☒

2. Have you ever been treated for or advised that you had any of the following: heart, lung, nervous, kidney, or liver disorder; high blood pressure; drug abuse, including alcohol; cancer or tumor; AIDS, or any disorder of your immune system; diabetes?

   First Applicant: Second Applicant:
   Yes ☐   No ☒   Yes ☐   No ☒

These answers are true and complete to the best of my knowledge and belief. To determine my insurability, I authorize any health care provider or insurance company to give any information about me or my physical or mental health.

FIRST APPLICANT'S SIGNATURE   SECOND APPLICANT'S SIGNATURE

_____   _____

Printing a Form

After the form fields in a form document have been filled in, the form can be printed in the normal manner. In some situations, you may want to print just the data (not the entire form) or print the form and not the fill-in data.

If you are using a preprinted form that is inserted in the printer, you will want to print just the data. Word will print the data in the same location on the page as it appears in the form document. To print just the data in a form, click Tools and then Options. At the Options dialog box, click the Print tab. At the Options dialog box with the Print tab selected, click Print data only for forms in the Options for current document only section (this inserts a check mark in the check box), and then Click OK. Click the Print button on the Standard toolbar. After printing only the data, complete similar steps to remove the check mark from the Print data only for forms check box.

To print only the form without the data, you would click File and then New, and then click the *General Templates* hyperlink in the New Document Task Pane. At the Templates dialog box, select the desired template document in the list box, and then click OK. With the form document displayed on the document screen, click the Print button on the Standard toolbar, and then close the document.

HINT

Form field shading does not print.

exercise 3

PRINTING ONLY DATA IN A FORM DOCUMENT

1. Open EWd C07 Ex02.
2. Print only the data in the form fields by completing the following steps:
   a. Click Tools and then Options.
   b. At the Options dialog box, click the Print tab.
   c. At the Options dialog box with the Print tab selected, click Print data only for forms in the Options for current document only section. (This inserts a check mark in the check box.)
   d. Click OK.
   e. Click the Print button on the Standard toolbar.
3. After printing, remove the check mark from the Print data only for forms option by completing the following steps:
   a. Click Tools and then Options.
   b. At the Options dialog box with the Print tab selected, click Print data only for forms in the Options for current document only section. (This removes the check mark from the check box.)
   c. Click OK or press Enter.
4. Close EWd C07 Ex02 without saving the changes.

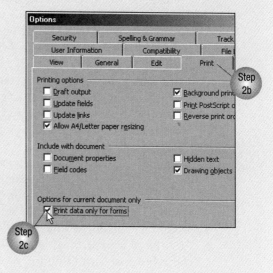

Protect Form

Editing a Form Template

When a form template is created and then protected, the text in the template cannot be changed. If you need to make changes to a form template, you must open the template document, unprotect the document, and then make the changes. After making the changes, protect the document again.

To unprotect a template document, click the Protect Form button on the Forms toolbar to deactivate it. You can also unprotect a document by clicking Tools and then Unprotect Document. Make any necessary changes to the document and then protect it again by clicking the Protect Form button on the Forms toolbar or by clicking Tools and then Protect Document.

exercise 4

EDITING A TEMPLATE FORM

1. Add the text shown in figure 7.4 to the XXX Template Document form template by completing the following steps:
   a. Click the Open button on the Standard toolbar.
   b. At the Open dialog box, click the down-pointing triangle to the right of the Look in option box. From the drop-down list that displays, click the drive where the *Templates* folder is located. (If you have Microsoft Office installed on a hard-drive system, click *(C:)*, double-click *WINDOWS*, double-click *Application Data*, double-click *Microsoft*, and then double-click *Templates*. If this is not the correct path, try clicking *(C:)*, double-clicking *Program Files*, double-clicking *Microsoft Office*, and then double-clicking *Templates*. This path will vary if you have only Word installed and not Microsoft Office. If you are using Word on a network system, check with your instructor to determine the location of the *Templates* folder.)
   c. With the *Templates* folder selected, click the down-pointing triangle to the right of the Files of type option box (located at the bottom left corner of the dialog box), and then click *All Files*.
   d. Double-click *XXX Template Document* in the list box (where *XXX* indicates your initials).
   e. With the XXX Template Document form template displayed on the document screen, display the Forms toolbar.
   f. Unprotect the document by clicking the Protect Form button on the Forms toolbar.
   g. Add the paragraph and the check boxes shown in figure 7.4 to the form.
   h. Protect the document again by clicking the Protect Form button on the Forms toolbar.
   i. Save the document with the same name (XXX Template Document).
2. Print and then close XXX Template Document.

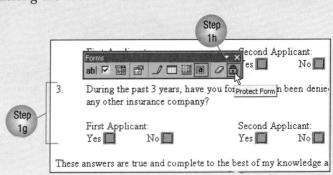

WORD

3. Change to the *Word Chapter 07E* folder on your disk by completing the following steps:
   a. Click the Open button on the Standard toolbar.
   b. At the Open dialog box, click the down-pointing triangle to the right of the Look in option box, and then click *3½ Floppy (A:)* (this may vary depending on the drive where your disk is located).
   c. Double-click *Word Chapter 07E* in the list box.
   d. Click the down-pointing triangle to the right of the Files of type option box (located at the bottom left corner of the dialog box) and then click *Word Documents*.
   e. Click the Cancel button.

FIGURE

7.4 **Exercise 4**

3. During the past 3 years, have you for any reason been denied life insurance by any other insurance company?

First Applicant: Second Applicant:

Yes ☐   No ☐   Yes ☐   No ☐

Customizing Form Field Options

A drop-down list, text box, or check box form field is inserted in a document with default options. You can change these default options for each form field. Options at the Drop-Down Form Field Options dialog box can be used to create form fields with drop-down lists.

Creating Form Fields with Drop-Down Lists

When creating form fields for a form document, there may be some fields where you want the person entering the information to choose from specific options, rather than keying the data. To do this, create a form field with a drop-down list. To do this, display the *Templates* folder, and then open the template document. Unprotect the template document, key the field name, and then click the Drop-Down Form Field button on the Forms toolbar. After inserting the drop-down form field, click the Form Field Options button on the Forms toolbar. This displays the Drop-Down Form Field Options dialog box shown in figure 7.5.

Drop-Down
Form Field

Form Field
Options

FIGURE

7.5 *Drop-Down Form Field Options Dialog Box*

Key the option you want to display in the drop-down list and then click the Add button.

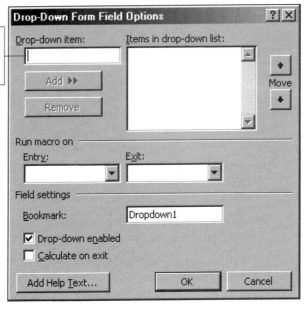

At the Drop-Down Form Field Options dialog box, key the first option you want to display in the drop-down list, and then click the Add button. Continue in this manner until all drop-down list items have been added and then click OK or press Enter to close the Drop-Down Form Field Options dialog box. Protect and then save the template document. A drop-down form field in a form document displays as a gray box with a down-pointing arrow at the right side of the box. You can remove drop-down items at the Drop-Down Form Field Options dialog box by selecting the item in the Items in drop-down list box and then clicking the Remove button.

When filling in a form field in a form template document that contains a drop-down list, position the insertion point in the drop-down form field, and then click the down-pointing triangle at the right side of the form field. At the drop-down list of choices that displays, click the desired choice.

HINT
Insert a drop-down list box to restrict choices to those in the list box.

HINT
Use the Move arrow buttons to move the most frequently selected item to the first position.

HINT
To remove an item in the Items in drop-down list box, click the item and then click the Remove button.

Changing Text Form Field Options

To change options for a text form field, position the insertion point on the text form field you want to change and then click the Form Field Options button on the Forms toolbar. This displays the Text Form Field Options dialog box shown in figure 7.6.

FIGURE

7.6 *Text Form Field Options Dialog Box*

Change the type of text to be inserted in the form field with options from this text box.

Specify an exact measurement for a form field at this text box.

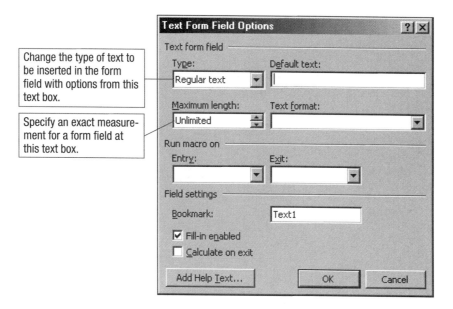

At the Text Form Field Options dialog box, you can change the type of text that is to be inserted in the form field. The default setting at the Type option box is *Regular text*. This can be changed to *Number, Date, Current date, Current time,* or *Calculation*.

If you change the Type option, Word will display an error message if the correct type of information is not entered in the form field. For example, if you change the form field type to *Number* in the Type option box, only a number can be entered in the form field. If something other than a number is entered, Word displays an error message, the entry is selected, and the insertion point stays in the form field until a number is entered.

If a particular text form field will generally need the same information, key that information in the Default text text box. This default text will display in the form field. If you want to leave the default text in the form document, just press the Tab key or the Enter key when filling in the form. If you want to change the default text, key the new text over the default text when filling in the form.

With the Maximum length option at the Text Form Field Options dialog box, you can specify an exact measurement for a form field. This option has a setting of *Unlimited* by default.

Formatting options for text in a form field can be applied with options at the Text format option box. For example, if you want text to display in all uppercase letters, click the down-pointing triangle at the right side of the Text format option box, and then click *Uppercase* at the drop-down list. When you key text in the form field while filling in the form, the text is converted to uppercase letters as soon as you press the Tab key or Enter key. The Text format options will vary depending on what is selected in the Type option box.

HINT
You can specify a default entry in a text form field.

Changing Check Box Form Field Options

Check Box form field options can be changed at the Check Box Form Field Options dialog box shown in figure 7.7. To display this dialog box, position the insertion point on a check box form field and then click the Form Field Options button on the Forms toolbar.

FIGURE

7.7 Check Box Form Field Options Dialog Box

Change the size of a check box by choosing Exactly and then keying the desired point size.

By default, Word inserts a check box in a form template document in the same size as the adjacent text. This is because Auto is selected at the Check box size section of the Check Box Form Field Options dialog box. If you want to specify an exact size for the check box, click Exactly, and then key the desired point measurement in the Exactly text box.

A check box form field is empty by default. If you want the check box to be checked by default, click the Checked option in the Default value section of the dialog box.

exercise 5

CREATING A FORM WITH TEXT FIELDS, CHECK BOXES, AND DROP-DOWN LISTS

1. Create the form shown in figure 7.8 as a template document named XXX EWd C07 Ex05 by completing the following steps:
   a. Click File and then New.
   b. Click the *General Templates* hyperlink in the New Document Task Pane.
   c. At the Templates dialog box with the General tab selected, make sure *Blank Document* is selected in the list box.
   d. Click Template in the Create New section at the bottom right corner of the dialog box and then click OK.
   e. At the document screen, make sure the default font is 12-point Times New Roman. (If it is not, display the Font dialog box, change the size to 12, and then click the

<u>D</u>efault button. At the question asking if you want to change the default font, click <u>Y</u>es.)

f. Turn on the display of the Forms toolbar.

g. Key the title of the form, **APPLICATION FOR PREFERRED INSURANCE,**
centered and bolded. Press the Enter key twice, turn off bold, and then return the paragraph alignment to left. Key **Date:**, press the spacebar once, and then insert a text form field that inserts the current date by completing the following steps:

1) Click the Text Form Field button on the Forms toolbar.
2) Click the Form Field Options button on the Forms toolbar.
3) At the Text Form Field Options dialog box, click the down-pointing triangle at the right side of the Type option box, and then click *Current date* at the drop-down list.
4) Click OK or press Enter to close the Text Form Field Options dialog box.
5) Press the right arrow key to deselect the field and move the insertion point to the right side of the field. (You can also position the mouse pointer immediately right of the field and then click the left mouse button.)

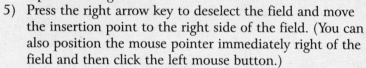

h. Press the Enter key twice, key **Name:**, press the spacebar once, and then create the form text field. Do the same for **Address:** and **Date of Birth:**.

i. Key **Social Security Number:** and then create a text form field that allows a maximum of 11 characters (the number required for the Social Security number including the hyphens) by completing the following steps:

1) Press the spacebar once after keying **Social Security Number:**.
2) Click the Text Form Field button on the Forms toolbar.
3) Click the Form Field Options button on the Forms toolbar.
4) At the Text Form Field Options dialog box, select *Unlimited* that displays in the <u>M</u>aximum length text box, and then key **11**.
5) Click OK or press Enter to close the Text Form Field Options dialog box.
6) Press the right arrow key to deselect the field and move the insertion point to the right side of the field. (You can also position the mouse pointer immediately right of the field and then click the left mouse button.)

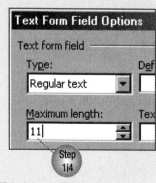

j. Press the Enter key twice, key **Gender:**, and then press the Tab key. Create the text and check boxes after *Gender:* as shown in figure 7.8.

k. After creating the check box after *Male,* press the Enter key twice, key **Nonprofit Employer:**, press the spacebar once, and then create a drop-down form field with three choices by completing the following steps:

1) Click the Drop-Down Form Field button on the Forms toolbar.
2) Click the Form Field Options button on the Forms toolbar.

3) At the Drop-Down Form Field Options dialog box, key **College** in the Drop-down item text box.
4) Click the Add button.
5) Key **Public School** in the Drop-down item text box.
6) Click the Add button.
7) Key **Private School** in the Drop-down item text box.
8) Click the Add button.
9) Click OK or press Enter to close the Drop-Down Form Field Options dialog box.
10) Press the right arrow key to deselect the field and move the insertion point to the right side of the field. (You can also position the mouse pointer immediately right of the field and then click the left mouse button.)

l. Press the Enter key twice, key **How are premiums to be paid?**, press the spacebar once, and then create a drop-down form field with the choices *Annually, Semiannually,* and *Quarterly* by completing steps similar to those in 1k.

m. Continue creating the remainder of the form as shown in figure 7.8.

n. After the form is completed, protect the document by clicking the Protect Form button on the Forms toolbar.

o. Close the Forms toolbar.

2. Save the document and name it XXX EWd C07 Ex05. (Use your initials in place of the *XXX*.)

3. Print and then close XXX EWd C07 Ex05.

FIGURE

7.8 *Exercise 5*

APPLICATION FOR PREFERRED INSURANCE

Date:

Name:

Address:

Date of Birth:

Social Security Number:

Gender: Female ☐   Male ☐

WORD

Nonprofit Employer: ░░░░░░░░

How are premiums to be paid? ░░░░░░░

1. Will this insurance replace any existing insurance or annuity?
   Yes ☐   No ☐

2. Within the past 3 years has your driver's license been suspended, revoked, or have you been convicted for driving under the influence of alcohol or drugs?
   Yes ☐   No ☐

3. Do you have any intention of traveling or residing outside the United States or Canada within the next 12 months?
   Yes ☐   No ☐

Signature of proposed insured:

_____   Date _____

FILLING IN A TEMPLATE FORM DOCUMENT

1. Create a form with the XXX EWd C07 Ex05 form template by completing the following steps:
   a. Click File and then New.
   b. Click the *General Templates* hyperlink in the New Document Task Pane.
   c. At the Templates dialog box, double-click *XXX C07 Ex05* (where your initials display instead of the *XXX*).
   d. Word displays the form document with the insertion point positioned in the *Name:* form field. Fill in the text and check boxes as shown in figure 7.9. (Press the Tab key to move the insertion point to the next form field. Press Shift + Tab to move the insertion point to the preceding form field.) To fill in the form fields with drop-down lists, complete the following steps:
      1) With the insertion point in the drop-down list form field, click the down-pointing arrow at the right side of the option box.
      2) Click the desired option at the drop-down list.
2. When the form is completed, save the document and name it EWd C07 Ex06.
3. Print and then close EWd C07 Ex06.

APPLICATION FOR PREFERRED INSURANCE

Date: (current date)

Name: Jennifer Reynolds

Address: 2309 North Cascade, Renton, WA 98051

Date of Birth: 12/18/63

Social Security Number: 411-23-6800

Gender: Female ☒   Male ☐

Nonprofit Employer: Public School

How are premiums to be paid? Quarterly

1. Will this insurance replace any existing insurance or annuity?
    Yes ☒   No ☐

2. Within the past 3 years has your driver's license been suspended, revoked, or have you been convicted for driving under the influence of alcohol or drugs?
    Yes ☐   No ☒

3. Do you have any intention of traveling or residing outside the United States or Canada within the next 12 months?
    Yes ☐   No ☒

Signature of proposed insured:

_____   Date _____

Creating Tables in a Form Template

A table can be very useful when creating a form with form fields. A table can be customized to create a business form such as an invoice or a purchase order. Figure 7.10 shows an example of a form you will create in exercise 7 using the table feature.

exercise 7

CREATING A FORM USING THE TABLE FEATURE

1. Create the form shown in figure 7.10 as a template document and name it XXX EWd C07 Ex07 (where *XXX* are your initials), by completing the following steps:
   a. Click File and then New.
   b. Click the *General Templates* hyperlink in the New Document Task Pane.
   c. At the Templates dialog box with the General tab selected, make sure *Blank Document* is selected in the list box.
   d. Click Template in the Create New section at the bottom right corner of the dialog box.
   e. Click OK or press Enter.
   f. Display the Forms toolbar.
   g. Click the Draw Table button on the Forms toolbar.
   h. Use the buttons on the Tables and Borders toolbar to draw the table lines as shown in figure 7.10.
   i. Change the text alignment to Align Center for specific cells by completing the following steps:
      1) Select the cells that will contain the text *Date, Description, Amount,* and *Ref #*.
      2) Click the down-pointing triangle at the right side of the Align Top Left button on the Tables and Borders toolbar.
      3) At the drop-down palette of choices, click *Align Center* (second option from the left in the second row).

   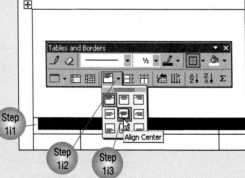

   j. After drawing the table, close the Tables and Borders toolbar.
   k. Key the text in the cells as shown in figure 7.10. Insert text form fields as shown in the figure. (To insert the three text form fields in the Date column, insert the first text form field and then press the Enter key. This moves the insertion point down to the next line within the cell. Continue in this manner until all three text form fields are inserted. Complete similar steps for the three text form fields in the Description, Amount, and Ref # columns.)
   l. After the table is completed, protect the document by clicking the Protect Form button on the Forms toolbar.
   m. Close the Forms toolbar.
2. Save the document and name it XXX EWd C07 Ex07. (Use your initials in place of the *XXX*.)
3. Print and then close XXX EWd C07 Ex07.

FIGURE 7.10 *Exercise 7*

GOOD SAMARITAN HOSPITAL
1201 James Street
St. Louis, MO 62033
(818) 555-1201

Account Number:

Invoice Number: Date:

Date	Description	Amount	Ref #

exercise 8

FILLING IN A TEMPLATE TABLE FORM

1. Create a form with the XXX EWd C07 Ex07 form template by completing the following steps:
   a. Click File and then New.
   b. Click the *General Templates* hyperlink in the New Document Task Pane.
   c. At the Templates dialog box, double-click *XXX C07 Ex07* (where your initials are displayed instead of the *XXX*).
   d. Word displays the form document with the insertion point positioned in the first form field. Fill in the text and check boxes as shown in figure 7.11. (Press the Tab key to move the insertion point to the next form field. Press Shift + Tab to move the insertion point to the preceding form field.)
2. When the form is completed, save the document and name it EWd C07 Ex08.
3. Print and then close EWd C07 Ex08.

GOOD SAMARITAN HOSPITAL
1201 James Street
St. Louis, MO 62033
(818) 555-1201

Account Number: 3423-001

Invoice Number: 342   **Date:** 04/30/02

Date	Description	Amount	Ref #
04/13/02	Bed linens	$984.50	5403
04/17/02	Hospital slippers	$204.00	9422
04/24/02	Hospital gowns	$750.25	6645

Protecting and Securing Documents

In a workgroup, you may want to distribute copies of a document to other members of the group. In some situations, you may want to protect your document and limit the changes that can be made to the document. If you create a document containing sensitive, restricted, or private information, consider protecting the document by saving it as a read-only document or securing it with a password. You can also consider adding a digital signature to a document to ensure that the document is not altered by someone else.

Protecting a Document

Use options at the Protect Document dialog box, shown in figure 7.12, to limit the kinds of changes a reviewer can make to the document. To display this dialog box, click Tools and then Protect Document. At the Protect Document dialog box, choose Tracked changes if you want changes made to the document to appear as tracked changes. If you choose the Comments option, a person can add comments to the document but changes cannot be made to the contents of the document. Choosing the Forms option protects a document to prevent changes to the document except in form fields or unprotected sections.

FIGURE

7.12 *Protect Document Dialog Box*

Read-only and password options are available at the Options dialog box with the Security tab selected or at the Security dialog box. Display the Options dialog box by clicking Tools and then Options. At the Options dialog box, click the Security tab and the dialog box displays as shown in figure 7.13. Display the Security dialog box by clicking the Tools button on the Save As dialog box toolbar and then clicking Security Options. The Security dialog box contains the same options as the Options dialog box with the Security tab selected.

FIGURE

7.13 *Options Dialog Box with the Security Tab Selected*

Protecting a Document with a Password

If you want to protect a document from being modified, key a password in the Password to <u>m</u>odify text box and then press Enter. At the Confirm Password dialog box, key the same password again and then press Enter. Follow the same basic steps to protect a document from being opened, except key a password in the Password to <u>o</u>pen text box. A password can contain up to 15 characters, can include spaces, and is case sensitive.

exercise 9

PROTECTING A DOCUMENT WITH A PASSWORD

1. Open Word Contract.
2. Save the document with Save As and name it EWd C07 Ex09.
3. Protect the document with a password by completing the following steps:
   a. Click <u>T</u>ools and then <u>O</u>ptions.
   b. At the Options dialog box, click the Security tab.
   c. Key your first name in the Password to <u>o</u>pen text box. (If it is longer than 15 characters, abbreviate it. You will not see your name—instead Word inserts asterisks.)
   d. After keying your name, press Enter.
   e. At the Confirm Password dialog box, key your name again (be sure to key it exactly as you did at the Save dialog box—including upper or lowercase letters), and then press Enter.
4. Save and then close EWd C07 Ex09.
5. Open EWd C07 Ex09, keying your password when prompted.
6. Close EWd C07 Ex09.

Step 3c

Identifying a Document as Read-Only

A document can be opened that is read-only. With a read-only document, you can make changes to the document but you cannot save those changes with the same name. Word protects the original document and does not allow you to save the changes to the document with the same name. You can, however, open a document as read-only, make changes to it, and then save the document with a different name. The documents in the folders you copy from the CD are read-only documents.

To indicate the document is a read-only document, display the Options dialog box with the Security tab selected, click the R<u>e</u>ad-only recommended check box, and then click OK. When you open a read-only document, clicking the Save button, or clicking <u>F</u>ile and then <u>S</u>ave causes the Save As dialog box to display where you can key a new name for the document.

1. Open a document, identify it as read-only, and then save it with a new name by completing the following steps:
    a. Display the Open dialog box with *Word Chapter 07E* the active folder.
    b. Open Word Notice 04.
    c. Click <u>T</u>ools and then <u>O</u>ptions.
    d. At the Options dialog box, click the Security tab. (Skip this step if the Security tab is already selected.)
    e. Click the <u>R</u>ead-only recommended check box to insert a check mark.
    f. Click OK to close the Options dialog box.
    g. Save the document with Save As and name it Demonstration.
2. Close the Demonstration document.
3. Open the Demonstration document. (When the message displays asking if you want to open the document as read-only, click the <u>Y</u>es button.)
4. Make the following changes to the Demonstration document:
    a. Change *Tuesday, October 22* to *Wednesday, October 23*.
    b. Change *9:00 – 11:30 a.m.* to *1:30 – 4:00 p.m.*
5. Save the document by completing the following steps:
    a. Click the Save button on the Standard toolbar.
    b. At the Save As dialog box, key **EWd C07 Ex10** and then press Enter.
6. Print and then close EWd C07 Ex10.

Options

User Information	
View	General
Security	Spellin

File encryption options for this do

Password to <u>o</u>pen: [ ]

File sharing options for this docu

Password to <u>m</u>odify: [ ]

☑ Read-only recommended

<u>D</u>igital Signatures... | Pro|

Step 1e

Creating and Applying a Digital Signature

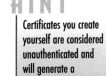
HINT

Certificates you create yourself are considered unauthenticated and will generate a warning.

With Microsoft Authenticode technology offered by Microsoft Office you can apply a digital signature to a document. A digital signature is an encryption-based electronic stamp you can apply to a macro or a document that vouches for its authenticity. Before applying a digital signature, you must obtain a signature. You can obtain a digital signature from a commercial certification authority or you can create your own digital signature using the Selfcert.exe tool. A certificate you create is considered unauthenticated and will generate a security warning.

Before creating and applying a digital signature, you or your system administrator must set up the Microsoft Exchange Server security features on your computer and you must obtain a keyword to your security file to digitally sign a document. Depending on how your system is set up, you might be prevented from using a certificate. Check with your instructor to determine if you should complete the optional exercise 11.

In the optional exercise 11, you will use the Selfcert.exe tool to create a digital signature and then apply that signature to a Word document. When a person opens the document, he or she will be able to view the certificate to identify who has authenticated the document.

(Note: Check with your instructor before completing this exercise. You may not be able to create a digital signature.)

1. Open Internet Explorer.
2. At the Internet Explorer window, click <u>F</u>ile and then <u>O</u>pen.
3. At the Open dialog box, click the B<u>r</u>owse button.
4. At the Microsoft Internet Explorer dialog box, change the Files of type option to *All Files*, and then navigate to the folder containing the SELFCERT.EXE tool. (This tool is probably located in the *C:\Program Files\Microsoft Office\Office* folder.)
5. Double-click the SELFCERT.EXE tool.
6. At the Open dialog box, click OK.
7. At the Create Digital Certificate dialog box, key your first and last name in the <u>Y</u>our name text box, and then click OK.
8. Close the Internet Explorer window.
9. With Word open, open the document named Word Legal 02.
10. Save the document with Save As and name it EWd C07 Ex11.
11. Apply a digital signature to the document by completing the following steps:
    a. Click <u>T</u>ools and then <u>O</u>ptions.
    b. At the Options dialog box, click the Security tab.
    c. Click the <u>D</u>igital Signatures button.
    d. At the Digital Signature dialog box, click the <u>A</u>dd button. (If a message appears asking if you want to continue signing without reviewing the document, click the <u>Y</u>es button.)
    e. At the Select Certificate dialog box, click the certificate in the list box containing your first and last name, and then click OK.
    f. At the Digital Signature dialog box, view the certificate by clicking the <u>V</u>iew Certificate button.
    g. At the Certificate dialog box, look at the certificate information, and then click the OK button.
    h. At the Digital Signature dialog box, click OK.
    i. At the Options dialog box, click OK. (Notice that the document name in the Menu bar is now followed by *(Signed)*.)
12. Close EWd C07 Ex11.

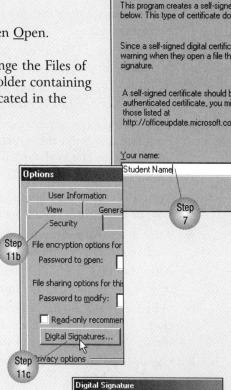

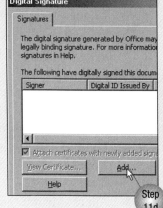

CHAPTER summary

➤ You can create your own forms with Word's form feature, thus eliminating the need for preprinted forms.

➤ A form is created as a template document that contains fill-in fields. Information based on the form template is keyed in the fields when a document is opened.

➤ A form document contains form fields where one of three actions is performed: text is entered, a check box is turned on or off, or information is selected from a drop-down list.

➤ Three basic steps are involved in creating a form: 1) create a form document based on a template and build the structure of the form; 2) insert form fields where information is to be entered at the keyboard; and 3) save the form as a protected document.

➤ Create a template document by clicking Template at the Templates dialog box.

➤ Word provides a Forms toolbar with buttons you can use to easily insert a text box, check box, or other form field into a form template document.

➤ After a template form document is created, protected, and saved, the template can be used to create a personalized form document.

➤ After the form fields have been filled in, the form can be printed in the normal manner, or you can print just the data from the Options dialog box with the Print tab selected.

➤ When a form template is created and then protected, the text in the template cannot be changed. To edit a template document, you must open the document, unprotect it, make the necessary changes, and then protect the document again.

➤ Use options at the Drop-Down Form Field Options dialog box to create form fields with drop-down lists.

➤ Change options for a text form field at the Text Form Field Options dialog box.

➤ Change check box form field options at the Check Box Form Field Options dialog box.

➤ Click the Draw Table button on the Forms toolbar and then draw table lines to create a form.

➤ Use options at the Protect Document dialog box to limit the kinds of changes a reviewer can make to a document.

➤ Specify a document as read-only or apply a password to a document with options at the Options dialog box with the Security tab selected.

➤ Apply a password to a document to protect it from being modified or to protect it from being opened.

➤ Apply a digital signature (an encryption-based electronic stamp) to a document to vouch for the authenticity of the document. Obtain a digital signature from a commercial certification authority or create your own using the Selfcert.exe tool.

COMMANDS review

Command	Mouse /Keyboard
Display New dialog box	Click File, New
Display Text Form Field Options dialog box	Position insertion point on text form field, then click Form Field Options button on Forms toolbar
Display Check Box Form Field Options dialog box	Position insertion point on check box form field, then click Form Field Options button on Forms toolbar
Display Drop-Down Form Field Options dialog box	Position insertion point on drop-down form field, then click Form Field Options button on Forms toolbar
Display Protect Document dialog box	Click Tools, Protect Document

CONCEPTS check

Completion: On a blank sheet of paper, indicate the correct term, command, or number for each item.

1. Generally, a form is created based on this default template document.
2. A fill-in form can include text boxes, check boxes, and/or these.
3. This is the third basic step performed when creating a form document.
4. To display the Text Form Field Options dialog box, position the insertion point on a text form field, and then click this button on the Forms toolbar.
5. To protect a document, click this button on the Forms toolbar.
6. If you want the user to fill in a form by choosing from specific options, create this type of form field.
7. To fill in a check box form field, move the insertion point to the check box, and then press this key on the keyboard.
8. The default setting for a text form field can be changed to *Number, Date, Current time, Calculation*, or this.
9. This is the default setting for the Maximum length option at the Text Form Field Options dialog box.
10. When filling in a form template document, press this key to move the insertion point to the next form field.
11. This Word feature can be used to create a business form such as an invoice or purchase order.
12. Create a password for a document with the Password to open option at this dialog box with the Security tab selected.

SKILLS check

Assessment 1

1. Create the form shown in figure 7.14 as a template document named XXX EWd C07 SA01. Insert text form fields and check box form fields in the document as shown in figure 7.14.
2. Protect the form.
3. Print and then close XXX EWd C07 SA01.

FIGURE

7.14 *Assessment 1*

GOOD SAMARITAN HOSPITAL
APPLICATION FOR FUNDING

Project Title:

Department Applying:

Facility: SFH ☐   LC ☐   SCC ☐

Contact Person(s):

Check the statement(s) that best describe(s) how this proposal will meet the eligibility criteria:

☐ Improved patient care outcomes

☐ Cost reduction

☐ Improved customer satisfaction

☐ Reduced outcome variation

☐ Compliance with quality standards

_____   _____
Signature   Date

_____   _____
Department   Extension

Assessment 2

1. Create a form with the XXX EWd C07 SA01 form template. Insert the following information in the form:

   Project Title: Quality Improvement Project

   Department Applying: Pediatrics

   Facility: (check SFH)

   Contact Person(s): Alyce Arevalo

   Check all of the statements describing the proposal except *Cost reduction*.

2. When the form is completed, save the document and name it EWd C07 SA02.
3. Print and then close EWd C07 SA02.

Assessment 3

1. Create the form shown in figure 7.15 as a template document named XXX EWd C07 SA03. Customize the table as shown in figure 7.15. Insert text form fields and check box form fields in the table shown in the figure.
2. Protect the form.
3. Print and then close XXX EWd C07 SA03.

LIFETIME ANNUITY

PROFESSIONAL LIABILITY INSURANCE APPLICATION

Name:

Address:

County: | **SSN:** | **DOB:**

Type of Deduction:
☐ Flat
☐ Participating

Deduction Amount:
☐ None   ☐ $2,500
☐ $1,000   ☐ $5,000

Check if this insurance is to be part of a program.
☐ AANA   ☐ AAOMS   ☐ APTA-PPS   ☐ None

Check your specific professional occupation.

☐ Chiropractor   ☐ Medical Technician
☐ Dental Anesthesia   ☐ Nurse
☐ Dental Hygienist   ☐ Nurse Practitioner
☐ Dietitian/Nutritionist   ☐ Occupational Therapist
☐ Laboratory Director   ☐ Optometrist
☐ Medical Office Assistant   ☐ Paramedic/EMT

Signature: | **Date:**

Assessment 4

1. Create a form with the XXX EWd C07 SA03 form template. Insert the following information in the form:

   Name: Steven Katori
   Address: 11502 South 32nd Street, Bellevue, WA 98049
   County: King
   SSN: 230-52-9812
   DOB: 11/20/60

   Type of Deduction: (check Flat)
   Deduction Amount: (check $1,000)
   Part of insurance program? (check None)
   Occupation: (check Nurse Practitioner)

2. When the form is completed, save the document and name it EWd C07 SA04.
3. Print and then close EWd C07 SA04.

Assessment 5

1. Delete the XXX Template Document form document created in exercise 1 by completing the following steps:
   a. Click File and then New.
   b. Click the *General Templates* hyperlink in the New Document Task Pane.
   c. At the Templates dialog box, position the arrow pointer on the *XXX Template Document* template form, and then click the *right* mouse button.
   d. From the pop-up menu that displays, click Delete.
   e. At the question asking if you want to delete the document, click Yes.
2. Complete similar steps to delete the other template documents created in this chapter containing your initials.

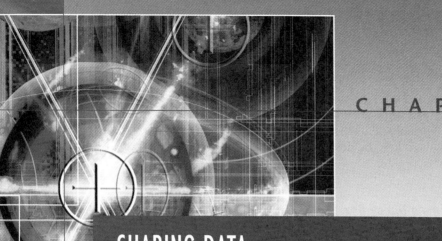

SHARING DATA

PERFORMANCE OBJECTIVES

Upon successful completion of chapter 8, you will be able to:
- Perform calculations on data in a table
- Import data from an Excel worksheet into a chart
- Open, link, and embed an Excel worksheet in a Word document
- Edit a linked worksheet
- Modify an embedded Excel worksheet
- Insert and modify hyperlinks
- Download and save a Web page and image
- Open and edit a saved Web page
- Insert a saved Web image in a Word document
- Send a document on a "round trip"

Word Chapter 08E

Data in one program in Microsoft Office can be seamlessly integrated into another program in Office. For example, data in an Excel worksheet or Excel chart can be inserted in a Word document. Integration is the process of completing a document by adding parts to it from other sources. In this chapter, you will learn how to import data from an Excel worksheet into a chart and how to open, link, and embed an Excel worksheet in a Word document.

Microsoft Office also allows integration of data between programs and Web sites. For example, you can download and save a Web page and then open and edit the Web page in Word. You can also insert hyperlinks that will quickly link you with sites on the Internet or to other documents or files.

Performing Calculations in a Table

You can create a table, which is similar to an Excel spreadsheet, with columns and rows containing data. You can insert values, total numbers, and insert formulas in a table in a manner similar to a spreadsheet. Performing calculations on data in a table is an important aspect of manipulating data.

Numbers in cells in a table can be added, subtracted, multiplied, and divided. In addition, you can calculate averages, percentages, and minimum and maximum

HINT

Click the Insert
Microsoft Excel
Worksheet button to use
Excel functions in Word.

values. Calculations can be performed in a Word table; however, for complex calculations, use a Microsoft Excel worksheet.

To perform a calculation in a table, position the insertion point in the cell where you want the result of the calculation to display, and then click Table and then Formula. This displays the Formula dialog box shown in figure 8.1. At this dialog box, key the desired calculation in the Formula text box, and then click OK.

FIGURE

8.1 **Formula Dialog Box**

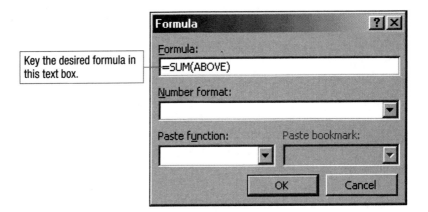

Key the desired formula in this text box.

Four basic operators can be used when writing formulas: the plus sign (+) for addition, the minus sign (hyphen) for subtraction, the asterisk (*) for multiplication, and the forward slash (/) for division. If there are two or more operators in a calculation, Word calculates from left to right. If you want to change the order of calculation, use parentheses around the part of the calculation to be performed first.

In the default formula, the SUM part of the formula is called a *function*. Word provides other functions you can use to write a formula. These functions are available with the Paste function option at the Formula dialog box. For example, you can use the AVERAGE function to average numbers in cells. Examples of how formulas can be written are shown in figure 8.2.

The numbering format can be specified at the Formula dialog box. For example, if you are calculating money amounts, you can specify that the calculated numbers display with two numbers following the decimal point. To specify the numbering format, display the Formula dialog box, and then click the down-pointing triangle to the right of the Number format option. Click the desired formatting at the drop-down list that displays.

Cell E4 is the total price of items.

Cell B4 contains the quantity of items, and cell D4 contains the unit price. The formula for cell E4 is =**B4*D4.** (This formula multiplies the quantity of items in cell B4 by the unit price in cell D4.)

Cell D3 is the percentage of increase of sales from the previous year.

Cell B3 contains the amount of sales for the previous year, and cell C3 contains the amount of sales for the current year. The formula for cell D3 is =**(C3-B3)/C3*100.** (This formula subtracts the amount of sales last year from the amount of sales this year. The remaining amount is divided by the amount of sales this year and then multiplied by 100 to display the product as a percentage.)

Cell E1 is the average of test scores.

Cells A1 through D1 contain test scores. The formula to calculate the average score is =**(A1+B1+C1+D1)/4.** (This formula adds the scores from cells A1 through D1 and then divides that sum by 4.) You can also enter the formula as =**AVERAGE(LEFT)**. The AVERAGE function tells Word to average all entries left of cell E1.

Modifying Table Formats

Modify the table format with options from the Table drop-down menu. With the drop-down menu options, you can perform such functions as insert/delete rows and/or columns, split and/or merge cells, apply autoformats, and customize the table with options from the Table Properties dialog box.

exercise

MODIFYING A TABLE AND CALCULATING SALES

1. Open Word Table 01.
2. Save the document with Save As and name it EWd C08 Ex01.
3. Make the following changes to the table:
   a. Position the insertion point in any cell in the top row and then insert a row above by clicking Table, pointing to Insert, and then clicking Rows Above.
   b. With the new top row selected, merge the cells by clicking Table and then Merge Cells.

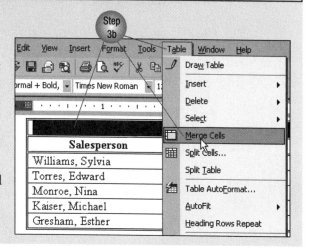

c. Key the company name, **EVERGREEN PRODUCTS**, bolded and centered in the new top cell.

d. Position the insertion point in any cell in the bottom row (row 7) and then insert a row below by clicking T<u>a</u>ble, pointing to <u>I</u>nsert, and then clicking Rows <u>B</u>elow.

e. Position the insertion point in cell A8 (in the new row), turn on bold, and then key **Total**.

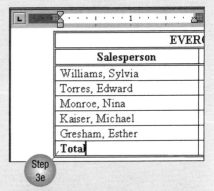

4. Insert a formula in cell B8 that calculates first half total sales by completing the following steps:

a. Position the insertion point in cell B8.

b. Click T<u>a</u>ble and then F<u>o</u>rmula.

c. At the Formula dialog box, make sure =*SUM(ABOVE)* displays in the <u>F</u>ormula text box.

d. Click the down-pointing triangle at the right side of the <u>N</u>umber format text box, and then click the third option from the top of the drop-down list.

e. Click OK to close the dialog box.

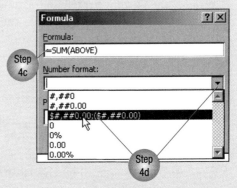

5. Move the insertion point to cell C8 and then insert a formula to calculate total sales for the second half by completing steps similar to those in step 4.

6. Save, print, and then close EWd C08 Ex01.

exercise 2

1. Open Word Table 01.

2. Save the document with Save As and name it EWd C08 Ex02.

3. Insert a column to the right side of the table by completing the following steps:

a. Position the insertion point in any cell in column C.

b. Click T<u>a</u>ble, point to <u>I</u>nsert, and then click Columns to the <u>R</u>ight.

c. Move the insertion point to cell D1 and then key **Average**.

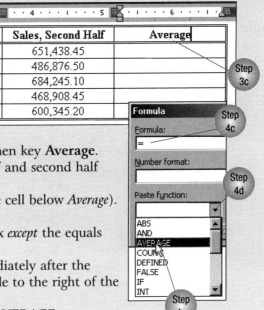

4. Insert a formula in cell D2 to average first half and second half sales by completing the following steps:

a. Position the insertion point in cell D2 (the cell below *Average*).

b. Click T<u>a</u>ble and then F<u>o</u>rmula.

c. Delete the formula in the <u>F</u>ormula text box *except* the equals sign.

d. With the insertion point positioned immediately after the equals sign, click the down-pointing triangle to the right of the <u>P</u>aste function text box.

e. At the drop-down list that displays, click *AVERAGE*.

W O R D

f. With the insertion point positioned between the left and right parentheses, key **left**.

g. Click the down-pointing triangle to the right of the Number format text box and then click the third option from the top at the drop-down list.

h. Click OK or press Enter.

5. Position the insertion point in cell D3 and then press F4 (the Repeat command).

6. Position the insertion point in cell D4 and then press F4.

7. Position the insertion point in cell D5 and then press F4.

8. Position the insertion point in cell D6 and then press F4.

9. Fit the table to the contents by clicking T<u>a</u>ble, pointing <u>A</u>utoFit, and then clicking Auto<u>F</u>it to Contents.

10. Save, print, and then close EWd C08 Ex02.

If changes are made to numbers in cells that are part of a formula, select the result of the calculation, and then press the F9 function key. This recalculates the formula and inserts the new result of the calculation in the cell. You can also recalculate by completing the following steps:

1. Select the number in the cell containing the formula.
2. Click T<u>a</u>ble and then F<u>o</u>rmula.
3. At the Formula dialog box, click OK or press Enter.

RECALCULATING AVERAGE SALES

1. Open EWd C08 Ex02.
2. Save the document with Save As and name it EWd C08 Ex03.
3. Make the following changes to the table:
   a. Change the number in cell C2 from *651,438.45* to *700,375.10*.
   b. Change the number in cell B5 from *412,209.55* to *395,960.50*.
   c. Position the mouse pointer in cell D2, click the left mouse button, and then press F9. (Pressing F9 recalculates the average.)
   d. Click the number in cell D5 and then press F9.
4. Save, print, and then close EWd C08 Ex03.

Importing Data

Microsoft Office suite contains a program named Excel, which is a complete spreadsheet program. While numbers can be calculated in a Word table, for extensive calculations, use Excel. In this section, you will import and modify data from Excel into a chart and import, modify, and create worksheets in a table.

If Excel is not available, you will still be able to complete many of the exercises in this section. Two Excel worksheets have already been created and are available in the *Word Chapter 08E* folder. To import and edit a worksheet, you will need access to Excel. Before completing exercises in this section, check with your instructor.

Importing Data into a Chart

Data in an Excel worksheet can be imported into a chart. To do this, you would complete these basic steps:

Import File

1. Click Insert and then Object.
2. At the Object dialog box with the Create New tab selected, double-click *Microsoft Graph Chart* in the Object type list box. (You will need to scroll down the list to display this program.)
3. With the default datasheet and chart displayed, click the Import File button on the Graph Standard toolbar.
4. At the Import File dialog box, double-click the desired worksheet name.
5. At the Import Data Options dialog box, shown in figure 8.3, specify whether you want the entire worksheet or a specific range of cells, and then click OK.
6. Click in the document screen outside the chart and datasheet to return to the document and view the chart.

FIGURE

8.3 *Import Data Options Dialog Box*

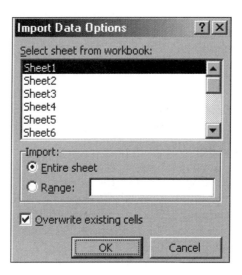

Edit data in a chart created with Excel data in the normal manner. Open Graph by double-clicking the chart. Make the desired changes in the datasheet and then click outside the datasheet to close Graph.

1. Open and save an Excel worksheet by completing the following steps:
   a. Open Excel by clicking the Start button on the Taskbar, pointing to *Programs*, and then clicking *Microsoft Excel*.
   b. In Excel, click the Open button on the Standard toolbar.
   c. At the Open dialog box, make sure the *Word Chapter 08E* folder on your disk is the active folder, and then double-click *Excel Worksheet 01*.
   d. With Excel Worksheet 01 open, click File and then Save As.
   e. At the Save As dialog box, key **Excel C08 Ex04** and then press Enter.
   f. Click File and then Close to close Excel C08 Ex04.
   g. Click File and then Exit to exit Excel.
2. In Word, import Excel C08 Ex04 into a chart by completing the following steps:

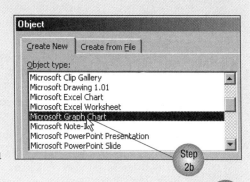

   a. At a clear document screen, click Insert and then Object.
   b. At the Object dialog box with the Create New tab selected, double-click *Microsoft Graph Chart* in the Object type list box. (You will need to scroll down the list to display this program.)
   c. With the default datasheet and chart displayed, click the Import File button on the Graph Standard toolbar.
   d. At the Import File dialog box, make sure the *Word Chapter 08E* folder on your disk is the active folder, and then double-click *Excel C08 Ex04*.
   e. At the Import Data Options dialog box, make sure Entire sheet is selected in the Import section, and then click OK.
   f. Click in the document screen outside the chart and datasheet to return to the document and view the chart.

3. Save the document and name it EWd C08 Ex04.
4. Print EWd C08 Ex04.
5. With EWd C08 Ex04 still open, revise data in the chart by completing the following steps:
   a. Double-click the chart.
   b. Click in the cell containing the number *795,460* and then key **590200**.
   c. Click in the cell containing the number *890,425* and then key **603565**.
   d. Click outside the datasheet to close Graph.
6. Save, print, and then close EWd C08 Ex04.

Importing a Worksheet into a Table

Several methods are available for importing a Microsoft Excel worksheet into a Word document. The methods include opening the worksheet into a Word document, linking the worksheet to a Word document, or embedding the worksheet as an object. Consider the following when choosing a method:

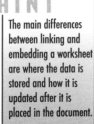
- Open an Excel worksheet in a Word document in situations where the worksheet will not need to be edited.
- Link an Excel worksheet with a Word document in situations where the worksheet is continually updated in Excel and you want the updates to appear in the Word document.
- Embed an Excel worksheet in a Word document in situations where the worksheet will be edited in the Word document.

exercise 5

OPENING A WORKSHEET IN A WORD DOCUMENT

1. At a clear document screen, open an Excel worksheet by completing the following steps:
   a. Click the Open button on the Standard toolbar.
   b. At the Open dialog box, change the Files of type option to *All Files*.
   c. Make sure *Word Chapter 08E* is the active folder.
   d. Double-click Excel Worksheet 01. (You may receive a message telling you that Microsoft Word needs a converter to display this file. If this message displays, you will need to install the converter feature.)
   e. At the Open Worksheet dialog box, make sure *Entire Workbook* displays in the Open document in <u>W</u>orkbook list box, and then click OK.

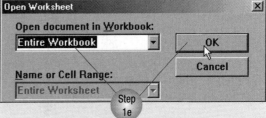

2. Make the following changes to the document:
   a. Press the Enter key three times. (This inserts blank lines above the worksheet and moves the worksheet down the screen.)
   b. Press the up arrow key once.
   c. Click the Bold button on the Formatting toolbar and then key **2002 REGIONAL SALES**.
   d. If gray gridlines do not display in the table, click in any cell in the table, click T<u>a</u>ble, and then Show Gridlines.
   e. Increase the size of the first column so the text does not wrap by completing the following steps:
      1) Position the mouse pointer on the column border between the first and second column (pointer turns into a left- and right-pointing arrow with a double line between).
      2) Hold down the Shift key and the left mouse button.
      3) Drag the column border to the right approximately 0.25 inch.
      4) Release the mouse button and then the Shift key.
3. Save the document with Save As and name it EWd C08 Ex05.
4. Print and then close EWd C08 Ex05. (The worksheet border gridlines will not print.)

2002 REGIONAL SALES

Region	1st Qtr.	2nd Qtr.
Northwest	300,560	320,250
Southwest	579,290	620,485
Northeast	890,355	845,380
Southeast	290,450	320,765

1. In Word, open Word Memo 02
2. Save the memo document and name it EWd C08 Ex06.
3. Link an Excel worksheet with EWd C08 Ex06 by completing the following steps:
   a. Open Excel by clicking the Start button on the Taskbar, pointing to *Programs*, and then clicking *Microsoft Excel*.
   b. In Excel, click the Open button on the Standard toolbar.
   c. At the Open dialog box, make sure the *Word Chapter 08E* folder on your disk is the active folder, and then double-click *Excel Worksheet 02*.
   d. With Excel Worksheet 02 open, click <u>F</u>ile and then Save <u>A</u>s.
   e. At the Save As dialog box, key **Excel C08 Ex06** and then press Enter.
   f. Select cells A1 through D7. (To do this, position the mouse pointer in cell A1, hold down the left mouse button, drag down to cell D7, and then release the mouse button.)
   g. Click the Copy button on the Standard toolbar.
   h. Make Word the active program (click the button on the Taskbar representing the Word document EWd C08 Ex06).
   i. With EWd C08 Ex06 open, position the insertion point between the first and second paragraphs of text in the body of the memo.
   j. Click <u>E</u>dit and then Paste <u>S</u>pecial.
   k. At the Paste Special dialog box, click *Microsoft Excel Worksheet Object* in the As list box.
   l. Click Paste <u>l</u>ink.
   m. Click OK to close the dialog box. (If you only see a border with no numbers inside, display the Options dialog box with the View tab selected and remove the check mark from the <u>P</u>icture placeholders check box, and then close the dialog box.)

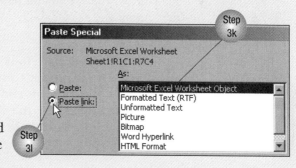

4. Save, print, and then close EWd C08 Ex06. (The worksheet border lines will not print.)
5. Exit Word.
6. With Excel the active program, close Excel C08 Ex06.
7. Exit Excel by clicking <u>F</u>ile and then E<u>x</u>it.

1. Open the Microsoft Excel program.
2. Open and edit Excel C08 Ex06 by completing the following steps:
   a. In Excel, click the Open button on the Standard toolbar.
   b. At the Open dialog box, make sure *Word Chapter 08E* on your disk is the active folder, and then double-click *Excel C08 Ex06*.
   c. Change some of the numbers in cells by completing the following steps:
      1) Position the mouse pointer (thick white plus sign) over the cell containing the number *$218,335* (cell C3) and then click the left mouse button.
      2) Key **230578** (over *$218,335*).
      3) Press the Enter key. (Notice that the number in cell D3 [the Difference column] automatically changed. This is because the cell contains a formula.)
      4) Change the number in cell B5 from *181,329* to *195,200*.
      5) Change the number in cell C7 from *197,905* to *188,370*. (Be sure to press the Enter key.)
   d. Save the revised worksheet by clicking the Save button on the Standard toolbar.
3. Close Excel C08 Ex06 by clicking File and then Close.
4. Exit Microsoft Excel by clicking File and then Exit.
5. Open Word and then open EWd C08 Ex06. (Notice how the numbers in the worksheet are updated to reflect the changes made to Excel C08 Ex06.)
6. Save the document with Save As and name it EWd C08 Ex07.
7. Print and then close EWd C08 Ex07.

	A	B	C	D
1		SALES FIGURES		
2	**State**	**Projected**	**Actual**	**Difference**
3	Florida	$238,450	230578	($20,115)
4	Georgia	$198,549	$210,698	$12,149
5	Alabama	$181,329	$175,320	($6,009)
6	Louisiana	$195,480	$156,700	($38,780)
7	Mississippi	$189,450	$197,905	$8,455

Step 2c2

HINT

Linking can help minimize the size of a Word document.

Linking does not have to be between two different programs—documents created in the same program also can be linked. For example, you can create an object in a Word document and then link it with another Word document (or several Word documents). If a change is made to the object in the original document, the linked object in the other document (or documents) is automatically updated.

1. At a clear Word document screen, open Word Memo 03.
2. Save the document and name it EWd C08 Linked Doc 1.
3. Change to the Print Layout view and then change the Zoom to *Whole Page*.
4. With EWd C08 Linked Doc 1 still open, open Word Table 04. Save the document with Save As and name it Word Table C08.
5. Copy and link the table by completing the following steps:
   a. With Word Table C08 the active document, select the table.
   b. Click the Copy button on the Standard toolbar.
   c. Click the button on the Taskbar representing EWd C08 Linked Doc 1.

d. With EWd C08 Linked Doc 1 the active document, click Edit and then Paste Special.

e. At the Paste Special dialog box, click *Microsoft Word Document Object* in the As list box, and then click Paste link.

f. Click OK to close the dialog box.

g. Move the table by completing the following steps:

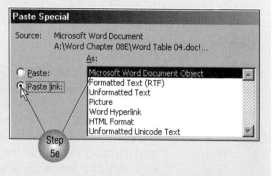

1) Make sure the Drawing toolbar displays.

2) Click the table once to select it (black sizing handles display around the table).

3) Click the Draw button on the Drawing toolbar, point to Text Wrapping, and then click Top and Bottom. (This change the sizing handles to white circles.)

4) Drag the table so it is positioned between the paragraph of text in the memo and the reference initials.

h. Change the Zoom back to *100%*.

6. Save and then print EWd C08 Linked Doc 01.

7. Change the name and title after TO: from *Kyle Suzenevich, Manager, Novelty Items* to *Regina Stewart, Manager, Catalog Services*.

8. Save the document with Save As and name it EWd C08 Linked Doc 2.

9. Print and then close EWd C08 Linked Doc 2.

10. Deselect the table and then print and close Word Table C08.

exercise 9

CHANGING DATA IN A LINKED OBJECT IN A WORD DOCUMENT

1. With Word the active program, open Word Table C08.

2. Make the following changes to the table in the document:

a. Change the following quantities in the On-Hand Qty. column:
Change *450* to *365*
Change *500* to *425*
Change *230* to *170*
Change *400* to *310*
Change *140* to *106*

b. Change the following quantities in the Weekly Usage column:
Change *85* to *67*
Change *60* to *45*
Change *34* to *20*

3. Save the edited document with the same name (Word Table C08).

4. Print and then close Word Table C08.

5. Open EWd C08 Linked Doc 1.

6. Change the date from *March 6, 2003* to *March 13, 2003*.
7. Save, print, and then close EWd C08 Linked Doc 1.
8. Open EWd C08 Linked Doc 2.
9. Change the date from *March 6, 2003* to *March 13, 2003*.
10. Save, print, and then close EWd C08 Linked Doc 2.

Insert Microsoft Excel Worksheet

Embed an Excel worksheet in a Word document using the Insert Microsoft Excel Worksheet button located on the Standard toolbar. Click this button and a grid displays below the button. This grid is similar to the grid that displays when you click the Insert Table button. Select the desired number of rows and columns and then click the left mouse button. This opens the Microsoft Excel program and inserts the worksheet in the document. Figure 8.4 shows the embedded worksheet you will create in exercise 10. The Excel toolbars and Formula bar are identified in the figure.

FIGURE

8.4 *Embedded Excel Worksheet*

When an Excel worksheet is inserted in a Word document using the Insert Microsoft Excel Worksheet button, Excel opens and all of the toolbars and Excel features are available for creating, modifying, or editing the worksheet. After creating or editing the worksheet, return to Word by clicking in the document screen, outside the worksheet.

WORD

exercise 10

1. At a clear document screen, click the Center button on the Formatting toolbar, click the Bold button, and then key the three lines of text shown at the beginning of figure 8.5.

2. With the insertion point positioned a triple space below the text (centered), create the text shown in the table in the figure as an Excel worksheet by completing the following steps:

    a. Click the Insert Microsoft Excel Worksheet button on the Standard toolbar.

    b. Drag down and to the right until four rows and four columns are selected on the grid. (The numbers below the grid display as *4 x 4 Spreadsheet*.)

    c. Click the left mouse button.

    d. Key the text in the cells as shown in figure 8.5. (Key the text in the cells in the same manner as you would in a table.)

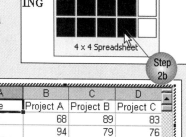

    e. When all of the text is entered in the worksheet, click in the document screen outside the worksheet.

3. Save the document and name it EWd C08 Ex10.

4. Print and then close EWd C08 Ex10.

F I G U R E

8.5 *Exercise 10*

MICROSOFT EXCEL TRAINING

Intermediate Session

Project Scores

Name	Project A	Project B	Project C
Riley	68	89	83
Kuo	94	79	76
Furgeson	54	76	56

One of the advantages to embedding an Excel worksheet in a Word document is the ability to modify the worksheet. To modify an embedded worksheet, open the Word document containing the worksheet, and then double-click the worksheet. This opens Microsoft Excel and provides all of the toolbars and editing features of Excel.

exercise 11

1. Open EWd C08 Ex10.
2. Save the document with Save As and name it EWd C08 Ex11.
3. Add a column to the worksheet, insert a calculation to average the project scores, and apply formatting by completing the following steps:
   a. Double-click the worksheet. (This opens Microsoft Excel.)
   b. Increase the size of the worksheet so columns E and F display by completing the following steps:
      1) Position the mouse pointer on the small square black sizing handle that displays in the middle at the right side of the worksheet until the pointer turns into a double-headed arrow pointing left and right.
      2) Hold down the left mouse button, drag to the right so the right border jumps twice (approximately 2 inches), and then release the mouse button.

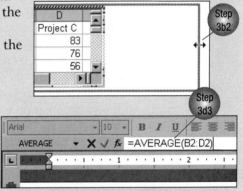

   c. Click once in cell E1 and then key **Average**.
   d. Insert a formula to calculate the average of the project scores by completing the following steps:
      1) Click once in cell E2.
      2) Click inside the white text box that displays immediately after an equals sign on the Formula bar. (The Formula bar displays above the Ruler. See figure 8.4.)
      3) Key **=AVERAGE(B2:D2)** and then press Enter.
   e. Copy the formula down to cells E3 and E4 by completing the following steps:
      1) Click once in cell E2 to make it active.
      2) Position the mouse pointer on the small black square that displays in the lower right corner of cell E2 until the pointer turns into a thin black cross. (The small black square is called the "fill handle.")

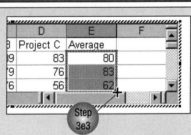

      3) With the mouse pointer displayed as a thin black cross, hold down the left mouse button, drag down to cell E4, and then release the mouse button.
   f. Decrease the size of the worksheet so column F is no longer visible by completing the following steps:
      1) Position the mouse pointer on the small square black sizing handle that displays in the middle at the right side of the worksheet until the pointer turns into a double-headed arrow pointing left and right.
      2) Hold down the left mouse button, drag to the left so the right border jumps once, and then release the mouse button.
   g. Apply the following formatting to the cells:
      1) Select cells A1 through E1.
      2) Click the Bold button and then the Center button on the Formatting toolbar.
      3) Select cells B2 through E4.
      4) Click the Center button on the Formatting toolbar.
   h. Click in the document screen outside the worksheet.
4. Save, print, and then close EWd C08 Ex11.

Creating Hyperlinks

A hyperlink is text or an object that you click to go to a different file, an HTML page on the Internet, or an HTML page on an intranet. Create a hyperlink in a Word document by keying the address of an existing Web page such as www.emcp.com. By default, the automatic formatting of hyperlinks is turned on and the Web address is formatted as a hyperlink (text is underlined and the color changes to blue). (You can turn off the automatic formatting of hyperlinks. To do this, display the AutoCorrect dialog box with the AutoFormat As You Type tab selected, and then remove the check mark from the Internet and network paths with hyperlinks check box.)

You can also create a customized hyperlink by selecting text or an image in a document and then clicking the Insert Hyperlink button on the Standard toolbar. At the Insert Hyperlink dialog box shown in figure 8.6, key the file name or Web site address in the Address text box, and then click OK. You can also use the Look in option to browse to the desired folder and file and then double-click the file name. To link to the specified file or Web page, position the mouse pointer on the hyperlink, hold down the Ctrl key, and then click the left mouse button.

Insert Hyperlink

FIGURE

8.6 *Insert Hyperlink Dialog Box*

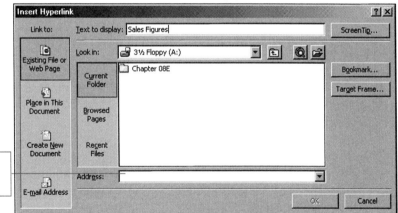

Key the file name or Web address site in this text box.

You can modify or change hyperlink text or the hyperlink destination. To do this, right-click the hyperlink, and then click Edit Hyperlink. At the Edit Hyperlink dialog box, make any desired changes, and then close the dialog box. The Edit Hyperlink dialog box contains the same options as the Insert Hyperlink dialog box.

HINT

Remove a hyperlink from text by right-clicking the hyperlink and then clicking Remove Hyperlink.

1. Open Word Memo 02.
2. Save the document with Save As and name it EWd C08 Ex12.
3. Create a hyperlink that will display the Excel Worksheet 02 spreadsheet in the Excel program by completing the following steps:
   a. Position the insertion point between the first and second paragraphs in the body of the memo.
   b. Key **Sales Figures**.
   c. Select *Sales Figures*.
   d. Click the Insert Hyperlink button on the Standard toolbar.
   e. At the Insert Hyperlink dialog box, click the down-pointing triangle at the right side of the Look in option and then navigate to the *Word Chapter 08E* folder on your disk.
   f. Double-click *Excel Worksheet 02* in the *Word Chapter 08E* folder on your disk. (This closes the Insert Hyperlink dialog box and displays the *Sales Figures* text as a hyperlink in the document.)
4. Display Excel Worksheet 02 by positioning the mouse pointer on the hyperlink text *Sales Figures*, holding down the Ctrl key, clicking the left mouse button, and then releasing the Ctrl key.
5. After looking at the data in Excel Worksheet 02, exit Excel by clicking File and then Exit.
6. Modify the hyperlink text by completing the following steps:
   a. Position the mouse pointer on the *Sales Figures* hyperlink, click the *right* mouse button, and then click Edit Hyperlink.
   b. At the Edit Hyperlink dialog box, select the text *Sales Figures* in the Text to display text box and then key **2002 Projected and Actual Sales**.
   c. Click OK.
7. At the memo document, position the mouse pointer over the *2002 Projected and Actual Sales* hyperlink, hold down the Ctrl key, click the left mouse button, and then release the Ctrl key.
8. Exit Excel by clicking File and then Exit.
9. Save, print, and then close EWd C08 Ex12.

In exercise 12, you created a hyperlink from a Word document to an Excel worksheet. You can also create a hyperlink in a Word document that will connect you to a specific Web site on the Internet.

1. Open Beltway Home Page.
2. Save the document with Save As and name it EWd C08 Ex13.
3. Apply a theme to the document by completing the following steps:
   a. Click Format and then Theme.
   b. At the Theme dialog box, click *Blends* in the Choose a Theme list box.
   c. Click OK.
4. Create a hyperlink so that clicking *Atlas Van Lines* displays the Atlas Van Lines Web page by completing the following steps:
   a. Select the text *Atlas Van Lines* that displays toward the end of the document (after a bullet).
   b. Click the Insert Hyperlink button on the Standard toolbar.
   c. At the Insert Hyperlink dialog box, key **www.atlasvanlines.com** in the Address text box.
   d. Click OK. (This changes the color of the *Atlas Van Lines* text and also adds underlining to the text.)
5. Complete steps similar to those in step 4 to create a hyperlink from *Bekins* to www.bekins.com.
6. Complete steps similar to those in step 4 to create a hyperlink from *United Van Lines* to www.unitedvanlines.com.
7. Save EWd C08 Ex13.
8. Jump to the hyperlink sites by completing the following steps:
   a. Make sure you are connected to the Internet.
   b. Hold down the Ctrl key, position the mouse pointer on the *Atlas Van Lines* hyperlink that displays toward the end of the document, click the left mouse button, and then release the Ctrl key.
   c. When the Atlas Van Lines Web page displays, scroll through the page, and then click on a hyperlink that interests you.
   d. After looking at this next page, click File and then Close.
   e. At the EWd C08 Ex13 document, hold down the Ctrl key, and then click the *Bekins* hyperlink.
   f. After viewing the Bekins home page, click File and then Close.
   g. At the EWd C08 Ex13 document, hold down the Ctrl key, and then click the *United Van Lines* hyperlink.
   h. After viewing the United Van Lines home page, click File and then Close.
9. Print and then close EWd C08 Ex 13.

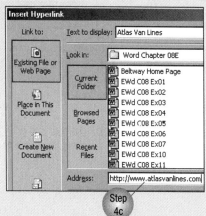

Step 4c

Downloading and Saving Web Pages and Images

The image(s) and/or text that displays when you open a Web page as well as the Web page itself can be saved as a separate file. This separate file can be viewed, printed, or inserted in another file. The information you want to save in a separate file is downloaded from the Internet by Internet Explorer and saved in a folder of your choosing with the name you specify. Copyright laws protect much of the information on the Internet. Before using information downloaded from the Internet, check the site for restrictions. If you do use information, make sure you properly cite the source.

To save a Web page as a file, display the desired page, click File on the Internet Explorer Menu bar, and then click Save As at the drop-down menu. At the Save Web Page dialog box, specify the folder where you want to save the Web page. Select the text in the File name text box, key a name for the page, and then press Enter or click the Save button. A Web page is saved as an HTML file. A folder is automatically created when the Web page is saved. All images in the Web page are saved as separate files and inserted in the folder.

Save a specific Web image by right-clicking the image and then clicking Save Picture As at the pop-up menu. At the Save Picture dialog box, key a name for the image in the File name text box and then press Enter.

exercise 14 — SAVING A WEB PAGE AND IMAGE AS SEPARATE FILES

1. Make sure you are connected to the Internet and then use Internet Explorer (or your default browser) to search for Web sites related to *Yellowstone National Park*.
2. When the search engine displays a list of Yellowstone National Park sites, choose a site that contains information about the park and also contains at least one image of the park.
3. Save the Web page as a file by completing the following steps:
   a. Click File on the Internet Explorer Menu bar and then click Save As at the drop-down menu. (These steps may vary if you are using a different browser.)
   b. At the Save Web Page dialog box, navigate (using the Save in option) to the *Word Chapter 08E* folder on your disk.
   c. Select the text in the File name text box, key **Yellowstone Web Page** and then press Enter.
4. Save the image as a separate file by completing the following steps:
   a. Right-click the image of the park. (The image that displays may vary from what you see to the right.)
   b. At the shortcut menu that displays, click Save Picture As.
   c. At the Save Picture dialog box, change the location to *Word Chapter 08E* folder on your disk.
   d. Select the text in the File name text box, key **Yellowstone Image**, and then press Enter.
5. Close Internet Explorer (or your default browser).

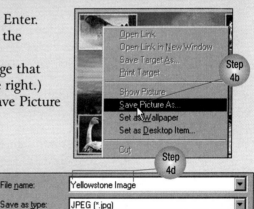

Opening and Editing a Saved Web Page

A Web page is saved as an HTML file. To open a Web page in Word, display the drive and/or folder where the page is located and then click the Open button on the Standard toolbar. At the Open dialog box, change the Files of type option to *All Files*, and then double-click the desired Web page file in the list box. Edit and save a Web page file in the normal manner.

exercise 15

OPENING AND EDITING A SAVED WEB PAGE

1. At a clear document Word screen, open the Yellowstone Web Page file by completing the following steps:
   a. Click the Open button on the Standard toolbar.
   b. At the Open dialog box, click the down-pointing triangle at the right side of the Files of type option box, and then click *All Files* at the drop-down list.
   c. Change to the *Word Chapter 08E* folder on your disk.
   d. Double-click *Yellowstone Web Page* in the list box. (Make sure you double-click the Yellowstone Web Page file and *not* the folder.)
2. Move the insertion point to the end of the Yellowstone Web page file.
3. Key your first and last name, press Enter, and then insert the current date.
4. Save the Web page file with Save As and name it EWd C08 Ex16.
5. Print and then close EWd C08 Ex16.

Inserting a Saved Image

Insert a Web image in a Word document by clicking the Insert Picture button on the Drawing toolbar or by clicking Insert, pointing to Picture, and then clicking From File. At the Insert Picture dialog box, specify the drive and/or folder where the image is located, and then double-click the image in the list box.

exercise 16

INSERTING A SAVED WEB IMAGE

1. At a clear document screen, insert a heading by completing the following steps:
   a. Click the Center button on the Formatting toolbar.
   b. Click the Bold button.
   c. Change the font size to 14 points.
   d. Key **Yellowstone National Park Image**.
   e. Press the Enter key twice.
2. Insert the Yellowstone image by completing the following steps:
   a. Click Insert on the Menu bar, point to Picture, and then click From File.
   b. At the Insert Picture dialog box, change the Look in option to the *Word Chapter 08E* folder on your disk, and then double-click *Yellowstone Image*.

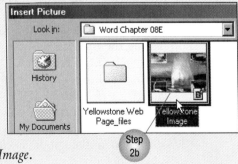

3. Save the document and name it EWd C08 Ex16.
4. Print and then close EWd C08 Ex16.

Sending a Document on a "Round Trip"

If you send a document on a company intranet, the person receiving the document will probably open and edit the document in the program in which it was created. For example, if you are sending a Word document to a colleague, he or she will open and edit the document in Word.

Situations may arise where you need to send a document to a person who does not have the program in which the document was created. In this situation, save the document in HTML file format. To do this, click File and then Save as Web Page. At the Save As dialog box, key a name for the document in the File name text box, and then click the Save button.

The person receiving the document does not need the originating program to view the document. The receiver can open the document in his or her Web browser (rather than the originating program). When the document is returned to you and opened in the originating program, all of the formatting and functionality of the document is retained. Office refers to this process as a "round trip." The document is saved in a specific program, saved in HTML file format, viewed in a Web browser, and then returned to the originating program without losing any formatting or functionality.

Edit with Microsoft Word

If the person receiving the document has the originating program, the receiver can open the document, edit it, and then save it. When you open a Word document in Internet Explorer, an Edit with Microsoft Word button is inserted on the Internet Explorer toolbar. Click this button and the document is opened in the Word program.

exercise 17

SENDING A DOCUMENT ON A ROUND TRIP

1. Open Word Contract.
2. Save the document as a Web page (in HTML file format) by completing the following steps:
   a. Click File and then Save as Web Page.
   b. At the Save As dialog box, key **Agreement** and then press Enter.
3. Close the Agreement Web page document.
4. Suppose that the Agreement Web page document is sent to you. Complete the following steps to view the document in your Web browser, open it in Word, make some changes, and then save the document again by completing the following steps:
   a. Close Microsoft Word.
   b. At your desktop, double-click the *Internet Explorer* icon.
   c. At the Internet Explorer window, click File and then Open.
   d. At the Open dialog box, click the Browse button.

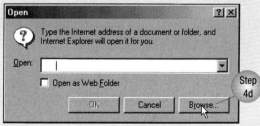

Step 4d

e. At the Microsoft Internet Explorer dialog box, navigate to the *Word Chapter 08E* folder on your disk, and then double-click *Agreement*.

f. At the Open dialog box, click OK. (This opens the Agreement Web page document in the Internet Explorer window.)

g. After viewing the document in Internet Explorer, edit the document by completing the following steps:

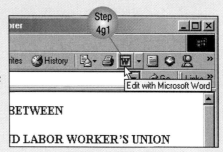

1) Click the Edit with Microsoft Word button on the Internet Explorer toolbar.

2) With the document open in Word, make the following changes:

a) Search for all occurrences of *LABOR WORKER'S UNION* and replace with *UNITED MANUFACTURER'S UNION*.

b) Search for all occurrences of *LWU* and replace with *UMU*.

c) Apply a theme of your choosing to the Web page document. *(Hint: Display the Theme dialog box by clicking Format and then Theme.)*

3) Save the document with the same name.

h. Close the Agreement Web page document and then exit Word.

i. Close the Internet Explorer window.

5. Open Word and then open the Agreement Web page document. (At the Open dialog box, make sure you change the Files of type option to *All Files* so the Agreement Web page document will display. With the Agreement Web page document open, notice that the changes you made to the document earlier are reflected in the document.)

6. Save the Agreement Web page document as a regular Word document by completing the following steps:

a. Click File and then Save As.

b. At the Save As dialog box, change the Save as type option to *Word Document*.

c. Select the text in the File name text box, key **Edited Agreement**, and then press the Enter key.

7. Print and then close the Edited Agreement document.

CHAPTER summary

➤ Calculate numbers in a table by inserting a formula in a cell at the Formula dialog box.

➤ Four basic operators are used when writing a formula: the plus sign for addition, the minus sign for subtraction, the asterisk for multiplication, and the forward slash for division.

➤ Recalculate a formula by clicking in the cell in the table containing the formula and then pressing F9.

➤ You can import data from an Excel worksheet into a chart in a Word document with Microsoft Graph Chart. This feature is available at the Object dialog box with the Create New tab selected.

➤ Several methods are available for importing a Microsoft Excel worksheet into a Word document such as opening the worksheet into a Word document, linking the worksheet to a Word document, or embedding the worksheet as an object.

➤ Open an Excel worksheet in a Word document in situations where the worksheet will not need to be edited. Link an Excel worksheet with a Word document in situations where the worksheet is continually updated. Embed an Excel worksheet in a Word document in situations where the worksheet will be edited in the Word document.

➤ A hyperlink is text or an object that you click to go to a different file or an HTML file on the Internet or on an intranet.

➤ To create a custom hyperlink, select the desired text in the document, and then click the Insert Hyperlink button on the Standard toolbar. At the Insert Hyperlink dialog box, make any desired changes, and then close the dialog box.

➤ Link to a specified file or site by positioning the mouse pointer on the hyperlink, holding down the Ctrl key, and then clicking the left mouse button.

➤ Modify or change hyperlink text or the hyperlink destination by right-clicking the hyperlink and then clicking Edit Hyperlink.

➤ You can save a Web page and/or text and images in a Web page as separate files. Save a Web page by clicking File on the Internet Explorer Menu bar and then clicking Save As. Save an image as a separate picture file by right-clicking the image and then clicking Save Picture As at the pop-up menu.

➤ Sending a document on a "round trip" means to save a document in a specific program, save it in HTML file format, view the document in a Web browser, and then return the document to the originating program without losing any formatting or functionality.

COMMANDS review

Command	Mouse/Keyboard
Display Formula dialog box	Table, Formula
Recalculate numbers in a table	Click in cell containing number, press F9
Display Object dialog box	Insert, Object
Display Insert Hyperlink dialog box	Click Insert Hyperlink button on Standard toolbar
Display Edit Hyperlink dialog box	Right-click hyperlink, click Edit Hyperlink

CONCEPTS check

Completion: On a blank sheet of paper, indicate the correct term, command, or symbol for each numbered item.

1. This is the operator for multiplication that is used when writing a formula in a table.
2. This is the operator for division that is used when writing a formula in a table.
3. This is the formula to multiply A1 by B1.
4. Recalculate a formula by clicking in the cell in the table containing the formula and then pressing this key.
5. The Microsoft Graph Chart feature is available at the Object dialog box with this tab selected.
6. Do this to an Excel worksheet you want inserted in a Word document when the worksheet will be continually updated.
7. Do this to an Excel worksheet you want inserted in a Word document when the worksheet will be edited in Word.
8. This term refers to text or an object that you click to go to a different file or an HTML file on the Internet or on an intranet.
9. To save a Web page as a file, display the desired page, click File on the Internet Explorer Menu bar, and then click this option at the drop-down menu.
10. Save a specific Web image by right-clicking the image and then clicking this option at the pop-up menu.
11. Sending a document on this means to save the document in a specific program, save it in HTML file format, view it in a Web browser, and then return it to the originating program without losing any formatting or functionality.

SKILLS check

Assessment 1

1. Open Word Table 05.
2. Save the document with Save As and name it EWd C08 SA01.
3. Insert a formula in cells D3, D4, D4, D5, D6, D7, and D8 that totals the first and second half sales.
4. Save, print, and then close EWd C08 SA01.

Assessment 2

1. Open Word Table 06.
2. Save the document with Save As and name it EWd C08 SA02.
3. Make the following changes to the table:
   a. Insert a new row at the top of the table.
   b. Merge the cells in the new row.
   c. Key **FUND RAISING EVENTS** centered and bolded in the new cell.
   d. Insert a formula in cells D3, D4, D5, and D6 that calculates the net profit. *(Hint: The Net Profit is Revenue minus Costs. At the Formula dialog box, change the Number format to the third option from the top of the drop-down list.)*
4. Save, print, and then close EWd C08 SA02.

Assessment 3

1. In Word, import Excel Worksheet 04 into a chart using Microsoft Graph Chart.
2. Save the document with Save As and name it EWd C08 SA03.
3. Print and then close EWd C08 SA03.

Assessment 4

1. Open Word Memo 04.
2. Save the document and name it EWd C08 SA04.
3. Open Excel and then open Excel Worksheet 03.
4. Save the worksheet with Save As and name it Excel C08 SA04.
5. Select cells A1 through C5, copy the cells, and then link the cells so the worksheet displays in EWd C08 SA04 between the first and second paragraphs. (Make sure you the Paste Special dialog box [and select the Paste link option in the dialog box].)
6. Save, print, and then close EWd C08 SA04.
7. Make Excel the active program, close Excel C08 SA04, and then exit Excel.

Assessment 5

1. Open the Microsoft Excel program.
2. Open Excel C08 SA04 and then make the following changes:
   a. Change the percentage in cell B3 from *8.3* to *8.4*.
   b. Change the percentage in cell C3 from *7.4* to *8.1*.
   c. Change the percentage in cell B5 from *17.4* to *17.3*.
   d. Change the percentage in cell C5 from *17.6* to *17.0*.

e. Save the revised worksheet by clicking the Save button on the Excel Standard toolbar.
3. Close Excel C08 SA04.
4. Exit Microsoft Excel.
5. Open Word and then open EWd C08 SA04. (Notice how the numbers in the worksheet are updated to reflect the changes made to Excel C08 SA04.)
6. Save the document with Save As and name it EWd C08 SA05.
7. Print and then close EWd C08 SA05.

Assessment 6

1. Open Word Memo 05.
2. Save the document with Save As and name it EWd C08 SA06.
3. Create the hyperlink *Total Sales* between the paragraph of text and the reference initials in the memo that will display the Excel Worksheet 04 spreadsheet (in the *Word Chapter 08E* folder on your disk) in the Excel program.
4. Click the *Total Sales* hyperlink to display Excel Worksheet 04 in Excel.
5. After looking at the data in Excel Worksheet 04, exit Excel.
6. Save, print, and then close EWd C08 SA06.

Assessment 7

1. Make sure you are connected to the Internet.
2. Search for information on mountain climbing.
3. Find a site that interests you and that contains at least one image (picture).
4. Save the Web page as a file named Climbing Web Page.
5. Save the image as a picture and name it Climbing Image. *(Hint: Right-click the image and then click* Save Picture As *at the pop-up menu.)*
6. Close Internet Explorer.

Assessment 8

1. At a clear document Word screen, open the Climbing Web Page file.
2. Move the insertion point to the end of the Web page and then insert your first and last name, the current date, and the current time.
3. Save, print, and then close Climbing Web Page.

Assessment 9

1. At a clear document screen, complete the following steps:
   a. Key a heading that is centered, bolded, and set in 14-point size and describes the Climbing Image.
   b. Insert the Climbing Image into the document below the heading. *(Hint: Click* Insert, Picture, *and then click* From File *to insert the image.)*
2. Save the document and name it EWd C08 SA09.
3. Print and then close EWd C08 SA09.

WORKPLACE Ready

ASSESSING proficiencies

In this unit, you learned to prepare specialized documents such as fill-in forms and documents with specialized tables such as tables of content, indexes, figures, and tables of authorities. You also learned about features for sharing documents within a workgroup and sharing data between programs.

(Before completing unit assessments, delete the Word Chapter 08E *folder on your disk. Next, copy to your disk the* Word Unit 02E *subfolder from the CD that accompanies this textbook and then make* Word Unit 02PE *the active folder.)*

Assessment 1

1. Open Word Survey.
2. Save the document with Save As and name it EWd U02 PA01.
3. Make changes to the document and track the changes by completing the following steps:
   a. Turn on tracking.
   b. Insert , *coursework,* between *study* and the word *and* in paragraph 2.
   c. Insert *computer* between *Using* and *technology* in paragraph 3.
   d. Display the Options dialog box with the User Information tab selected, change the name to *Justin Renquist* and the initials to *JR,* and then close the dialog box.
   e. Delete the words *knowledge and* in paragraph 2.
   f. Insert *and analyzing* at the end of the sentence in paragraph 4 (between *questioning* and the period).
   g. Turn off tracking.
   h. Display the Options dialog box with the User Information tab selected, change back to the information that displayed before you keyed *Justin Renquist* and the initials *JR,* and then close the dialog box.
4. Save, print, and then close EWd U02 PA01.

Assessment 2

1. Open EWd U02 PA01.
2. Save the document with Save As and name it EWd U02 PA02.
3. Accept or reject the following changes in the document:
   a. Reject the change deleting the words *knowledge and.*
   b. Accept the change inserting , *coursework,* between *study* and the word *and* in the second paragraph.

    c. Reject the change inserting *computer* between *Using* and *technology* in the third paragraph.

    d. Accept the change inserting *and analyzing* at the end of the sentence in the fourth paragraph (between *questioning* and the period).

4. Save, print, and then close EWd U02 PA02.

Assessment 3

1. Open Word Legal 03.
2. Save the document with Save As and name it EWd U02 PA03.
3. Create a version of the original document by completing the following steps:
    a. Display the Versions in EWd U02 PA03 dialog box.
    b. Click the <u>S</u>ave Now button to display the Save Version dialog box.
    c. At the Save Version dialog box, key **First draft of Notice** in the <u>C</u>omments on version text box.
    d. Click OK to close the dialog box.
4. Make the following editing changes to the document:
    a. Insert , *attorneys at law,* after *Garcetti & Donovan* in the paragraph that begins *YOU AND EACH OF YOU....*
    b. Insert the word *waive* before the words *the Sixty-Day Rule* in the paragraph that begins *YOU AND EACH OF YOU....*
    c. Delete the word *heretofore* in paragraph 4.
5. Create another version of the document with the comment *Second draft of Notice.*
6. Make the following editing changes to the document:
    a. Insert the words *in this Summons* at the end of the sentence in paragraph 4 (between *requested* and the period).
    b. Delete paragraph 3.
    c. Renumber paragraph 4 to paragraph 3.
7. Create another version of the document with the comment *Third draft of Notice.*
8. Open the First draft of Notice version of the document.
9. After viewing the first draft version, save the version as a separate document named Notice First Draft.
10. Close the Notice First Draft document.
11. Maximize the EWd U02 PA03 window.
12. Delete the second draft version of the document.
13. Save the document again with the same name (EWd U02 PA03).
14. Compare the Notice First Draft document with the latest version.
15. Save the document with Save As and name it EWd U02 Com Doc.
16. Print and then close EWd U02 Com Doc.
17. Close EWd U02 PA03.

Assessment 4

1. Open Word Report 06.
2. Save the document with Save As and name it Master Doc U02.
3. Make the following changes to the document:
   a. Change to the Outline view.
   b. Apply the following heading styles to the specified headings:

SECTION 1: COMPUTERS IN COMMUNICATIONS	= Heading 1
Telecommunications	= Heading 2
Publishing	= Heading 2
News Services	= Heading 2
SECTION 2: COMPUTERS IN ENTERTAINMENT	= Heading 1
Television and Film	= Heading 2
Home Entertainment	= Heading 2
SECTION 3: COMPUTERS IN PUBLIC LIFE	= Heading 1
Government	= Heading 2
Law	= Heading 2
Education	= Heading 2

   c. Make sure the Master Document View button on the Outlining toolbar is active.
   d. Create subdocuments by selecting the entire document and then clicking the Create Subdocument button on the Outlining toolbar.
4. Save and then close Master Doc U02
5. Open Master Doc U02 and then print the document. (At the prompt asking if you want to open the subdocuments, click No.)
6. Make the following changes to the document:
   a. Move the section 3 subdocument above the section 1 subdocument. (Make sure the dark gray horizontal line displays above the white square above the section 1 subdocument before releasing the mouse button.)
   b. Delete the section 2 subdocument.
7. Save and then print Master Doc U02.
8. Print Master Doc U02. (At the prompt asking if you want to open the subdocuments, click No.)
9. Close Master Doc U02.

Assessment 5

1. At a clear document screen, create the text shown in figure U2.1 as a concordance file.
2. Save the document and name it EWd U02 CF.
3. Print and then close EWd U02 CF.
4. Open Word Report 02.
5. Save the document with Save As and name it EWd U02 PA05.
6. Make the following changes to the document:
   a. Mark text for an index using the concordance file, EWd U02 CF.
   b. Compile the index at the end of the document.
   c. Mark the title and headings for a table of contents.
   d. Compile the table of contents at the beginning of the document.
7. Save the document and then print the table of contents and the index. (Check with your instructor to see if you should print the entire document.)
8. Close EWd U02 PA05.

message	Message
publication	Publication
design	Design
flier	Flier
letterhead	Letterhead
newsletter	Newsletter
intent	Design: intent
audience	Design: audience
layout	Design: layout
thumbnail	Thumbnail
principles	Design: principles
focus	Design: focus
balance	Design: balance
proportion	Design: proportion
contrast	Design: contrast
directional flow	Design: directional flow

Figure U2.1 • Assessment 5

Assessment 6

1. Create the table form shown in figure U2.2 as a template document named XXX U02 PA06 (where your initials are inserted in place of the *XXX*). Customize the table as shown in figure U2.2. Insert text form fields in the table as shown in the figure.
2. Print and then close XXX U02 PA06.

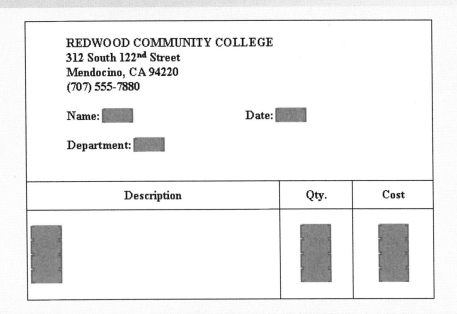

Figure U2.2 • Assessment 6

Assessment 7

1. Create a form with the XXX U02 PA06 form template. Insert the following information in the form:

   Name: Ronald Jarvis
   Date: (key the current date)
   Department: Public Relations

   Description: Transfer Brochure
   Qty.: 400
   Cost: $225.00

   Description: Technology Degree Brochure
   Qty.: 250
   Cost: $179.50

   Description: College Newsletter
   Qty.: 2,000
   Cost: $150.50

2. When the form is completed, save the document and name it EWd U02 PA07.
3. Print and then close EWd U02 PA07.

Assessment 8

1. Open Word Table 07.
2. Save the document with Save As and name it EWd U02 PA08.
3. Make the following changes to the table:
   a. Insert a new row at the bottom of the table.
   b. Key **Total** in cell A6 (the first new cell at the left).
   c. Insert a formula in cell B6 that totals first quarter sales. *(Hint: At the Formula dialog box, change the Number format to the third option from the top of the drop-down list.)*
   d. Insert the same formula in cells C6, D6, and E6.
4. Save, print, and then close EWd U02 PA08.

Assessment 9

1. Open Word Document 08.
2. Save the document and name it EWd U02 PA09.
3. Open Excel and then open Excel Worksheet 05.
4. Save the worksheet with Save As and name it Excel U02 PA09.
5. Select cells A1 through D9, copy the cells, and then link the cells so the worksheet displays in the EWd U02 PA09 between the paragraph of text in the document and the name *Michael Kingston*. (Make sure you the Paste Special dialog box [and select the Paste link option in the dialog box].)
6. Save, print, and then close EWd U02 PA09.
7. Make Excel the active program, close Excel U02 PA09, and then exit Excel.

Assessment 10

1. Open the Microsoft Excel program.
2. Open Excel U02 PA09 and then make the following changes:
   a. Change the number in cell D3 from *98,244* to *80,932*.
   b. Change the number in cell D5 from *34,264* to *28,096*.
   c. Change the number in cell D7 from *45,209* to *37,650*.
   d. Save the revised worksheet by clicking the Save button on the Excel Standard toolbar.
3. Close Excel U02 PA09.
4. Exit Microsoft Excel.
5. Open Word and then open EWd U02 PA09. (Notice how the numbers in the worksheet are updated to reflect the changes made to Excel U02 PA09.)
6. Save the document with Save As and name it EWd U02 PA10.
7. Print and then close EWd U02 PA10.

Assessment 11

1. Open Word Document 08.
2. Save the document with Save As and name it EWd U02 PA11.
3. Create the hyperlink *Quarterly Sales* between the paragraph of text and the name *Michael Kingston* that will display the Excel Worksheet 05 spreadsheet (in the *Word Unit 02E* folder on your disk) in the Excel program.
4. Click the *Quarterly Sales* hyperlink to display Excel Worksheet 05 in Excel.
5. After looking at the data in Excel Worksheet 05, exit Excel.
6. Save, print, and then close EWd U02 PA11.

WRITING activities

The following writing activities give you the opportunity to practice your writing skills along with demonstrating an understanding of some of the important Word features you have mastered in this unit.

Activity 1

Situation: You manage a small business research company and are interested in learning more about how businesses use overnight or express shipping. Create a fill-in form template containing the information shown in figure U2.3 that you plan to mail to selected small businesses. You determine the layout of the form and the types of form fields needed.

SHIPPING INFORMATION

1. What is the title of the person at your company who is most responsible for selecting small-package carriers?
   President/Owner
   Chief Financial Officer
   Controller
   Purchasing Manager
   Other

2. Does the person indicated above have access to a personal computer for use in shipping?   Yes   No

3. How do you currently ship overnight letters or packages?
   Ground
   Domestic air express
   Neither

4. Do you receive a discount rate for domestic air express shipping?   Yes   No

5. Does your company ship or receive international express letters or packages?
   Yes   No

6. If you currently do not ship or receive internationally, do you plan to do so within:
   Next month
   Next 6 months
   Next year
   Not likely

Figure U2.3 • Activity 1

After creating the form template, save the template document as XXX U02 Act01. Use the XXX U02 Act01 form template to create a fill-in form. You make up information to fill in the form fields. After the form is filled in, save it and name it EWd U02 Act01. Print and then close EWd U02 Act01.

Activity 2
1. Display the Templates dialog box.
2. Delete the following template form documents:
   XXX U02 PA06 (where your initials display rather than XXX)
   XXX U02 Act01 (where your initials display rather than XXX)
3. Close the Templates dialog box.

Activity 3

In this unit, you learned about copying, linking, and embedding objects in a document. Read the situations below and then write a report on which of the following procedures you would choose for the described situation:

Copy and paste   Copy and link   Copy and embed

Situation 1: Each week you prepare a memo in Word to your supervisor that includes an Excel worksheet. The memo includes information about the number of products sold by your division, the current number of products on hand, and the number of products on order. This memo (with the worksheet) is updated each week. Which of the three procedures would you use for including the worksheet in the memo? Why?

Situation 2: Each year, you prepare an annual report for your company in Word that includes several Excel worksheets. This report and the worksheets are very different from year to year. Which of the three procedures would you use for including the worksheets in the report? Why?

Situation 3: You travel to various companies showing a PowerPoint presentation to prospective customers. The presentation includes several charts showing information such as quarterly sales figures, production figures, and projected sales. These charts are updated quarterly. Which of the three procedures would you use for including the charts in the presentation? Why?

Save the report document containing your responses to the three situations and name the document EWd U02 Act03. Print and then close EWd U02 Act03.

INTERNET project

Researching Job Opportunities

Make sure you are connected to the Internet and then use a search engine (you choose the search engine) to search for companies offering employment opportunities. Search for companies offering jobs in a field in which you are interested in working. Find at least three Web sites that interest you and then create a report in Word about the sites that includes the following:

- Site name, address, and URL
- A brief description of the site
- Employment opportunities

Create hyperlinks from your report to each of the three sites and include any other additional information pertinent to the sites. Apply formatting to enhance the document. When the document is completed, save it and name it EWd U02 Internet Project. Print and then close EWd U02 Internet Project.

JOB study

Developing Staff Guidelines for Reading Technical Manuals

As a staff member of a computer e-tailer, you are required to maintain cutting-eduge technology skills, including being well versed in the use of new software programs such as Office XP. Recently, you were asked to develop and distribute a set of strategies for reading technical and computer manuals that the staff will use as they learn new programs. In addition, you are to create a form to survey your staff regarding the publication and its contents. The project is co-sponsored by EMCParadigm Publishing, which will provide additional information at its Web site.

Use the concepts and techniques you learned in this unit to create the guidelines and survey form as follows:

1. Create a baseline draft by keying the text in figure U2.4. Use Word's versioning feature to save a version of this draft.
2. Edit the document. Use Word's track changes feature to highlight all changes in the document as you edit:
   a. Change all occurrences of "computer manuals" to "technical and computer manuals."
   b. Format the document with appropriate heading and list styles.
   c. Insert at least two comments regarding the content and/or format of the document.
   d. Insert the EMCP logo attractively into the document. (Connect to your ISP and go to www.emcp.com. Download the EMCP logo located in the upper right-hand corner of the Web page.)
   e. Include page numbers, a hyperlink to www.emcp.com, and your name attractively formatted in a footer.
   f. Generate a table of contents.
3. Prepare draft and final copies. Save the revised document as a new version. Print one copy of the document with the tracking visible. Accept all of the changes, save the document as the final version, and print one copy.
4. Create a survey form. Use Word's form feature to create a survey form document based on a template. Each member of your staff who received a copy of the guidelines prepared above will complete the form. The goal of the form is to help you determine whether or not the guidelines were helpful to your staff and whether or not they would like to see similar publications in the future. Add additional questions as you think appropriate. Be creative. Include text boxes, check boxes, and pull-down lists. Save the form as a protected document and print one copy.

Strategies for Reading Computer Manuals

Understand Your Reading Goal

When you use a computer manual, your reading goal usually is to find out how to do something or how to complete a task. Preview the material and review your reading goals for this course session. You may be learning how to do a mail merge or how to organize your computer files. Keep the larger task in mind as you follow each of the "hands-on" steps.

The hands-on tasks in computer manuals are often set up in one of the following ways. Review how the information in your text is organized:

Text presents detailed, sequential directions around tasks to be completed.

Text presents sequenced illustrations or pictures around task to be completed.

Text presents the software functions and provides factual details about how they work.

Text provides general guidelines but not specific steps on how to complete a task.

Will you be guided every step of the way or are you encouraged to experiment or practice using trial and error?

Know the Text Structure

Look over the structure of the text. Is there a glossary? Is there a help section? Does the index look exhaustive?

Skim the table of contents and introduction or preface for an overview of the text.

Look at the headings to see where information is located or how the information is organized: the main headings and the subheadings that follow. Thumb through the pages to see where the diagrams are, where the descriptions are, and how the hands-on steps are listed.

Use the table of contents. Look at how the table of contents is structured and get a general understanding of the new technical skills you will be learning.

Use the index to look up a specific command or feature of the software. Study the subtopics and cross-references provided.

Begin the Hands-On Work as Soon as Possible

Computer instruction manuals are designed to launch you into hands-on action as early as possible. Go ahead and start on a lesson and do not be concerned if you make mistakes. You will learn as much or more by correcting your mistakes as when you follow the steps correctly.

Focus on just what you need to know in order to get started. You will learn more by doing than by just reading. Think about what you already know about the topic as you begin.

When you have completed a sequence of steps, go back, read the side text, and review the screen illustrations.

Use Effective Reading Strategies

Use effective skimming techniques. Skim sections for key words and labels to determine the relevance of the information. The material may or may not provide information necessary for completing your immediate task.

Turn the headings into questions that require answers.

Mark important information in the margins. Ask yourself questions and note terms not understood.

Use the Visual Aids to Help You Understand

Carefully read the callouts, titles, or notes that help explain the illustrations. Stop to think about why the illustration is important.

Try to connect the words with the illustrations and the screen captures. Read a few steps and then examine the illustration. Then continue reading the steps. Returning periodically to the illustration. Ask yourself: "What is this illustration saying that the words do not?"

State the visual information in words. Illustrations provide new information. Try to state that information in your own words.

Improve Your Technical Vocabulary
To communicate effectively on the job, you will need to speak the language of computers. It is important to learn the specialized terminology and incorporate it into your own speech and writing. As you read, estimate the meaning of the word from the context.
Write down new meanings of common abbreviations and acronyms. Compare your definition with the one provided in the glossary.

Remember What You Have Learned
Rewrite the steps on note cards using your own words. Read the notes out loud.
Write the steps of a difficult procedure using a visual diagram or flowchart.
Repeat any sequence of steps on an item that caused you difficulty.
Complete the supplementary and end-of-chapter problems. If you really want to master the software steps, work backwards. Complete the end-of-chapter assignments or one of the items that requires you read the Online Help feature. Then write the steps needed to solve the problem for a learner new to the software.
Go back and answer any questions that you wrote in the margins.

Figure U2.4 • Reading Strategies Document

INDEX